AF323289

Europe and the United States

Europe and the United States

<hr>

THE EMERGING SECURITY PARTNERSHIP

Franz Oswald

PRAEGER SECURITY INTERNATIONAL
Westport, Connecticut • London

Library of Congress Cataloging-in-Publication Data

Oswald, Franz, 1947–
    Europe and the United States : the emerging security partnership / Franz Oswald.
        p.   cm.
    Includes bibliographical references and index.
    ISBN 0–275–98975–5
    1. Security, International.   2. Europe—Foreign relations—United States.
3. United States—Foreign relations—Europe.   I. Title.
JZ5588.O89 2006
355'.031091821—dc22   2005035391

British Library Cataloguing in Publication Data is available.

Library of Congress Catalog Card Number: 2005035391
ISBN: 0–275–98975–5

First published in 2006

Praeger Security International Publishers, 88 Post Road West, Westport, CT 06881
An imprint of Greenwood Publishing Group, Inc.
www.praeger.com

Printed in the United States of America

The paper used in this book complies with the
Permanent Paper Standard issued by the National
Information Standards Organization (Z39.48–1984).

10 9 8 7 6 5 4 3 2 1

Contents

Preface

At the center of a profound redefinition of the West since 1991 is the recasting of the roles in the transatlantic relationship. "Because of the measured pace of developments in Western Europe, there has been a tendency to assume that somehow only the East, not the West, would be in for a massive redefinition."[1] It was obvious that the end of the Soviet Union in 1991 meant the end of the bipolar conflict of the Cold War period. It was less obvious that the West could not remain what it had become after 1945, a U.S.-led global alliance in a bipolar world. Instead, a multipolar world is emerging in which the United States and a European Union (EU) of more than 500 million people will be preeminent among a handful of great powers. And after half a century of military presence in Europe, the United States can return to the much older objective of minimizing entanglements in European affairs.

Comparing the international system to a multilevel chessboard, Joseph S. Nye made the distinction between a unipolar distribution of power on the military chessboard and the multipolarity on the economic chessboard.[2] Yet these two chessboards do not just coexist—they interact. Global economic competition with the United States and Japan has motivated Europeans to build a vast unified EU market. This has not only rebalanced the competition on the economic chessboard. The creation of a unified economic actor with the potential of becoming a strategic actor is bound to affect the military chessboard as well.

In the post-1991 security environment, Europe is much safer than it had been through most of the twentieth century. Therefore, the EU can, without much risk, begin to assume responsibility for security in Europe, while the United States, without much risk, can reduce its military involvement in Europe and pursue national interests in other regions. While transatlantic economic

interdependence continues, to the benefit of both sides, the security relationship is undergoing a redefinition, at a measured pace but nevertheless profound.
The transatlantic tensions during the crises in Bosnia and Kosovo, at the time
of the intervention in Afghanistan, after the terrorist attacks of September 11,
2001, and around the war in Iraq of 2003 are all part of this redefinition of
transatlantic relations, leading from the asymmetrical relationship of the Cold
War to a more balanced security partnership of the future.

I am obliged to Charles Doran and other power cycle theorists[3] for the
insight that subtle changes in relative power have to be accommodated by
renegotiating the roles of international actors. This approach is more relevant
to the current redefinition of the West than the question of whether there was
anywhere "the challenger" preparing to line up against the hegemon.

For giving me the opportunity to develop my ideas on European security, I am grateful to my colleagues and students during my involvement both
in the Graduate Studies in Strategy and Defence of the Australian National
University (2002–04) and in the Graduate Studies in International Relations
program at Curtin University of Technology, Perth. Last but not least, I want
to thank Peter Shearman and the Contemporary Europe Research Centre
at the University of Melbourne for bringing together a small but dedicated
group of Australian academics interested in European security.[4]

Abbreviations

ACP	African, Caribbean, and Pacific
AFSOUTH	Allied Forces Southern Europe
BAe	British Aerospace Systems
CEE	Central and Eastern Europe
CESDP	Common European Security and Defense Policy
CFE	Conventional Forces in Europe Treaty
CFR	Council on Foreign Relations
CFSP	Common Foreign and Security Policy
CINCSOUTH	Commander in Chief Southern Europe
CIS	Commonwealth of Independent States
CJTF	Combined Joint Task Forces
DCI	Defense Capabilities Initiative
EADS	European Aeronautics Defence and Space Company
EC	European Community
EDEM	European Defense Equipment Market
EDITB	European Defense Industrial and Technological Base
EEC	European Economic Community
EEC/EC/EU	three stages of European integration taken together
EFTA	European Free Trade Association
EMU	Economic and Monetary Union
EPU	European Political Union
ERRF	European Rapid Response Forces
ESDI	European Security and Defense Identity
ESDP	European Security and Defense Policy
ESS	European Security Strategy

EU	European Union
FRG	Federal Republic of Germany
GATT	General Agreement on Tariffs and Trade
GDP	Gross Domestic Product
GNP	Gross National Product
IGC	Intergovernmental Conference
ILSA	Iran-Libya Sanctions Act
IMF	International Monetary Fund
JSF	Joint Strike Fighter
KLA	Kosovo Liberation Army
MEADS	Medium Extended Air Defense System
NAFTA	North American Free Trade Association
NATO	North Atlantic Treaty Organization
OSCE	Organization for Security and Cooperation in Europe
PfP	Partnership for Peace
PNAC	Project for the New American Century
SAA	Stabilization and Association Agreement
SDI	Strategic Defense Initiative
SHAPE	Supreme Headquarters of Allied Powers in Europe
TAFTA	Transatlantic Free Trade Association
UNPROFOR	United Nations Protection Force
WEU	West European Union
WTO	World Trade Organization

Introduction: Recasting Transatlantic Relations—New Roles for the United States and Europe

For more than 40 years, during the Cold War, the United States and Western Europe were one another's most important allies. However, in the first decade of the twenty-first century, the transatlantic partnership is going through a rapid and profound transformation. Deep tensions in the transatlantic relationship became visible in the lead-up to the Iraq War of 2003, but the recasting of roles started earlier when the Cold War ended in 1991. At the moment of its greatest success, the future of the transatlantic alliance was under a cloud. The North Atlantic Treaty Organization (NATO) had won the Cold War when an exhausted Soviet Union disintegrated, but soon the question arose whether the alliance would go out of business. Until 1991, the United States and Europe were on one side in the Cold War confrontation. Their roles within the partnership had been set in the late 1940s, when Western Europe was weak and exhausted by World War II and the United States had reached global economic and military supremacy. Since then, Europe's economies had recovered and been integrated into an economic bloc. With the end of the Soviet Union, Western Europe was no longer threatened and Eastern Europe no longer separated by the Iron Curtain. In this new security environment, the powerful economic bloc resulting from European integration should also be capable of looking after European security without involving the United States. A new security partnership between Europe and the United States is replacing the security dependency of the Cold War period.

The tensions between the United States and the European Union (EU) triggered by disagreements over the Iraq War were expressions of a deeper challenge to the transatlantic allocation of roles. Within the EU, the renegotiation of the transatlantic relationship was accompanied by disputes between Atlanticists such as Great Britain and Poland on one side and Europeanists such as France and Germany on the other. Since 1991, the EU had been redefining its role: the economic bloc began to claim a geostrategic role with responsibility for security in Europe. The United States was also reconsidering its role: the only superpower could continue its leadership in European security through the NATO alliance, or it could leave Europe alone while pursuing global interests in other regions. Renegotiating these roles was linked to an assessment of the international balance of power. Was post-1991 U.S. supremacy permanent or transient? Was the unipolar moment the beginning of a unipolar era where Europe would be a junior ally of the United States as before or perhaps even an irrelevant region ignored by U.S. unilateralists? Or would the unipolar moment be replaced by a multipolar world in which U.S. preeminence was relativized by several global players including the EU? Behind the daily events covered by journalists, a fundamental redefinition of the roles of Europe and the United States was taking place. The change of 1989–91 meant that the international system resulting from 1945 was coming to an end. This involved more than the disintegration of the Soviet Union and the end of the Cold War. The end of the post-1945 international system also meant the transformation of what had been "the West" for almost half a century. The current recasting of the transatlantic relationship implies the end of the unified and U.S.-led West, a substantial reduction of U.S. involvement in Europe, and increasing EU responsibility for European security.

THE END OF THE POST-1945 PERIOD IN "THE WEST"

One central aspect of the post–World War II international system came to an end in 1991: the bipolar confrontation between the United States and the Soviet Union. Another important outcome of 1945 was changing more slowly: the primacy of the United States in the West and in the whole international system outside the Soviet bloc. The sudden collapse of the Soviet Union left the United States as the only military superpower. On the other hand, the preeminence of the United States in the West was being weakened by gradual changes, especially by Europe's emancipation from the post-1945 military protectorate. "Because of the measured pace of developments in Western Europe, there has been a tendency to assume that somehow only the East, not the West, would be in for a massive redefinition."[1]

The redefinition of the West was gathering pace in the late 1990s. Since the end of the Cold War, the EU had deepened its economic integration further by completing the Single Market in 1992 and introducing the euro currency in 1999. But the EU was also moving beyond economic integration: a common foreign and security policy was initiated in 1991, a European Rapid Response Force was started in 1999, and the EU conducted its first military crisis management missions abroad in 2003. Europeans have been taking on more responsibility for European security, and by 2015–20, Europe's security emancipation should be completed.

The unprecedented supremacy of the United States within the West was institutionalized in the mid-1940s when the older established powers, Britain and France, were exhausted and the aggressive challenges by Germany, Japan, and Italy had failed. The economic supremacy of the United States was consolidated with the Bretton Woods conference of 1944, and military primacy was given permanence in NATO. This alliance consolidated U.S. leadership in Western Europe by transforming past rivals into a military protectorate. For U.S. historian David Calleo, NATO was "the rather elaborate apparatus by which we have chosen to organize the American protectorate in Europe." Although NATO's secretary-general was always a European, the Supreme Allied Commander was always an American general who "has never been the first servant of the Council, but the viceroy of the American president."[2]

The decline of post-1945 U.S. leadership in "the West" is less visible than the sudden and spectacular collapse of the Soviet role as leader of the Eastern bloc. Nevertheless, there is enough evidence to suggest that the asymmetrical relationship between the United States and Europe is also coming to an end. The economic and military superiority of the United States after 1945 was more spectacular than its military supremacy after 1991. In 1945, the former great powers of Europe were reduced to a military protectorate under U.S. supervision while the United States inherited parts of collapsing European empires. This change in the balance of power between Europe and the United States was a less prominent but nevertheless intended outcome of U.S. involvement in World War II. Neoconservative polemicist Robert Kagan, in his 2002 essay "Power and Weakness," remembered that President Roosevelt's objectives in World War II included not only the defeat of Nazi Germany and militaristic Japan but also the reduction of Great Britain and France to the second rank.[3] As a pleasing side effect of World War II, the British Empire was transformed into a junior partner dependent on U.S. arms technology and loans and the British pound was replaced as world currency by the U.S. dollar at the Bretton Woods conference of 1944. Other ambitious powers, such as France, Germany, and Japan, found themselves reduced to sheltering in U.S.-led alliances.

The asymmetrical relationship between the United States and Western Europe corresponded to the balance of power as it existed in 1949, when NATO was founded. However, half a century later, the balance of power between the transatlantic friends has changed. Europe has completed its economic emancipation from post-1945 dependency, whereas security dependency continued beyond the 1991 collapse of the Soviet Union. In world trade, Europe has become a global actor. On the other hand, the EU has only begun to claim a role in security policy, displaying rather limited operational power so far but enjoying massive potential power.

Joseph S. Nye, who argued that "the World War II effect had largely worked its way through the international system by the early 1970s," suggested a different historical perspective.[4] The United States had emerged stronger after the war, whereas Europe had been devastated. Predictably, Europe recovered, and U.S. supremacy diminished somewhat compared to the post-1945 position. Yet, according to Nye, this rebalancing in favor of Europe was quite limited. "The World War II effect lasted for about a quarter of a century and most of the decline worked its way through the system by the mid 1970s and then stabilized."[5] Nye's argument can be accepted regarding economic growth rates, which were higher in Europe during postwar recovery until the 1970s and did not surpass U.S. growth rates after that. However, Nye underestimates implications working their way through the international system much more slowly. First, even after growth rates had leveled off, Europe's economic weight increased further through enlargement and deeper integration. Second, the role allocation in the transatlantic security partnership was institutionalized in 1949 and reflected the World War II effect even after 1991 since U.S. leadership in NATO had not ended in the early 1970s. The post–World War II allocation of roles began to change only after the end of the Soviet Union and with the development of the EU's Common Foreign and Security Policy since 1991.

Europe's uneven emancipation created the EU as autonomous economic actor in world trade. The unfinished half of Europe's emancipation consisted in creating an autonomous foreign and security policy. Some U.S. leaders will experience the end of their responsibility for European security as a loss. Yet the current rebalancing of transatlantic relations will free the United States of European entanglements, bringing back an older objective of U.S. foreign policy. The asymmetrical roles in the transatlantic alliance will give way to a balanced security partnership, creating a new framework for future economic and cultural interdependence.

Relations between the United States and Europe have entered a new phase, characterized by the ambition of the EU to supplement its economic strength with autonomy in security matters. This clashes with U.S. claims for continued leadership in European security. If this renegotiation of roles is carefully managed, transatlantic cooperation will continue in a new form, whereas mismanagement of this adjustment could damage transatlantic economic, cultural, and security cooperation. Transatlantic interdependency is deep enough to ensure that the relationship will survive problems such as U.S. unilateralism prevailing during President George W. Bush's first term.

Six decades after World War II, the U.S. military presence in Europe has been reduced from more than 300,000 at the end of the Cold War to 60,000 to 70,000. In June 2004, U.S. Army Chief of Staff General Peter Schoomaker announced further reductions, and in April 2005, the U.S. Army announced plans to reduce U.S. forces in Europe from 62,000 to 24,000 in the next five to ten years.[6] The post-1945 engagement of the United States in Europe was a long but passing period in the history of transatlantic relations. As far as Europe is concerned, the United States is returning to an older policy of avoiding entanglements. Future crises in Europe will be left to the Europeans to sort out. The transatlantic alliance is being transformed from a collective defense organization against an external threat into a security community ensuring peaceful relations among NATO members and associates.

U.S. LEADERSHIP AFTER 1945: EUROPE AS MILITARY PROTECTORATE

The centerpiece of the transatlantic relationship was the military alliance united during the Cold War by the Soviet threat. The NATO alliance, founded in 1949, incorporated Western Europeans in a global network of alliances. The roles of the transatlantic partners were clearly asymmetrical. The United States exercised leadership, while European allies were grateful to enjoy protection. The United States contributed nuclear capabilities and leadership, while Europeans supplied conventional forces for NATO's central front in Europe. The expression "providing leadership" presents hegemony as a community service, as a sacrifice by the leader for the benefit of junior allies. Yet while U.S. leadership provided protection, it also transformed West Europeans into dependent allies. Several decades after World War II, "the far western tip of the Eurasian continent still" remained "an American military protectorate."[7]

The asymmetrical relation between the United States and NATO–Europe was a result of a unique 1940s distribution of power. Henry A. Kissinger argued in the 1960s that the relation had to be renegotiated, to some extent, as Europe had recovered economically. The "temporary loss of Europe's ability to play an effective international role" could not be expected to last.[8] He suggested adjustments in NATO's role allocations, but by no means did he envisage an end to U.S. leadership. Other methods to bolster U.S. hegemony were suggested by Zbigniew Brzezinski. "In brief, for the United States, Eurasian geostrategy involves the purposeful management of geostrategically dynamic states and the careful handling of geopolitically catalytic states. . . . To put it in a terminology that hearkens back to the more brutal age of ancient empires, the three grand imperatives of imperial geostrategy are to prevent collusion and maintain security dependence among the vassals, to keep tributaries pliant and protected, and to keep the barbarians from coming together."[9] It was somewhat inconsistent that Brzezinski also proposed that "an America that truly desires a united and hence also a more independent Europe will have to throw its weight behind those European forces that are genuinely committed to Europe's political and economic integration."[10] On the one hand, Brzezinski searched for ways of prolonging U.S. hegemony by keeping the vassals disunited; on the other, he deplored the "brutal fact . . . that Western Europe, and increasingly also Central Europe, remains largely an American protectorate," commenting that this was "not a healthy condition"[11] and obviously had to be overcome.

Kissinger's argument of the 1960s can be extended beyond his intentions and applied to transatlantic relations after 1991. The post-1945 weakness of

Europe and unprecedented U.S. supremacy were indeed the outcome of a unique situation. In the 1960s, relative power had already shifted noticeably, but it has shifted even more in the four decades since. Thus, any renegotiation of roles was likely to go further than envisaged in 1966. Brzezinski's "vassals" had become confident and united enough to move beyond the outdated post-1945 military protectorate toward a new transatlantic security partnership.

DIFFERENTIAL SECURITY FOR NATO PARTNERS

The argument for the Europeanization of European security can be strengthened by remembering that the United States and Western Europe enjoyed very uneven levels of security even while NATO was united by the Soviet threat. Before 1991, the underlying tensions over differential security were contained by a shared threat perception. While these tensions remained latent before 1991, in the post–Cold War security environment of "multi-faceted" and "multi-directional" risks,[12] differences in threat perceptions between the United States and Europe caused severe divisions. During the Cold War, geography was the main cause of differential security within NATO. Western Europe shared land borders with the Soviet bloc, whereas the United States found itself in a much safer location on the other side of the Atlantic Ocean. This implied different security outcomes for the United States and Europe under all strategies adopted by NATO. Before 1991, the problem of differential security never grew virulent enough to split the transatlantic alliance, but it indicated that NATO's cohesion would be severely tested without a unifying external threat. The post-1991 transatlantic rift was always more than a clash of personalities or styles; it had structural causes in the post-1991 security environment and the changed balance of power between the United States and a unifying European bloc.

BETWEEN MILITARY UNIPOLARITY AND ECONOMIC MULTIPOLARITY

Central to the argument of this book is the observation that there was a significant difference between the distribution of economic power and the distribution of military power in the post-1991 international system. After the disintegration of the Soviet Union, there was only one military superpower: the United States. However, there was clearly a multipolar distribution of economic power. This observation contradicts Robert Kagan's simplistic assessment of Europe as weak and the United States as strong. Instead, one has to distinguish clearly between U.S. supremacy on the military chessboard and a more balanced multipolar competition on the economic chessboard, to use Joseph S. Nye's metaphor of a multilevel chess game.[13]

During the Cold War, the bipolarity of the international system had already been complicated by an economic multipolarity coexisting with military bipolarity. More pertinent to the current argument, there was also a significant difference between the bipolar distribution of military power and the one-sided distribution of economic potential between the superpowers. The Soviet Union attempted to match the superior military potential of the United States, but because of the inferiority of the Soviet economy, the military effort was not sustainable. The imbalance between economic potential and military ambitions exhausted the Soviet Union and resulted in its demise as a superpower. In post-1991 great-power rivalries, a different discrepancy of economic potential and military power is at work. The United States is still a formidable economic power although no longer as clearly superior to Europe and Japan as in 1950. This relative parity of economic power raises the question whether the military supremacy of the United States will remain sustainable. The United States can still be perceived as the only superpower because of its unchallenged military supremacy and its relative economic preeminence. However, European integration has unified a huge economic potential, making it possible for the EU to claim a geostrategic role.

NO SINGLE CHALLENGE TO U.S. HEGEMONY BUT MULTIPLE CHANGES IN RELATIVE POWER

European integration did not create "the challenger," but the EU figures prominently among the multiple challenges to U.S. hegemony. Power cycle theory, instead of concentrating on the interaction between a hegemon and a challenger, "focuses on the rise, maturation, and decline in capability of each state relative to all other states . . . in the relevant system."[14] This draws attention to smaller changes of relative power, not just to the question whether the EU, Japan, China, or another power will be the next challenger of U.S. supremacy. The latter is the focus of "transition theory," which "argues that the rising challenger in an international system tends to contest the largest state," and of "hegemonic stability theory," which "argues reversely that a declining hegemon tends to make a preventive war against the challenger to sustain its dominant position."[15] Power cycle theory, on the other hand, highlights gradual changes of relative power requiring adaptation of the roles and ambitions of actors in the international system.

Gradual change in the transatlantic relationship has reached a turning point. The United States accepted the EU as economic equal in the World Trade Organization, the International Monetary Fund, and the World Bank but insisted on a leading role in European security through NATO. The EU, on the other hand, has grown into an economic superpower, claiming a commensurate security role. Roles claimed by states and roles ascribed to them by others are the subjective side of the balance of power. When potential power and operational power of states change, the claimed and ascribed roles of states need to be adjusted. Role claims can be exaggerated and based, misguidedly, on past strength or expectations of future strength. Role claims can also be understated compared to potential power, for example, in the case of Japan and Germany in the second half of the twentieth century. On the other hand, ascribed roles can be inappropriate if the power of other states is under-estimated, corresponding to exaggerated views of one's own power. In particular, claiming continued U.S. leadership in NATO and ascribing a junior role to Europe could be based on memories of the distribution of power in 1949 and habitual perceptions out of tune with present reality.

The roles in the transatlantic alliance were institutionalized in the late 1940s, reflecting U.S. military and economic supremacy. These roles were only marginally adjusted during the Cold War in spite of Europe's growing economic power. After the end of the Cold War, neoconservative unilateralists ascribed a reduced role to an allegedly weak Europe. Others argued for the maintenance of existing asymmetrical relations. However, should the EU grow to unite almost 600 million people, roles would need significant adjustment. The asymmetrical relationship of the late 1940s would have to be change into a symmetrical relationship of equals.

Understanding Europe's uneven emancipation from post–World War II dependence will enable U.S. policymakers to shape better transatlantic relations instead of squandering goodwill in a vain attempt to retain the asymmetrical transatlantic relations of the late 1940s. Unilateral use of military supremacy not only squandered U.S. economic resources and soft power[16] but also accelerated the EU's search for an autonomous security role. Instead of relying on military means, the United States could use its preeminence to shape a stable framework for a multipolar future.[17] This should include accepting the EU not only as an economic bloc but also as an emerging security actor. Instead of trying to extend the unipolar moment into a unipolar era, the United States could use post-1991 primacy to guide the transition to a multipolar world.

Changes in relative power require adjustments in the claimed and ascribed roles of the United States and other relevant actors. The United States is still enjoying the aftereffects of the post-1945 moment of economic unipolarity, whereas the full impact of the rise of Japan and Europe as economic competitors on U.S. power still has to be felt. While Joseph S. Nye noted the difference between U.S. supremacy on the military chessboard and the more balanced, multipolar competition on the economic chessboard,[18] a stronger claim is made here: economic multipolarity has the potential to transform military unipolarity. The unipolar moment of post-1991 military supremacy will be affected by multiple challenges, including the claim of the European bloc to take charge of European security.

EUROPEAN SECURITY AFTER 1991: THE UNITED STATES REDUCING EUROPEAN ENTANGLEMENTS

The central contentious issue in transatlantic relations is currently the responsibility for European security. In the nineteenth century, European powers wanted to find security against one another in a balance of power game of shifting alliances and escalating arms races. For decades, stability was achieved, but European rivalries ended in the devastation of World War I and World War II. After 1945, the United States and the Soviet Union shared responsibility for security in a divided Europe. In 1991, when the Soviet Union withdrew from Central and Eastern Europe, NATO under U.S. leadership became the security framework for all of Europe. However, the EU had achieved such a level of economic integration that deeper political integration and a security role for the EU had become possible.

The most likely outcome of this situation is that the United States will disengage from Europe in order to concentrate on commitments in other parts of the world. This will imply a quiet retreat from security leadership in Europe, leaving it to the EU to act as a security community within and as crisis manager at its periphery. After half a century of security leadership, the United States will revert to the role of the centuries before 1945: the policy of avoiding entanglements in European conflicts. Yet this withdrawal will not be total. Even after the end of a significant U.S. military presence in Europe, the United States will play a role in European security as a partner in a large security community anchored by a transformed NATO alliance. The redefinition of the transatlantic relationship "will probably result in the further weakening of what remains of the American 'empire,'" although a "continued role of the US as the ultimate arbiter in Europe" is still conceivable.[19] However, it is more likely that the post-1945 security dependency will be replaced by a balanced transatlantic partnership.

SECURITY EMANCIPATION WITHOUT MAKING EUROPE "THE CHALLENGER"

The following chapters analyze changes in the roles of the transatlantic partners since 1991. Chapter 1 discusses the allocation of roles in the transatlantic partnership, the roles that the United States and Europe claim for themselves and ascribe to the other. Chapter 2 outlines the economic emancipation of Europe from post-1945 weakness. European integration and its combined economic potential created the opportunity for the EU's future geostrategic role.

Chapter 3 discusses the reasons for the longevity of the NATO alliance and its survival beyond the completion of its primary purpose with the end of the Soviet Union. Chapter 4 assesses the contradictory effects of NATO's new tasks. They gave the alliance a new lease of life, but they also contributed to the end of NATO as a collective defense alliance by transforming it into a security community.

Chapter 5 shows the development of the EU's Common Security and Defense Policy from the early institutional prerequisites to the formation of armed forces and the first EU missions. The emerging EU responsibility for European security is the greatest challenge to post-1945 U.S. leadership in Europe. The period of ambiguity, during which European defense efforts could be interpreted as contributions both to a stronger NATO and to European autonomy, will last for another decade because the reorientation of Germany's *Bundeswehr* from its Cold War tasks is so much slower than the reform of British or French forces.

Chapter 6 presents the changes of U.S. engagement in Europe during the presidencies of Bill Clinton and George W. Bush. While the transatlantic rift had become visible and, at times, acrimonious between 2001 and 2004, there was a surprising amount of continuity in gradual U.S. disengagement since 1991. Finally, chapter 7 outlines the geostrategic potential of an enlarged EU and the likely framework of future transatlantic relations. Europe's uneven emancipation will be completed with the end of post-1945 security dependence in addition to the change in relative economic power since 1950. The United States can be free of European entanglements once more, and a new transatlantic security partnership can provide a stable framework for future economic and cultural interdependence.

CHAPTER 1

Why Europe Matters: Roles in the Transatlantic Relationship

EUROPE'S CHANGING ROLE

The transatlantic relationship, together with Europe's division by the Iron Curtain, has been the single most important determinant of Western Europe's role in the international system since 1945. And after 1991, with the retreat of the Soviet Union/Russia from its sphere of influence, the transatlantic relationship extended its defining power to Central and Eastern Europe (CEE). In turn, the momentous changes transforming Europe in 1989–91 could not but affect the transatlantic relationship. Since 1991, on both sides of the Atlantic, a variety of role conceptions for Europe and the United States has been under discussion. This diversity of role conceptions contributed to inconsistent and changing policies but also illustrated the options available in the current renegotiation of roles.

Europe has been dismissed as weak and irrelevant by U.S. neoconservatives and unilateralists during the Bush administration's first term, while others have argued that Europe was still relevant as indispensable ally, economic competitor, and potential geostrategic rival. This diversity in U.S. assessments is not surprising because the international role of Europe changed considerably several times in the past hundred years and has been changing once more since 1991. Therefore, any understanding of Europe's role cannot rely on simple extrapolation of earlier periods. This applies to images derived from pre-1945 history but also to those extrapolating Europe's Cold War role.

For a century, from 1815 to 1914, the concert of European great powers, guided by British hegemony, was central to world politics. The rivalry among European powers was contained for decades in a system of alliances, but it erupted in two world wars from 1914 to 1945, reduced the exhausted European powers to the second rank, and brought about the dominance of two superpowers, the United States and the Soviet Union. During the bipolar confrontation of the United States and the Soviet Union, Europe was divided into spheres of influence of the two superpowers responsible for security in Western and Eastern Europe, while European powers were allocated roles as junior allies in the North Atlantic Treaty Organization (NATO) and the Warsaw Pact, respectively. However, since 1991, Europe's emancipation from post-1945 dependence has entered a new phase: after four decades of economic emancipation, Europe was taking steps toward security emancipation. This involved a redefinition of Europe's role in the transatlantic relationship and of the U.S. role in Europe.

This chapter presents the mutual role conceptions of the transatlantic partners. The question of whether the United States needs Europe and vice versa is approached in a comparison of several answers to the question. Together with this range of role conceptions, their underlying assumptions regarding the relative power of the European Union (EU) and the United States are discussed. Since claimed roles and ascribed roles are influenced by perceptions (and misperceptions) of relative power, the role conceptions are assessed for their adequacy as responses to observable changes of relative power.

U.S. ROLE CONCEPTIONS

The roles played by states in the international arena depend on but are not directly determined by their power. Instead, claimed roles (role conceptions about self) and ascribed roles (role conceptions for others) are negotiated and constructed on the basis of past, present, and future power, but they are also affected by past and present role conceptions. Objective power is very hard to estimate because it depends on diverse factors of varying relevance in different situations. Finding appropriate role constructions is even harder because rational assessment can be overwhelmed by flattering memories of past supremacy or comforting hopes for future grandeur. An additional difficulty is the need to adjust roles to the ongoing change of relative power, even if this change does not amount to a counterhegemonic challenge on which hegemony theory tends to focus.

During the second half of the twentieth century, the role of European powers such as Britain, France, Germany, or Italy was that of junior allies of the United States in the NATO alliance. This was still the benchmark for roles ascribed to Europe by U.S. analysts after the Cold War. Some continued to regard Europeans as valuable junior allies capable of more burden sharing, aiding the United States no longer against the Soviet Union but against global terrorism. Others saw a diminished relevance of Europe, irrelevant as military nonentity and even no longer relevant as the likely central theater of war. On the other hand, there were those noticing an increased importance of Europe, either as junior ally making a greater contribution or as indispensable (but still junior) ally and partner in the West. A minority went further, suggesting that the United States should accept Europe as equal partner and autonomous actor in an emerging multipolar world.

Habits of Half a Century: U.S. Leadership and Burden-Sharing European Allies

For half a century, the role of the United States had been to provide leadership and superior military capabilities to NATO while European allies contributed conventional forces to the alliance. The United States had been the indispensable nation and NATO–Europe the indispensable ally, and together they formed the most powerful alliance on the globe. This role conception became habitual and shaped the perceptions of politicians and military officers. As a prized possession in the post-1945 US global sphere of influence, "Europe is America's essential geopolitical bridgehead on the Eurasian continent. America's geostrategic stake in Europe is enormous. Unlike America's links with Japan, the Atlantic alliance entrenches American influence and military power directly on the European mainland." Therefore, the transatlantic alliance was essential for U.S. power since "without close transatlantic ties, America's primacy in Eurasia promptly fades away."[1]

A more flexible characterization of these roles was offered by Henry Kissinger. Even before becoming national security adviser to President Nixon in the 1970s, he was aware of the relative decline of U.S. supremacy compared to the unique and transitory situation immediately after World War II, although the United States remained by far the stronger partner.[2] He advocated a rebalancing of the Atlantic Alliance by granting the Europeans a somewhat greater role in return for more burden sharing. Thus, Kissinger was an early witness for the relative rise of Europe. Nevertheless, Kissinger expressed a "paternalistic view of Europe's importance"[3] in his proposed Atlantic charter. In stating that "diplomacy . . . is essentially conducted by traditional nation states," he implied that the United States could act as hegemon in bilateral relations with European nations and ignore the EEC as a bloc. He clearly delimited Europe's modest role: "The United States has global interests and responsibilities. Our European allies have regional interests."[4] Later he underestimated the cumulative effect of European integration since the 1960s, especially the qualitative change during the 1990s, after the Cold War. He continued to regard Europe as junior partner when he suggested a "Transatlantic Free Trade Area" and an "Atlantic Steering Group" in order to supplement the military alliance by closer economic and political coordination.[5]

Continuity of roles was also suggested by Robert Wilkie, adviser to Republican U.S. Senate Leader Trent Lott and previously adviser to Senator Jesse Helms. Unlike Kagan's neoconservative polemic dismissal of NATO allies, Wilkie's article reflected the thinking about the role of Europe among more traditional U.S. Republicans: "In sum, the onus for the successful transition of the Atlantic Alliance to the grim realities of the 21st century is on the

Europeans. For six decades they have prospered under the American nuclear umbrella and behind our trip-wire conventional presence on the continent."[6] In this view, major modifications of the transatlantic alliance were not considered necessary. Wilkie merely presented a new version of the demand for greater burden sharing without, however, offering a greater share in the control of NATO in return for greater European contributions.

This American conception of Europe's role had firm roots in the experiences of the Cold War period. However, after 1991, it was losing credibility, first because Europe was no longer facing a major military threat and second because U.S. disengagement had already been taking place throughout the 1990s in spite of regular assertions by all sides that NATO and U.S. leadership still constituted the unchanging bedrock of European security.

Unilateralists Dismissing an Alliance with Europe

In the neoconservative perspective of Robert Kagan, NATO–Europe was no longer the indispensable ally. With absolute U.S. supremacy in a unipolar world, even the asymmetrical roles of the previous 50 years overestimated Europe's potential. A weak Europe was not even strong enough to be a useful junior ally in NATO. If U.S. supremacy was greater than ever before, the transatlantic alliance would either be lopsided (with Europeans as very junior partner), or it would become irrelevant because a supreme United States did not need a weak Europe. According to unilateralists, the United States was better off without meddling European allies demanding influence but not contributing military capabilities. In a unipolar era, the only superpower no longer needed Europe and had to focus on other regions.

The assumption that Europe was weak and irrelevant while the United States enjoyed unchallenged supremacy suggested that the United States could act unilaterally, neither fearing competitors nor requiring allies. Only weak countries needed foreign policies centered on multilateralism and international law and institutions, with a preference for the use of nonmilitary instruments, according to Kagan. On the other hand, strong countries such as the United States were able to face a harsh world of conflicts and were better off using their military strength. European weakness attempted to entangle U.S. strength in a net of institutions, rules, and multilateral negotiations, but the United States should overcome this. In the nineteenth century, European powers still ruled the world; in the late twentieth century, Europe was still at the center of world politics in a passive sense, as the potential battlefield in an all-out war between the United States and the Soviet Union. However, after 1991, Europe had lost even this passive "strategic centrality."[7] Thus, the United States should ignore Europeans and their foreign policies born out of weakness.

This assessment of Europe's potential by Kagan was an echo of an argument heard earlier from neoclassical economists claiming that the welfare state and regulated labor markets were undermining Europe's long-term competitiveness. Europe was bound to suffer from so-called Eurosclerosis because Christian Democrats, Social Democrats, and Greens had guided Europe's economic policies away from the pure gospel of deregulation and monetarism. The facts of economic history over half a century did not support this view, but economic dogma obscured facts. In 1950, the United States alone produced twice the total of Western Europe's industrial production. By 2000, Western Europe's economies equaled that of the United States. Just like the neoclassical arguments against the social market economy had failed to appreciate Europe's economic potential, now Kagan's arguments failed to notice the EU's geostrategic potential.

The Project for the New American Century and Krauthammer's "Unipolar Era"

Kagan's role conception for the United States and Europe corresponded to the views of the Project for the New American Century (PNAC) think tank, arguing that it was desirable and possible to perpetuate the "American Century" announced by Henry Luce in the 1940s. The twenty-first century would be dominated by the United States even more than the twentieth if the United States only pursued its destiny energetically. This opportunity was, according to the 1997 Statement of Principles of the PNAC, being wasted by the Clinton administration's "cuts in foreign affairs and defense spending" and its "inconstant leadership," making it "increasingly difficult to sustain American influence around the world."[8] Members of PNAC, including Donald Rumsfeld, Richard Cheney, and Paul Wolfowitz, who were to become prominent members of the Bush administration, were less interested in balanced budgets than in U.S. primacy backed by overwhelming military strength. Their disdain for Clinton's budget-driven policies resulted in a strategy ignoring budgetary restraints, adopted by the incoming Bush administration in 2001.

In its first term, the Bush administration followed the Euro-skeptic and unilateralist views articulated by PNAC. The lesson drawn from the Kosovo crisis of 1998–99 was that Europe was weak and meddlesome; it could be dealt with by dividing Atlanticist "new Europe" from recalcitrant "old Europe." At best, the alliance could be used as a toolbox to assemble coalitions of the willing when needed.

Critics of the PNAC position suggested that U.S. supremacy was limited in its quality and duration. Therefore, the United States had to husband resources by practicing a more restrained hegemony. In particular, the transatlantic alliance had to be renewed as a more balanced partnership; otherwise, it could become irrelevant because the EU would not need the United States. The PNAC position presupposed a very unipolar distribution of power between the United States and the rest of the world. However, if the strategies proposed by PNAC and adopted by the Bush administration were based on an overestimation of U.S. potential power, the result would be a costly waste of resources. By alienating allies, an overly ambitious PNAC strategy could shorten the unipolar moment by squandering U.S. soft power, especially the acceptance of U.S. leadership by allied elites. Indeed, the escalating budget deficits of the Bush administration signaled the need to return to a more budget-driven strategy as practiced by the Clinton administration so despised by PNAC.

In reality, the United States was "preeminent, not omnipotent," whereas the overly ambitious neoconservative strategy was "premised on a radically inflated view of American power."[9] The unjustified "assumption that U.S. primacy is here to stay" was breeding complacency and unilateralism.[10] Contrary to PNAC expectations, the unilateralist approach would squander the foundations of U.S. primacy. The overestimation of temporary U.S. supremacy by the Bush administration was bound to backfire by provoking other powers into counterbalancing, and the transition to multipolarity would be unnecessarily acrimonious. However, the intellectuals around PNAC and U.S. leaders in the Bush administration were fully convinced that unilateralism was justified in a unipolar era, while European weakness had rendered the transatlantic alliance irrelevant.

If unipolarity was here to stay, the confident unilateralism advocated by PNAC was a feasible strategy for the Bush administration. On the other hand, if "global politics has . . . moved from the bipolar system of the Cold War through a unipolar moment—highlighted by the Gulf War—and is now passing through one or two uni-multipolar decades before it enters a truly multipolar 21st century,"[11] then the United States should adopt a more multilateralist stance, preparing for a role as one of several great powers. Samuel P. Huntington argued that "the United States could find life as a major power in a multipolar world less demanding, less contentious, and more rewarding than it was as the world's only superpower."[12]

Transatlantic Habits Renewed: An Essential Ally under Benign Hegemony

While unilateralists were happy to reduce NATO to a toolbox for coalitions of the willing, a variety of other voices still appreciated the value of the transatlantic alliance as a vehicle for U.S. leadership. For example, if the world was to be shaped by a "clash of civilizations," as suggested by Huntington,[13] Europe's relevance as ally had even increased after 1991. During the Cold War, the global alliance network led by the United States had been held together by a shared opposition to the Soviet bloc, but after the end of ideological conflicts, Huntington expected that cultural fault lines were to shape international conflicts. Huntington's expected pattern of conflict also implied future alliance options. The West could no longer be a global anticommunist alliance but was bound to shrink to a core sharing a Christian-European civilization with the United States. This implied that Europe was the most significant ally, more indispensable than middle powers such as Canada or Australia, and more reliable than Japan with its East Asian culture.

The transatlantic alliance had been the centerpiece of international order during the Cold War, and it was still the most important alliance of the United States even after 1991. Kissinger claimed that it was "not an exaggeration to say that the future of democratic government as we understand it depends on whether the democracies bordering the North Atlantic manage to revitalize their relations in a world without Cold War."[14] He deplored the transformation of NATO from an alliance into a collective security arrangement and questioned the European duplicity of relying on U.S. efforts without much burden sharing while also challenging U.S. leadership. Instead, he proposed a vision for a future transatlantic relationship in a changed security environment. Extending the New Atlanticism of President George H. W. Bush and the New Transatlantic Agenda of President Clinton, Kissinger suggested a combination of an Atlantic Steering Group for political coordination, NATO for military coordination, and a Transatlantic Free Trade Association as a vehicle of economic integration, eventually to be merged with the North American Free Trade Association (NAFTA).

This arrangement had the implied purpose of making sure that the economic emancipation of Europe did not undermine overarching U.S. control over European security. NATO was to be reinforced, while the EU's security role was to remain subordinate. At the same time, the strength of the EU as an economic bloc speaking with one voice in the World Trade Organization (WTO) was to be softened by integrating it with NAFTA. While Kissinger rejected the European tactic of forming a caucus and then confronting the United States with an inflexible united position, his model suggested that the United States and Europe communicate in a U.S.-dominated forum.

Perpetuating U.S. leadership by making limited concessions to Europe was Kissinger's response to increased European economic power in the 1960s. More than 30 years later, he was once more suggesting limited role adjustments. Kissinger's new transatlantic agenda attempted to perpetuate U.S. security leadership by relaxing the reins of subordination while trying to tie Europe's economy into a transatlantic free trade area. Binding Europe's economy to the United States at a time when past U.S. economic supremacy had not disappeared completely was perhaps also capable of preventing deeper European integration by diluting the EU in a larger North Atlantic Free Trade Area, together with the United States, Canada, and Mexico.

U.S. Leadership through Institutions and Soft Power

In contrast to neoconservative assumptions of unlimited supremacy, G. John Ikenberry pointed out that the United States was "preeminent, not omnipotent."[15] Implicitly criticizing the hubris of Richard Cheney and Donald Rumsfeld, he suggested that U.S. supremacy was limited in its strength and duration. Instead of carefully husbanding U.S. power resources, the Bush administration's unilateralism and military adventures unintentionally shortened the unipolar moment, bringing U.S. hegemony to an unnecessarily fast end. By contrast, Ikenberry pointed to the example of Presidents Roosevelt and Truman, who had translated the U.S. supremacy of the mid-1940s into stable global leadership through institution building. American self-restraint in operating through multilateral institutions such as the United Nations, the Bretton Woods framework, and NATO achieved a favorable "institutional bargain" because it resulted in willing acceptance of U.S. leadership by a global network of allies.[16] Roosevelt's multilateralism was a method of institutionalizing supremacy. This achievement was threatened by a Bush administration opting for the deceptive benefits of unilateralism since 2001.

American leadership depended not only on military supremacy but also on "soft power."[17] The latter included not only the pervasive influence of U.S. media and popular culture but also the legitimacy of U.S. primacy and the willingness of other countries to follow the lead of the United States. This goodwill was being wasted by the exclusive reliance of the Bush administration on military supremacy. Such unilateralist arrogance was provoking counterbalancing behavior and accelerated the end of U.S. primacy. Instead of relying solely on military power, a more enduring form of U.S. hegemony could be pursued using many sources of power, including stable institutionalized leadership, the goodwill of allies, and the consensual legitimacy achieved through consultation.

Critics of neoconservative unilateralism allocated to Europe a relevant role as indispensable ally. Yet they still envisaged Europe as junior partner in an alliance led by the United States without acknowledging the post-1991 potential for European autonomy. The post-1945 role of Europe was only marginally upgraded to that of an essential helper in the coming clash of civilizations.

U.S. Hegemony with Greater Concessions: "Europe First"—Dialogue with the EU

More concessions to European role claims were suggested in the "Europe-first" approach articulated by researchers at the Brookings Institution. Unlike neoconservative unilateralists, they regarded the transatlantic alliance as essential for U.S. foreign policy. And unlike traditional Atlanticists advocating continuity in the alliance, they argued for major adjustments in the roles of the transatlantic partners. The greatest concession by the United States was to be a willingness to deal with Europeans as a bloc, not as a loose collection of individual states. This shift toward EU–U.S. dialogue envisaged a much more equitable transatlantic relationship than the traditional preference for NATO as a forum underlining U.S. leadership. Even Zbigniew Brzezinski, who had earlier argued that hegemony could be prolonged by keeping the vassals divided, argued for adapting alliance structures. "As Europe gradually and hesitantly unifies, the internal structure and processes of NATO will have to adjust. . . . One cannot someday have a truly united Europe and yet have an alliance that remains integrated on the basis of one superpower plus fifteen dependent powers. . . . NATO will have to be altered on the basis of a 1 + 1 (US + EU) formula."[18]

This Europe-first approach implied an end to the "NATO-first" option with its entrenched asymmetrical roles, the United States as leader, and Europeans as junior allies. While it was still possible to prolong past asymmetrical roles within NATO or in bilateral relations with EU members, it was no longer advisable to do so. Instead, it could be more productive to accept a diminished leadership role in a less unequal relation with the EU as a whole. Ivo Daalder and James M. Goldgeier also questioned a "Russia-first" approach, that is, the continued Cold War pattern of prioritizing relations with the other military superpower while relegating Europe to a junior role. In the Europe-first approach, the United States should deal with the EU bloc as a whole instead of trying to exercise bilateral influence on each European nation separately.[19] While it might be successful in the short run, it would create long-term costs of resentment without being able to stop the eventual outcome. The United States should accept that the EU was acting as a bloc and becoming a powerful partner in a more symmetrical relationship.

Accepting the EU as relevant partner while also continuing U.S. primacy was a difficult balancing act. Brzezinski welcomed EU expansion because a "larger Europe will expand the range of American influence." Yet the EU should not create "a Europe politically so integrated that it could soon challenge the United States on geopolitical matters of high importance to America elsewhere, particularly in the Middle East." Obstructing greater European unity "could prove calamitous for stability in Eurasia and thus also for America's own interest."[20] Therefore, the EU had to be accepted as regional stabilizer but prevented from becoming a challenger.

The Europe-first approach with its softening of U.S. leadership could satisfy European Atlanticists by giving them a more respected role in the transatlantic alliance and extend U.S. hegemony by making it more benign and nonthreatening. The transatlantic relationship could be adapted taking into account S. Walt's argument that antihegemonic counterbalancing would emerge only if hegemony was perceived as threatening but not automatically from a hegemonic balance of power itself.[21] The United States as benign, nonthreatening hegemon would be welcome to European Atlanticists but was unlikely to satisfy Europeanist desires for autonomy, except as a transitory position on the way to a balanced partnership.

U.S. Shaping Transition to Multipolarity: Partnership with an Autonomous EU

Contrary to the expectation that the unipolar moment was turning into a lasting unipolar era, the United States had to prepare for a soft landing after the end of unipolarity, according to Charles A. Kupchan. In his view, the leadership role of the United States in Europe was coming to an end. Accepting this gracefully could lay the foundation for good relations between the

United States and Europe in the coming multipolar world. "While they have the luxury of doing so, the United States and its main regional partners should begin to imagine life after Pax Americana."[22] The end of U.S. leadership in Europe was also envisaged by Ted Galen Carpenter of the Cato Institute. "Washington's preeminence began in the context of a Western Europe that was devastated and demoralized by World War II and had to face a potentially lethal security threat. It is unrealistic to believe that, more than half a century later, a prosperous, capable and confident Europe will forever defer to the United States."[23]

The grand strategy of the United States had the task of managing the transition to multipolarity. Instead of wasting energy on the counterproductive attempt to perpetuate primacy, the United States "should get ahead of the curve and seek to shape the global transition that is now under way and picking up speed."[24] Even now, when still strong enough to bypass international institutions, the United States should take a multilateralist approach. Institutions consolidated now would be even more useful in the future when the United States was likely to need them. Therefore, the United States should exercise strategic restraint and cede space to the emerging European rival willingly. Instead of practicing unilateralism and isolationism in a contradictory combination, the United States should adopt a new restrained internationalism.

Europe was already the most significant emerging competitor of the United States. The EU's economic potential already rivaled the United States, and the EU was an emerging strategic actor. While China's challenge depended on further decades of high economic growth, the EU's economic potential already equaled that of the United States. This existing potential merely had to be integrated and translated into increasingly unified foreign policy. "Europe will soon catch up with America not because of a superior economy or technological base, but because it is coming together, amassing impressive resources and intellectual capital possessed by its constituent states."[25] In this situation, it would be unwise if U.S. leaders tried to continue past role claims. Instead, U.S. grand strategy should move ahead of the curve, make the most of unipolarity while it lasted, and shape an institutional framework for a multipolar world.

Renewing the Alliance: Council on Foreign Relations Multilateralism versus PNAC Unilateralism

On the one hand, the practitioners of unilateralism in the Bush administration and their intellectual backers in PNAC suggested that the only superpower did not need the alliance with weak and meddlesome Europeans. On the other hand, there was a variety of voices arguing that the transatlantic alliance should be continued, repaired, renewed, or rebalanced. A blend of these voices contributed to a 2004 report by a task force of the influential Council on Foreign Relations (CFR) reminding U.S. leaders that Europe was an indispensable ally. The report highlighted that the United States and the EU were one another's most important economic partners in trade and foreign direct investment. The economic interdependence across the North Atlantic surpassed all other interregional economic relations. Furthermore, cooperation should extend beyond economics to security issues. Even after the Cold War, the transatlantic alliance was still necessary. Conflicts of interest should not be exacerbated by polemical rhetoric. Instead of deepening the transatlantic rift, an effort should be made to renew the alliance.[26]

The CFR report recommended that personality clashes and stylistic differences should be overcome in order to renew the alliance. This was put into practice in early 2005 when President George W. Bush and Secretary of State Condoleezza Rice visited several European capitals[27] signaling a certain shift away from the earlier unilateralist disdain for Europe.

EUROPEAN ROLE CONCEPTIONS

Atlanticist Habits of Half a Century: European Security Needs U.S. Leadership

On the European side, options ranged from the French ambition to develop *Europe puissance*, or an autonomous geostrategic actor equal to the United States, to the Atlanticist acceptance of benign U.S. hegemony. In the view of European Atlanticists, U.S. leadership in NATO not only had been welcome during the Cold War but was still essential to guarantee Europe's security. NATO had to be retained as security framework for Europe, implying continued U.S. leadership. This view was shared by the United Kingdom, Denmark, and other Atlanticists among the old EU members. Strong Atlanticist views were also held among the governments of CEE countries joining the EU in May 2004. The future role of Europeans was that of reliable partners in an alliance led by the United States. The greater economic potential of Europe should be used for a more effective military contribution to NATO. Europe still needed the United States, but Europeans had to spend more on "burden sharing" and closing the "capabilities gap" in order to earn the right to be consulted by the United States.

Yet in the renegotiation of transatlantic roles since 1991, the most fundamental fact was that the old Atlanticism was coming to an end. Neither for the United States nor for Western Europeans would transatlantic security relations remain as important as they had been from 1949 to 1989. This could be accepted by unilateralists and primacists in the United States without much sorrow, and on the European side, the end of Atlanticism was readily acceptable for Europeanists (and Gaullists). Accepting it will be much more painful for those who warned against the deepening of the transatlantic rift, against the willful damage inflicted by Rumsfeld's unilateralism and French *Europe puissance* rhetoric.

Atlanticists wanted the United States involved as Western European balancer. Conflicts between European powers, especially German ambitions to challenge the established powers Britain and France, had been the main cause of war in the early twentieth century. In the foundation years of the transatlantic alliance, memories of World War II were still lively, and Western Europeans appreciated that U.S. military presence was a guarantee against a revival of German nationalist ambitions. One can assume that this aspect of U.S. presence in Europe even resonated with Soviet leaders and generals. Half a century later, Atlanticists still wanted the United States as Western European balancer. In early 1990, when German unification was imminent, British Prime Minister Margaret Thatcher and her advisers were alarmed enough to discuss the threat potential of a united Germany. Some still assumed that U.S. disengagement from Europe could still unleash German ambitions to dominate Europe, a fear appearing not only in the imagination of French novelist Alain Crémieux but also in articles by experts on international relations.[28]

This justification for continued U.S. leadership in European security was, however, questionable. Several decades of European integration had habituated Germans to a multilateral approach. When German unification in 1990 awakened the fear of renewed instability, French President Mitterrand and German Chancellor Kohl took the initiative to suggest deeper European integration in order to avoid renationalization of European security. Deeper integration was to include monetary union as well as a common foreign and security policy in order to make Germany even more European. Thus, the traditional Atlanticist method of inviting the United States as European balancer could be superseded by the new Europeanist method of absorbing Germany into an EU functioning as security community. The more the EU integrated and adopted a security role, the less U.S. presence in Europe would be necessary to prevent German nationalist ambitions.

The Netherlands was an example of a smaller Western European country welcoming U.S. engagement as a counterbalance against possible domination by continental neighbors France and Germany. However, even Dutch politicians felt that Atlanticist options became less feasible as the United States gradually withdrew from Europe[29] and less urgent as France and Germany were tied into European integration.

For Atlanticists, the United States was also a cultural model, a liberal corrective against European nationalism and traditionalism on the right but also against European radicalism and socialism on the left. In the 1950s, the United States was not only technologically most advanced and militarily the strongest. It was also a model of liberal democracy with an appealing modern culture. While the terms "modern," "progressive," and "Western" were used synonymously with "American," Europe needed the transatlantic link to be fully part of the West. Yet the debate about a transatlantic value gap around the time of the Iraq War of 2003 indicated that European intellectuals no longer perceived "the West" as an undivided value community. At the level of popular opinion, positive attitudes to the United States declined among Europeans from the historically high levels of the 1950s, while intellectuals discovered a value gap. For many Europeans, the United States was now characterized by fundamentalist evangelical religiosity, the death penalty, questionable presidential elections (as in 2000), the absence of significant Social Democratic and Green parties, environmental recklessness, and insular ignorance of the world outside the United States. No longer a country of political, intellectual, and moral progress, United States showed symptoms of backwardness and could no longer be the role model for "the West."

In spite of this recent discovery of a transatlantic value gap, Atlanticists views were widely held among European politicians and voters whose attitudes had been shaped by NATO's role during the Cold War decades. The particular strength of Atlanticist opinions in several countries was signaled in the Letter of Eight (late January 2003) and the Letter of Ten (early February 2003), in which leaders of a number of current and prospective EU members expressed their support for President Bush and rejected France's and Germany's attempt to block the invasion of Iraq in the UN Security Council. Indeed, U.S. experts expected Atlanticism in the EU to grow stronger with the inclusion of new CEE members in May 2004.[30]

Bridging Role for Britain: "Special Relationship" with the United States

In the case of the United Kingdom, a general Atlanticist orientation was bolstered by the "special relationship" with the United States. This gave the United Kingdom an important "bridging role" between the United States and continental Europe. Skeptical observers claimed that the special relationship was more self-deception than reality. It allowed Britain the feeling that it was not just a part of Europe but could play a global role on its own, not through the EU. It also gave Britain the impression that it had influence on U.S. decision making. British prime ministers from Harold Macmillan to Tony Blair valued the special relationship. While the United Kingdom no longer had the weight to act as a global power, it still had a distinctive role to play, a "pivotal role," in the words of Tony Blair.[31] By placing the United Kingdom halfway between the United States and continental Europe, these British leaders hoped to maximize British influence on the United States while also enhancing Britain's role in Europe as the only EU member with a global perspective and special access in Washington. Thus, British Atlanticists saw not only general benefits for all members of the transatlantic alliance but also more specific benefits for Britain. The bridging role promised to give the United Kingdom significance far greater than any deeper involvement in the EU.

Yet the United Kingdom's influence on U.S. decision making appeared to be marginal, and its distance from European integration did not strengthen British claims for a leading role in Europe. Britain on its own was too small to be heard in Washington, whereas a unified European voice would have influence. William Wallace, an academic linked to Britain's third party, the Liberal

Democrats, regarded the special relationship as self-delusion, recommending instead closer cooperation with EU partners.[32] However, both the ruling Labour Party and the Conservatives continued the habitual special relationship together with half-reluctant membership in the EU.

New Atlanticists in CEE: Belonging to the West through Alliance with the United States

The new members of NATO and the EU in CEE adopted strongly Atlanticist positions. Especially Poland expected much from joining NATO in 1999. After long historical experiences with Russian and German domination and aggression, Poland regarded very close links with the United States as essential guarantees of security and sovereignty. In Western Europe, after the security dependence of the preceding decades, U.S. hegemony had become less necessary and less welcome no matter how benign it was; for CEE countries, on the other hand, after "the direct hegemony of their neighbours," their newly won sovereignty was hardly threatened by a "situation in which the hegemon is a far away country and a non-imperialistic liberal democracy."[33] For Western Europeans, the EU was a vehicle of emancipation from post-1945 U.S. hegemony; yet for Poland especially, benign U.S. hegemony was an insurance against Russia and Germany, whereas the EU could easily fall under the hegemony of the "Franco-German monster"[34] if the United States stopped acting as balancer.

Furthermore, Atlanticism also promised Poland a special role as the leading country in CEE in a special relationship with the United States. "At the beginning of the 1990s the US was seen mainly as a security provider, now the ties are perceived more as a political asset that might increase Poland's role in Europe, especially as a counterbalance to Franco-German leadership."[35] Poland saw itself "fast emerging as the US' key ally and its protégé in the east."[36] It accepted "a $3.8 billion loan from the US Congress to purchase 48 F-16s from Lockheed Martin." This "choice in defence procurement of US rather than European systems is a firm expression of Warsaw's Atlanticist credentials."[37]

However, disappointment was setting in much faster and much more dramatically than in Western Europe, where Atlanticism had lasted six decades. "The Atlanticism of the CEE states may have begun to erode as a consequence of their costly and largely unrewarded involvement in Iraq," although they "will certainly support the continuation of the US's involvement in European security."[38]

A second reason for ebbing Atlanticism in CEE was the changing nature of NATO. By the time Poland, the Czech Republic, and Hungary joined in 1999, it was no longer the military alliance the new members imagined it to be. While especially Poland expected NATO to retain an anti-Russian posture, the alliance made an effort to strengthen Russia's association with NATO in order to soften the perception that NATO expansion constituted a threat to Russia.

Poland "believed that the Atlantic Alliance's ultimate strength rested on its collective defense commitment" and "wanted to join a NATO in which the leading role of the US would never be questioned." Thus, Poland opposed French–German initiatives because "ESDP [European Security and Defense Policy] must not challenge the US presence and role on the continent and must be kept within a NATO framework." Yet Polish fears that NATO was becoming an "organization for collective security at the expense of its central defense mission" were coming true in spite of efforts to prove that Poland "was a staunch ally of the US and its leadership role in the alliance."[39]

Doubts about Atlanticism grew quickly as the Polish government realized that a special relationship with the United States was not a viable strategy. By 2005, Poland had second thoughts about its involvement in Iraq and about the purchase of F-16 fighters from Lockheed Martin. The government intended to withdraw troops from Iraq before the end of 2005 because popular support was declining and Polish business had not been able to sign big contracts in Iraq. Regarding the F-16 purchase, U.S. promises of technology transfer and contracts for Polish companies had disappointing outcomes. After a costly but rather fast apprenticeship, Poland began to turn to the realization that its interests were in Europe. "Poland—and this is a sea-change in the attitude—clearly recognizes that in the course of time, the EU will become the equal partner of NATO. Important is, however, that it will be a natural process driven by a common-sense since any political haste or institutional competition may result in undermining NATO as well as the CESDP [Common European Security and Defense Policy]."[40]

Two factors will, in the long run, dampen the Atlanticist enthusiasm of CEE states: first, the reduction of the U.S. military presence in Europe as an indicator of NATO's transformation into a looser security community, and, second, the long-term effect of cooperation in the EU reducing historical fears between neighbors and making a common security policy more credible.

Europe Puissance Counterbalancing U.S. Hyperpower

French foreign policy had, for half a century, pursued the objective of creating a European bloc capable of playing a global role independent of the superpowers. In President Charles de Gaulle's vision of a "Europe of nations," other states would eventually rally behind France's bid to reclaim a role on the world stage. The Gaullist approach to European integration advocated intergovernmental cooperation by sovereign nations rather than building supranational institutions. Yet the Gaullist vision of a geostrategic role for Europe could not be realized without deep European integration involving a sacrifice of French sovereignty incompatible with Gaullism. The other flaw of the Gaullist vision was that Western Europe was still too weak and disunited in de Gaulle's time to claim a global role successfully. Nevertheless, driven by a mixture of Gaullist and Europeanist motives, France persistently worked for *Europe puissance* during the Cold War and even more so after 1991.

French Foreign Minister Hubert Védrine described the United States as "hyperpower"[41] that needed to be counterbalanced. Therefore, the EU had to work for a transition to a multipolar world, not out of anti-American sentiments but for the sake of stability. In a unipolar world, the United States was a problem, but in a multipolar world, relations with a preeminent United States could be positive. For Europeans, the unilateralism of the Bush administration in its first term did much to give credibility to the description of the United States as hyperpower. In the United States, the Védrine option provoked heated opposition and much anti-French rhetoric from neoconservatives. Even calmer responses, such as the 2004 report of the task force of the CFR, warned that "casting the EU as a counterweight to the United States, even if only for rhetorical purposes," would "surely fuel transatlantic tension."[42]

The desirability of the Védrine option depended on a perception of the United States as an overbearing hyperpower. The viability of counterbalancing, however, presupposed the decline of U.S. supremacy and the creation of EU political unity. For the promoters of *Europe puissance*, U.S. foreign policy was deeply flawed. Old U.S. traditions, such as exceptionalism, Manichaeanism, and unilateralism, together with the new facts of military supremacy and the radical terrorist threat, created "a temptation to behave imperially," turning into frustration when interventions turned into quagmires.[43] In response to such shortcomings, Europeans should try to moderate U.S. mood swings by close transatlantic cooperation while also developing European military capacities.

The U.S. tradition of exceptionalism accepted "entangling alliances" only when the United States could dominate them. Foreign policy in the United States turned multilateralist only after victorious wars while still reserving the right to act unilaterally. After September 11, 2001, blunt unilateralism prevailed, unmitigated by the instrumental use of multilateralism. Even U.S. experts arguing for multilateral and pro-European policies saw multilateralism only as an avenue to minimize costs and were still in favor of unilateralism when it counted.

The U.S. military avoided "civilian tasks" such as peacekeeping, preferring instead high-altitude bombing: "Such use of air power could in particular reduce the risk of ground combat, of becoming bogged down in a Vietnam-type of quagmire and of 'mission creep' leading to the military taking on unrewarding, dangerous 'civilian' tasks. Even prior to the war in Kosovo, military or ex-military authors like presidential candidate Bush's adviser John Hillen, justified . . . reluctance to become involved in peacekeeping, with the catch-phrase 'superpowers don't do [i.e., clean] windows.' "[44] This claim that superpowers were above mundane tasks was, according to Pierre Hassner, a weakness. A country that relied on high-altitude bombing and Special Forces was not capable of peacekeeping, interposition and nation building.

The events of September 11, 2001, had made U.S. foreign policy more simplistic: "In two hours" these events "gave Bush a foreign policy that can be summed up in three words: war on terrorism. . . . In a way it could be said that the relative ignorance of the outside world shared by George Bush and the majority of Americans meant that they were immediately . . . on the same frequency: the incomprehensible bolt from the blue of 11 September was bound to herald a radically new era and an uncompromising enemy to be eradicated—radically. . . . 'We have found our mission,' George Bush declared."[45]

Opposing such flawed policies was not only desirable but also viable. At first impression, the supremacy of a hyperpower would condemn counterbalancing to failure, inviting instead "bandwagoning," that is, minor powers rallying behind an overwhelmingly powerful leader. Yet the advocates of *Europe puissance* were encouraged by claims that U.S. power was in relative decline. American supremacy was real enough to warrant counterbalancing but not durable enough to make it hopeless. According to French writer Emmanuel Todd, the U.S. empire was declining, and its unilateral use of superior military force was no more than "theatrical militarism."[46] From 1990 to 1995, the United States downgraded its global military involvement trying to balance the trade deficit, whereas remilitarization since 1999 was a response to "growing economic vulnerability."[47] The success of Emmanuel Todd's best seller signaled a widespread willingness to find symptoms of the relative decline of U.S. power, although Todd's "obituary" exaggerated this relative decline to proclaim the imminent demise of U.S. hegemony. Finally, the *Europe puissance* option was also predicated on the success of the EU's common foreign and security policy proclaimed in 1991.

If the United States could be understood as a hyperpower with a sense of mission but with limited understanding of the world outside, then the most appropriate response had to be *Europe puissance*. If U.S. supremacy was serious but not durable and if the EU succeeded with a Common Foreign and Security Policy (CFSP) and ESDP, counterbalancing was a viable option. Then a multipolar power constellation could be achieved in which the United States was no longer tempted by hyperpower hubris, accepting instead a balanced transatlantic relationship.

Movable Compromise: Juggling Atlanticist and Europeanist Options

It was desirable and possible to combine Atlanticism and European integration: this was the guideline characterizing West German foreign policy since the 1950s. Close relations with the United States and reconciliation with France demonstrated that the Federal Republic of Germany (FRG) had become part of the West. In the early 1990s, united Germany renewed its commitment to multilateralism through NATO and the EU. The FRG promoted the expansion of NATO into CEE as well as deeper European integration.

In the past, these two objectives had occasionally clashed, as in 1963, when an Atlanticist preamble was attached by Germany's parliament to the Elysée Treaty,[48] intended by President de Gaulle and Chancellor Adenauer to be the beginning of a Franco-German core of independent European power. Nevertheless, the FRG had always pursued close relations with both the United States and France. It was only between 1998 and 2003, from the Kosovo crisis to the Iraq War, that reconciling Atlanticism and Europeanism became difficult once more, when NATO's viability as military alliance was seriously questioned while the EU began to implement a common security and defense policy (ESDP).

For other countries, the balancing of Atlanticist and Europeanist priorities took a different form. France promoted *Europe puissance* consistently but also rejoined NATO's military committee in December 1995, having participated in NATO's political organs only since 1966. Britain's Euro-skepticism prevented it from joining the common currency in 1999, and its Atlanticist orientation made it the major ally of the United States in the 2003 Iraq War. Yet Britain also advanced European defense integration as far as it was compatible with NATO's primacy. Britain's position had shifted toward accepting autonomous EU capabilities in the British–French St Malo agreement of 1998. It shifted even further when Britain first rejected the 2003 Tervuren proposal of EU military headquarters independent of NATO but later agreed with France and Germany to establish an EU planning cell. "But in a measure of the proposal's sensitivity, the three countries did not use the word 'headquarters,' in order to avoid the impression that the military structure could compete with the North Atlantic Treaty Organization."[49] This gave the EU its own capacity to plan military missions without, however, openly challenging NATO's primacy.

The Netherlands was a founding member of the EEC but always clearly Atlanticist in security policy. However, a slow shift occurred toward an acceptance that U.S. military presence was declining and U.S. involvement in Europe changing. In Poland, Atlanticism had peaked in 2003 and began to decline with the disappointment about meager rewards for joining the so-called coalition of the willing in Iraq.[50]

In spite of these observable shifts, it was still an exaggeration to pronounce "the end of Atlanticism."[51] To varying degrees, the Atlanticists of Europe still regarded the United States as guarantee against a Russian threat, as balance against possible German or French–German dominance in the EU, and as leader in the fight against global threats. In the slow-moving development of European security architecture, neither Atlanticist traditions nor Europeanist counterbalancing intentions were clearly predominant. Instead, the 25 EU members achieved a movable compromise, retaining a transatlantic alliance as security community while gradually Europeanizing the responsibility for security in Europe.

The disputes between Europeanists (France, Germany, Belgium, and Luxembourg), Western European Atlanticists (Britain, the Netherlands, and Denmark), and new CEE Atlanticists flared up occasionally as in late January and early February 2003 with the Letter of the Eight and the Letter of the Ten signaling Atlanticist support for the United States and rejection of the French and German attempts to block the Iraq War in the UN Security Council. However, such conflicts between "old Europe" and "new Europe" did not stop the gradual development of the ESDP. Without openly challenging the role of the United States in Europe, the EU was filling the space left by the quiet disengagement of the United States from Europe. The security role of the EU grew slowly because there were many practical difficulties, because the Atlanticists of Europe agreed only slowly, and because offending the United States had to be avoided.

While Atlanticists feared that French demands for an autonomous *Europe puissance* could be driving the United States out of Europe, in reality the reduction of the U.S. military presence in Europe was driven by changing U.S. priorities after the end of the Cold War. "It is therefore not unlikely that those Europeans who continue to advocate strong transatlantic bonds— the British and the CEE states—are in fact fighting a losing battle. . . . In other words, whatever view prevails in the EU, transatlantic relations may be weakening anyway."[52] The efforts of European Atlanticists to strengthen the European pillar of NATO were, de facto, contributions to a stronger and autonomous ESDP.

GENERATIONAL EXPERIENCE: THE CHANGING PSYCHOLOGY OF TRANSATLANTIC RELATIONS

In the 1950s, the transatlantic alliance had been without alternative, but in the 1990s, U.S. involvement in European crises had become optional and an autonomous European security policy conceivable. This change was caused by structural factors, such as the post-1991 security environment and the new U.S.–EU balance of power, but it was also accompanied by changing attitudes on both sides of the Atlantic. In the German case, analysts observed generational change reducing the closeness between the United States and Germany. Until 1998, the generation of Chancellor Kohl and Foreign Minister Genscher led the government of the FRG. Their formative years included the experience of World War II as very young men. For the generation reaching adulthood after 1945, the United States was the liberator from Nazism, protector from Soviet communism, a cultural model, and an impressively rich country. Yet for the generation growing up in the 1960s and 1970s, the United States was a flawed country involved in late-colonial wars abroad, and associated with unsavory regimes such as the Greek military dictatorship (1967–74) and General Pinochet's Chile (1973–90). And since 1998, this generation, personalized in Chancellor Gerhard Schröder and Foreign Minister Joschka Fischer, was heading Germany's government.

With the change of generations, American leadership was becoming less welcome not only for European leaders but also for the general public. This change intensified between 2001 and 2003. Pro-U.S. feelings in Europe reached a peak in response to the terrorist attacks of September 11, 2001. However, this wave of sympathy subsided when European voters disagreed with President

Bush's drive for a war in Iraq. For 40 years, the United States had been perceived as guarantor of European security and freedom, but between 2001 and 2003, the Bush administration created a negative image. Voters began to prefer a superpower role for the EU to continued U.S. leadership.

Similar generational change occurred in the United States. The first President Bush had been the last of a long series of U.S. presidents whose entire political career had been shaped by the Cold War experience, with its focus on the Soviet Union and European security. The younger President Bush, on the other hand, conducted foreign policy in a post–Cold War environment, with European security requiring less attention. He also represented the demographic shift in the United States away from the East Coast with its European affinities toward the South and the West, more interested in Latin America and the Asia–Pacific region.

The psychological foundations for the roles of the allies in the transatlantic alliance were laid in the 1940s and 1950s. These deep loyalties eroded somewhat in the strategic debates of the 1960s, 1970s, and 1980s, but acceptance of NATO and U.S. leadership was still overwhelming. For postwar leaders from Eisenhower to President George H. W. Bush in the United States and from Adenauer to Kohl, NATO had been the foundation of European security and transatlantic unity. However, for the generation of President George W. Bush and Chancellor Schröder, NATO was a historical relic not ideally suited for contemporary priorities.

RELATIVE POWER: THE OBJECTIVE BASE OF ROLE CONCEPTIONS

Whether unilateralism or Atlanticism prevailed in the United States or whether Europeanism or Atlanticism won out in Europe, the success of any of these options depended not only on the eloquence of their advocates or the psychology of generational experience. Of course, role conceptions are affected by habits, wishful thinking, limited information, and reluctance to acknowledge uncomfortable information. Yet role conceptions lack practical value if they do not take into account the international balance of power. Relative power was calculated by most U.S. experts in comparing different nation-states since states were indeed the most relevant actors in the international system. However, there was one relevant exception. When comparing Europe to other actors, it was no longer enough to consider individual European nation-states such as France, Germany, Italy, Spain, or the United Kingdom. It was also necessary to compare the United States, China, or Japan with the EU as a whole. The EU was not merely a free trade area but a unique case of intensive regional integration; it was integrated to such an extent that it can be considered as a unitary actor in some policy fields.

In geoeconomic terms, the EU was already a unitary actor. The balance of relative power in world trade negotiations showed the United States and the EU to be roughly equal, with Japan a distant third. In international finance, the introduction of the euro currency created a unitary actor in the European Central Bank. In geostrategic terms, on the other hand, the EU was not a unitary actor, as the nation-states of Europe have jealously guarded security and defense as the core of national sovereignty not to be usurped by the European level. However, in 1991, the EU began to move toward a CFSP, and since 1999, the EU has become a military actor on a small scale. The involvement of EU personnel in crisis interventions outside EU territory was much larger than that of any other power except the United States.

The EU was exercising soft power through economic and diplomatic instruments, and it was becoming a geostrategic actor capable of implementing the Petersberg Tasks of crisis management defined by the West European Union in 1992. A serious underestimation of Europe's actual soft power and potential military power contributed to neoconservative advocacy of U.S. unilateralism. Even those in the United States regarding Europe as an indispensable ally underestimated the growth of Europe's potential compared to 1949. Psychologically, it was so much easier to continue claiming unqualified U.S. leadership, as if the balance of power within the West had not changed since NATO's foundation. Nevertheless, European integration had changed the balance of power between the transatlantic allies compared to the late 1940s, and acknowledging this fact could overcome comforting but unrealistic role conceptions.

NONCORRESPONDENCE OF MILITARY AND ECONOMIC STRENGTH

A key difficulty in analyzing the balance of power is the discrepancy between relative economic power and relative military strength. In broad terms and in the long run, economic and military power tend to correspond to one another; however, this correspondence does not apply in every situation. In the case of post-1945 Japan and Germany, their international role was underpinned by substantial economic power without corresponding military power. On the other hand, the Soviet Union was a military superpower without the corresponding economic potential. The EU has been described as an economic giant and a military dwarf. This may not have been perfectly correct because EU member states spent more on defense budgets than China, Japan, and Russia combined. Nevertheless, it was a fact that the EU's economic capabilities were much more impressive than the military forces of its members.

In the case of the United States, we also find a certain noncorrespondence of military and economic power after 1991. In the late 1940s, the United States produced about 50 percent of the entire global industrial production; it was also a military superpower unmatched by any other country. This military supremacy was limited to the extent that the Soviet Union achieved nuclear "parity," which rendered U.S. nuclear superiority less useful because of the stalemate of mutual assured destruction. The United States won the military competition of the Cold War because it was always far ahead in the economic competition with the Soviet Union, the military power of which could not be sustained without the required economic power.

After the Cold War, great power competition took on a different format. In the competition with Europe and Japan, the United States was far ahead in military power but not in economic strength. This unevenness lent itself to misjudgments and flawed decisions: it suggested reliance on military means because they were available, not because they were necessarily appropriate. The ambitious role claims of the PNAC were predicated on U.S. military supremacy but overestimated what remained of past economic supremacy. On the other hand, if the limitation of U.S. economic resources was taken into account, the option of benign institutionalized hegemony exercised with self-restraint seemed more appropriate. For Europeanists, the ambition for *Europe puissance* went hand in hand with the assumption that U.S. military supremacy could not be sustained because of diminished economic supremacy.

CAN THE UNITED STATES MANAGE A SOFT LANDING IN MULTIPOLARITY?

The roles of Europe and the United States in the transatlantic alliance depended on the future structure of the international system. If the unipolar moment was really extending into a unipolar era, the only superpower could confidently either neglect a Europe lacking military capabilities or demand that European allies contribute more to the out-of-area missions required by the global role of the United States. In a hypothetical unipolar era, U.S. grand strategy would have to prevent the rise of challengers and the formation of counterhegemonic alliances between China, Japan, India, and Russia. Regarding Europe, the United States would have to encourage divisions between the Europeanist core and the Atlanticists in Eastern and Western Europe. Widening the EU into a large free trade area too complex to allow deeper integration could prevent it from becoming a geostrategic actor. American-owned media in the United Kingdom could campaign against Britain ever joining the euro currency. Thus, U.S. foreign policy had instruments available to resist any challenge by the EU. On the other hand, in the more likely case that the unipolar moment was to be replaced by a multipolar structure, such resistance would be not only futile but also costly and counterproductive. Instead of alienating Europeans by neglecting or dividing them, the United States should encourage EU autonomy. After all, the loss of transatlantic leadership would be compensated by gaining a close ally and partner in shaping future multipolarity. Instead of squandering the post-1991 unipolar moment, "America must devise a grand strategy for the transition to a world of multiple power centres now,"[53] including the acceptance of Europe as global player emancipated from post-1945 dependency.

The practice of the Clinton administration was characterized by a combination of continued leadership claims with some concessions to the Europeans. The United States acknowledged the need for Europe to take on more responsibility while still insisting on continued U.S. leadership, getting involved in Europe only reluctantly, and, last but not least, also hinting at U.S. withdrawal. Since 2001, the practice of the Bush administration combined the unilateralist impulse to go it alone, the isolationist impulse to neglect Europe, and the desire to continue control over European security through NATO. Yet the effort not to relinquish leadership was undermined by the withdrawal of U.S. troops from Europe, continuing under the first President Bush, President Clinton, and the younger President Bush.

"Asking that the United States prepare for and manage its exit from global primacy, however, is a tall order. Great powers have great difficulty accepting their mortality."[54] It was a tall order to expect a hegemonic power to manage the transition into multipolarity with grace. Indeed, the Bush administration's misplaced confidence in unending unipolarity exacerbated transatlantic tensions and alienated allies. Such tensions were not inevitable since hegemony in itself did not have to provoke counterhegemonic alliances as long as the hegemon was not perceived as threatening. Yet in 2003 and 2004, the perceptions of the United States in Europe, among elites and among the public, turned distinctly less positive. The claimed role of the United States as unchallenged leader and unilateral actor no longer corresponded to the distribution of potential power.

The most ambitious role claims for the United States assessed Europe as weak and expected lasting U.S. supremacy. Less ambitious role claims acknowledged that the United States was "preeminent, not omnipotent," implying that Europe was clearly a necessary ally. This allocation of roles was also preferred by European Atlanticists seeking a role as important and capable allies while welcoming continuing U.S. leadership in the transatlantic alliance. More ambitious claims by Europeanists aimed for a role as *Europe puissance*, strong enough to be autonomous in European regional security. This range of role conceptions was being negotiated under the conditions of military unipolarity and economic multipolarity. American military supremacy suggested that Europe no longer mattered after the Cold War. On the other hand, the economic potential and the degree of political unity achieved by the EU suggested that the United States would have to accommodate the European bloc as more or less equal geostrategic actor in the foreseeable future.

CHAPTER 2

Europe's Uneven Emancipation: Economic Giant under U.S. Umbrella

Europe's economic integration since the 1950s was the precondition for the second part of its emancipation, that is, the Europeanization of European security beginning in the 1990s. Two wars within three decades (1914–18 and 1939–45) had devastated the economies of Europe. Yet European integration transformed this collection of exhausted countries into an economic giant rivaling the gross domestic product (GDP) of the United States. The low point of 1945 was brought about by a combination of great power rivalries and, virtually, a European civil war involving the end of authoritarian monarchies, the transition to liberal and social democracy, communist revolutions, and a fascist backlash in a variety of countries. These 30 years of turmoil brought to an end a period of European economic preeminence. In the nineteenth century, Britain and other European countries had been the industrial leaders of the world. Before World War I, Europe's combined output still surpassed that of the United States, although U.S. industrial production was already greater than that of any European nation. After 1945, however, U.S. industrial production greatly surpassed the European total.

The self-inflicted European catastrophe of 1914–45 resulted in a period of economic weakness and strategic dependence. However, in the 1950s, Europe's economy began to recover. In addition, economic integration through the European Economic Community (EEC; later the European Community [EC] and the European Union [EU]) transformed the small and medium-sized national markets into one large European domestic market. Thus, the catastrophic decline inflicted as result of World Wars I II was overcome by postwar recovery and European economic integration.

The economic development of the past 50 years challenged two stereotypes. The image of perpetually antagonistic nation-states corresponded to the facts of the nineteenth and the early twentieth centuries, while the "junior ally" stereotype reflected the Cold War experience. Yet these two images are insufficient to understand the long-term change in the role of European states. "Realist" nation-state competition does not have to be a permanent characteristic, and the junior ally role was characteristic of a rather short historical period, from 1949 to 1991. European integration since the 1950s has gradually changed the role of European states beyond these two stereotypes. Integration has not replaced the nation-states by a European federation; however, it has reduced nation-state rivalries to such an extent that wars between France and Germany, for example, have become inconceivable. Nation-states have also learned to pursue their national interests through multilateral cooperation. Therefore, the end of the Cold War division of Europe did not result in the return of past rivalries or in the renationalization of foreign and defense policies.

European economic integration has served as the framework of economic recovery and growth, allowing each of the European nations to have more potential power than in 1950. It has also created a single European market allowing EU members to function as one combined economic power in world trade. The junior ally role corresponded to the balance of power within the West during the early Cold War period. It was still inevitable in the later Cold War period while the Soviet Union still existed, although Europe's economic weight had already recovered compared to the late 1940s. However, after the end of the Soviet Union and after the formation of the European Single Market, the junior ally role had become obviously obsolete in the economic field and started to unravel in security policy as well.

1945: EUROPE'S ECONOMIC LOW—MOMENT OF GREATEST U.S. ECONOMIC SUPREMACY

The institutional framework for post–World War II international politics was established at the moment of greatest U.S. economic and military supremacy in the 1940s. This primacy was consolidated by President Roosevelt and his successor, Truman, into an institutionalized hegemony.[1] It did not depend on unilateralism and disdain for international institutions as practiced by U.S. neoconservatives since 2001. On the contrary, it relied on the formation of institutions through which U.S. primacy could be exercised effectively, with limited costs, enjoying broad legitimacy, willing acceptance by allies, and the prospect of lasting many years. Unchallenged and enduring U.S. leadership was accepted by others as it corresponded to the balance of power within the West at that time. And this role allocation was reinforced by the external factor of Soviet power threatening Western Europe.

In 1945, Europe was an economic wreck and had reached the low point in its economic trajectory. Not only defeated Germany and Italy were devastated, but victorious Britain and France were economically exhausted as well. The United States, on the other hand, had entered the European war rather late and did not experience any destruction on the U.S. mainland. The United States had already been the greatest industrial power around 1900; however, the devastation of Europe in two world wars gave U.S. economic supremacy a new dimension. "By virtue of emerging from World War II unscathed, the United States was the world's preeminent power, with its GNP [gross national product] accounting for more than half the world economy."[2] In 1944, the Bretton Woods conference set a framework for world trade and finance establishing the U.S. dollar as the anchor currency of world trade. The British pound had enjoyed this leading role in the nineteenth and early twentieth centuries but had to relinquish it, as Britain's economy was exhausted by the war and its colonial empire disintegrating. In 1945, the United Nations was founded, and in 1949, the North Atlantic Treaty Organization (NATO) was formed, the strongest component of a U.S.-led global network of military alliances. This institutionalization of U.S. supremacy made it more durable than any simple reliance on unilateral use of superior force could have done.

In this moment of greatest European weakness and greatest U.S. economic and military supremacy, the United States created an international framework for Europe's economic recovery and provided stability as guarantor and supervisor of European security. While security dependency continued for half a century, Europe's economic weakness of the late 1940s was overcome much earlier, with U.S. support. Western Europe's economic recovery, like Japan's, was in the strategic interest of the United States in the incipient Cold War with the Soviet Union. In contrast to World War I, defeated Germany was not burdened with reparations after 1945 by the Western Allies because a different conflict was more important than any possible conflict with Germany. While East Germany had to pay reparations to the Soviet Union, West Germany was included in the European Recovery Program established by the United States. A successful Western European economy was more attractive for the United States as trading partner and as ally in the Cold War. Economic stability could erode the influence of communist parties in France and Italy, and it was a prerequisite for a European contribution to the transatlantic military alliance. It was only decades later, when the EU became a serious economic competitor, that the United States experienced negative effects of European recovery.

Economic integration strengthened and unified the EEC until it spoke with one voice in world trade. On the other hand, in security matters, Western Europe remained a multitude of junior partners in NATO relying on the U.S. nuclear umbrella. Yet the transformation of Europe into an economic superpower was bound, eventually, to have spillover effects, beginning to transform the military dwarf into a strategic actor more commensurate with the EU's economic power.

After 1991, a window of opportunity opened for Europe's security emancipation. Responsibility for European security was shifting from the United

States to Europe; at the same time, it was moving from the nation-states to the EU. The window of opportunity had opened because after 1991 there was no threat to Europe from any state or group of states. The diversity of post-1991 threats posed new challenges, but major wars were unlikely. Europe did not face any immediate existential threat; therefore, the EU had the time and opportunity to develop autonomous military capabilities.

Decades of economic integration made it possible for the EU to consider a common security and defense policy. The economies of the EU were strong enough to afford military expenditure and to sustain a European Defense Industrial and Technological Base (EDITB) to supply EU forces. At the same time, EU economies were so integrated that national governments could begin to imagine integrated EU armed forces. The ambitions of EU leaders as well as the disengagement of the United States from Europe contributed to a development using the economic potential of the EU to create a relevant strategic actor.

EUROPE AS ONE DOMESTIC MARKET: FROM CUSTOMS UNION TO SINGLE CURRENCY

One important outcome of European economic integration was the formation of a gigantic domestic market. In the eighteenth century, a unified French or English nation-state provided business with a sizable domestic market more capable of accommodating industrial and commercial development than the multitude of political units and fragmented markets of Germany or Italy. In the twentieth century, the size of the U.S. and Japanese domestic markets allowed companies to grow and to conquer world markets from a home base much larger than that of German, French, English, or Italian companies. However, European integration gave business a domestic market rivaling the United States and Japan in size. One result of European integration is that "the U.S. economy is no longer the single dominant economy," in a comparison of regional economic blocs, although it is still "the world's richest and most productive national economy,"[3] in a comparison between nations. The sheer size of the EU's domestic market has allowed more European companies to grow to an internationally competitive size. Out of the biggest 500 multinational companies, 185 were still based in the United States, but 126 were European and 108 Japanese. Thus, "American-based multinationals" were "only a fraction—and a diminishing one—of all multinationals."[4]

In the 1950s, two competing concepts for European economic integration were put into practice. On the one hand, the six founders of the EEC set out to create a customs union, to adopt a common agricultural policy, and to embark on an open-ended process of integration. On the other, Britain and six other countries started the European Free Trade Association (EFTA), implementing a much more limited concept of economic integration. EFTA was meant to be no more than a free trade area for industrial goods, without an agricultural policy and not envisaging any deeper economic integration.

The competition between these two models was decided within a few years. Britain abandoned its EFTA partners, applied for membership in the EEC in 1961, and became a member in 1973, together with Denmark and Ireland. Thus, the EEC's concept of deepening economic integration prevailed and shaped the development from EEC to EC and EU.

Economic integration went through several main stages. The EEC became a functioning customs union by 1968, having removed internal tariff barriers and established a common external tariff. Between 1986 and 1992, the EC created the European Single Market by removing nontariff barriers and established freedom of movement not only for the import and export of goods but also for services, capital, and labor. Furthermore, between 1991 and 1999, the EU achieved monetary union by introducing the euro currency for 12 of its 15 member countries.

This process of deepening economic integration was not guided by a long-term plan but evolved over time in incremental steps. In the absence of federalist blueprints, participants in European integration followed the logic of functionalism.[5] Agreements on policies in specific areas created a habit of cooperation and the requirement to think through the implications of previously adopted policies. Functional integration meant that adopting one policy would lead to the adoption of further policies in the same field, perhaps even to integration in other fields. Removing customs barriers made it easier for business to operate across the borders of member states. It was only consistent that the end of tariff barriers pointed to the subsequent removal of nontariff barriers. And a single integrated market could operate much better with one currency, thus eliminating the problem of fluctuations between more than a dozen national currencies. The spillover effect of each common economic policy suggested further integration. The integrated market of 1992 and the single currency of 1999, managed by the European Central Bank, made deeper economic integration, including tax harmonization, more plausible. It was not necessary but plausible that deep economic integration could also facilitate closer political union and a common foreign and security policy.

ENLARGEMENT OF THE EU FAR BEYOND SIX FOUNDERS

The model of deepening economic integration was successful for the EEC's founding members, but it also attracted an increasing number of other countries. Initially, the EEC had six members in 1957, while the competing EFTA was founded by seven members in 1960. Very soon, the most important member of EFTA, the United Kingdom, applied to join the EEC. In 1973, the EEC grew to nine members with the inclusion of Great Britain, Denmark, and Ireland. A second wave of applicants brought membership to 12 when Greece joined in 1981, followed by Spain and Portugal in 1986. In 1990, East Germany was included in the Federal Republic of Germany, thus enlarging the EU without adding a new member country. The end of the Cold War also made it easier for countries with a tradition of neutrality and nonalignment to join the EU. Thus, in 1995, the inclusion of Austria, Finland, and Sweden increased membership to 15. Finally, 10 countries in Central and Eastern Europe and in the Mediterranean joined in May 2004, expanding membership to 25.

The population of the six EEC founders amounted to 167 million in 1957. Since then, the population of the EEC/EC/EU increased more through the accession of new member countries than through population growth. With the last round of expansion, in May 2004, EU membership increased from 15 countries with 381 million inhabitants to 25 countries with 455 million people, compared to 277 million for the United States, 145 million for Russia, and 127 million for Japan.[6] The EU domestic market was far larger than the Japanese economy and matched (or marginally surpassed) the U.S. GDP. Bulgaria and Romania were expected to join in 2007, adding 30 million people. Croatia and Turkey also have applied to join, and with the remaining successor states of Yugoslavia likely to follow, the total EU population could grow to 580 million. This enlargement of the EU was evidence of its success, but it also threatened to derail any further deepening of economic integration. Enlarged membership threatened to paralyze decision making because the institutions established by the six founders could hardly accommodate 25 members. Nevertheless, the fact that so many countries found the EU attractive enough to apply for membership was evidence that economic integration worked.

THE ECONOMIC WEIGHT OF THE EU

"Today the American and European economies are the world's largest, and they are likely to remain so for the foreseeable future."[7] The success of Japan and the rapid rise of the Chinese economy do not obliterate the plain fact that the United States and the EU each produce a quarter of the global GDP. In 2000 the EU's GDP was roughly equal to that of the United States and twice that of Japan. China was expected to surpass individual European powers within two decades. However, it would require several decades of uninterrupted rapid growth for China to match the EU's total GDP of 2000. For the time being, the economic weight of the EU was of a magnitude capable of underpinning the emerging role of the EU as geostrategic actor.

In 1960, the combined GDP of the six EEC founders amounted to $393 billion, that is, about 59 percent of the U.S. GDP of $666 billion, and in 1970, the EEC total was equal to 63 percent of U.S. GDP of $981 billion (in 1970 prices).[8] However, by 2000, even before the inclusion of 10 new members in 2004, the EU economy had come to match the U.S. economy. Between 1957 and 2000, the economic weight of the European bloc had caught up with the United States, stayed ahead of Japan, and surpassed that of the Soviet Union/ Russia. Admittedly, this success of the EU had been achieved not through superior growth rates but rather through a combination of EU enlargement and economic growth. Nevertheless, the outcome was the creation of an economic bloc, sharing with the United States leadership in the World Trade Organization (WTO), the International Monetary Fund (IMF), and the World Bank. It also created a gigantic domestic market enabling European companies to become global competitors.

In the medium term, "the United States could . . . find itself with a smaller 'home market' than rival blocs" if EU enlargement succeeded and if U.S. efforts to form a larger trading bloc remained limited to North and Central America. As the EU was forming closer economic relations with the South American Common Market grouping, Latin American countries had the option of reducing their dependence on the United States[9] and to maintain a distance from the U.S.-led North American Free Trade Association.

LABOR PRODUCTIVITY

After World War II, the technology used by U.S. industries was vastly superior, while the size of the domestic market and of major enterprises created economies of scale. Thus, U.S. labor productivity was superior to Europe's by a great margin. However, over the next decades, European industries modernized their equipment while they also enjoyed the economies of scale made possible by a larger integrated European market. Between 1950 and 1990, labor productivity of EU countries gradually closed the gap to U.S. productivity.

Taking U.S. labor productivity as the benchmark of 100 for the years 1950 and 1990, respectively, productivity per hour improved between 1950 and 1990 from 34 to 85 in Italy, from 45 to 102 in France, and from 35 to 95 in Germany.[10] The U.S. economy has, nevertheless, grown faster than Western European economies, but "the main factor driving higher U.S. economic growth" was "not greater productivity gains; it is a more rapidly expanding population." Another factor explaining differences in economic growth was "the disparity in the number of hours each worker worked. "In the last 30 years, the EU15 has made dramatic improvements in its relative productivity (in France, GDP per hour has gone from 73 to 105 percent of the U.S. figure), but its per capita GDP has remained just 70 percent that of the United States. This is explained by the fact that workers in the EU15, and in France in particular, log far fewer hours on the job than do U.S. workers." The outcome of these differences was that between 1970 and 2000, the GDP per hour worked in EU15 countries rose from 65 to 91 percent of US productivity. Yet because hours per person declined in the EU15 from 101 to 77 percent of U.S. hours, the resulting GDP per person for the EU15 changed only from 69 to 70 percent of U.S. figures between 1970 and 2000.[11]

Of course, it has to be taken into account that the U.S. economy was very capable of improving labor productivity by using information technology in the 1980s and 1990s. This short-term development has helped the United States retain or extend a residual advantage. However, it certainly has not reestablished the massive superiority prevailing in 1950. Furthermore, "U.S. investment in information technology (IT), which has been a key driver of productivity gains over the last decade, is likely to flatten out." On the other hand, EU companies "can now achieve quick gains by becoming 'fast followers' of their American counterparts."[12]

Whether the leading EU countries exactly matched U.S. labor productivity matters less here than the significant long-term shifts in relative economic power between 1950 and 2000. Residual differences in labor productivity were certainly much smaller than half a century earlier.

BALANCE OF TRADE AND INVESTMENT

Europe and the United States were one another's most important economic partners. This was true for the flow of imports and exports but also for foreign direct investment in both areas. These economic giants of similar overall size were bound together by a mutual dependence for trade and investment. "Transatlantic commerce approaches $2.5 trillion per year and employs directly or indirectly some twelve million workers in Europe and the United States."[13] While the U.S. current account deficit was "approaching a record-high 6 percent of GDP,"[14] most of which originated in U.S. trade with China and Japan, the EU enjoyed overall a slightly positive trade balance. American industries had a technological lead in selected sectors, but this did not translate broadly enough into competitiveness of U.S. exports in Europe and in the world market.

Foreign direct investment between these two regions surpassed investment streams between any other regions worldwide. In the eight years up to 2005, "Americans invested as much in the Netherlands as in Mexico and ten times as much as in China. During that time, Europeans invested more in Texas than Americans did in Japan. And today, American business invests 60 percent more in Eastern Europe than in China. . . . Conversely, Europe provides 75 percent of all investment in the United States, and it is far and away the biggest foreign source of American jobs."[15] In recent years, Europe was investing more in the United States than vice versa. This indicated a historical turnaround. Since the 1920s, the United States had invested much more in Europe, but now the United States was once more a capital importer and a net debtor, as in the nineteenth century. Europe's response to U.S. trade deficits differed from East Asian responses. Japanese and Chinese investors used their trade surplus to become creditors by buying fixed-interest U.S. securities. Europeans, on the other hand, tended to invest in U.S. equities, taking over U.S. companies and building subsidiaries of European companies. Thus, European ownership of productive assets in the United States broadly matched U.S. ownership of assets in Europe.

In the balance of trade and in mutual investments, there existed a rough equality of economic power. As economic powers of equal weight, the EU and the United States acted out their limited conflicts through the WTO without ever putting at risk their entire mutually beneficial trade relationship. It may be of interest in a different context to speculate whether the United States or the EU will have a competitive edge in the long run; however, it is more relevant here that their economic weight in 2000 was roughly equal, whereas in 1950, the United States had enjoyed vast supremacy. A massive shift in relative economic power had occurred since 1950, but the increase of Europe's relative power was not reflected in transatlantic security structures. For Europeans, this new balance of economic power suggested a renegotiation of security roles, although this depended on translating the EU's economic power into a coherent foreign and security policy.

THE EU AS GLOBAL ECONOMIC ACTOR

The EU was not only an arithmetic aggregate of massive economic figures. It was also an actor speaking with one voice in world trade. Its most important instrument was the Common Commercial Policy[16] regulating access of outsiders to its gigantic common market. The EU was also an important participant in the WTO (and in its predecessor, the General Agreement on Tariffs and Trade [GATT]). Another EU instrument affecting world trade was the Common Agricultural Policy. Although the individual member states of the EU were still sovereign governments acting according to their separate national interests, European integration had gone so far that the EU could be regarded as one unitary actor in trade matters, speaking on behalf of the member states and able to enter international agreements binding for EU members. The United States and the EU dominated international economic institutions. While the United States regularly nominated the president of the World Bank, the president of the IMF was nominated by EU countries. This method of personnel selection reflected the economic weight of the United States and the EU in relation to one another and in relation to all other countries.

THE EU'S SPHERE OF INFLUENCE

The European colonial powers Britain, France, the Netherlands, Belgium, Spain, and Portugal had lost their empires between the late 1940s and mid-1970s, but often they retained influence in former colonies. Since the Convention of Lomé (1975), the EU had developed formalized links to 71 African, Caribbean, and Pacific (ACP) countries, forming a vast sphere of influence tied to the EU through preferential trade links. Earlier, such links had been established with several former French colonies in Africa in the Conventions of Yaoundé (1963 and 1969).[17] The currencies of several African countries were linked to the French franc and have become linked to the euro since 1999. The EU and its members were also the largest donors of economic aid, ahead of Japan and the United States. Further influence was exercised through trade and investment. The Cotonou Partnership Agreement of 2000[18] modified the relations between the EU and the ACP countries (78 after the inclusion of East Timor in 2003).

Thus, the sphere of influence of the EU extended well beyond its immediate periphery. Members of the EU (with 450 million people in 2004), applicants for EU membership (another 110 million), and 78 ACP countries with preferential trade agreements formed a large area in which the influence of the EU was stronger than that of the United States and definitely stronger than that of Japan, China, India, or Russia. Even without EU military capabilities, the civilian power of the EU succeeded in securing its economic interests.

THE EURO AS SECOND WORLD CURRENCY

The introduction of the euro was, according to U.S. historian David Calleo, "the single most important event in European and transatlantic politics since the demise of the Soviet Union."[19] It was not just a matter of making life easier for tourists and businesses across Europe. Strategically, the euro meant that a bloc of 300 million people in 12 countries had left the dollar zone. Participant countries no longer had their currencies subject to fluctuations induced by a much larger U.S. dollar and disrupting intra-European trade streams. Instead, intra-European trade was insulated from external fluctuations, more or less like intra-U.S. trade.

The economic power of the EU was strengthened significantly with the introduction of the single European currency by 12 of its 15 members in 1999. The euro has not replaced the U.S. dollar as leading world currency, a role enjoyed since the 1944 Bretton Woods conference, when the leading role of the British pound ended. Nevertheless, the EU created a second world currency capable of becoming a regional lead currency for Europe and Africa and a second reserve currency worldwide. The euro could even grow into a role equal to the U.S. dollar, according to American financial expert Fred Bergsten: "A bipolar currency regime dominated by Europe and the United States, with Japan as a junior partner, will replace the dollar-centred system."[20]

Internal causes, together with the somewhat diminished role of the U.S. dollar as world anchor currency, had been leading the EEC toward monetary union since the 1970s. The completion of the customs union in 1968 had raised the question of the future course of EEC economic integration. European leaders began to experiment with ways of coordinating their currencies in the 1970s, when President Nixon's devaluation of the U.S. dollar provided an additional motive. As the costs of the Vietnam War diminished the superior competitiveness of the U.S. economy, a high exchange rate could not be sustained, and the convertibility of the U.S. dollar into a guaranteed quantity of gold came to an end. Yet attempts to stabilize exchange rates between European currencies by limiting fluctuation to a set maximum did not achieve their objective. On the contrary, they invited currency speculators to exploit the predictable behavior of central banks trying to hold divergent currencies within a target range. Only in the 1990s did EU leaders finally agree to go beyond currency coordination and introduce a single currency. When the previous mechanism of coordinating exchange rates experienced its last crisis with the British pound having to opt out of the exchange rate mechanism on September 16, 1992,[21] the Maastricht conference of 1991 had already adopted a timetable for the introduction of the euro and defined the conditions to be met by participants in order to join the common currency.

The benefits of having the only world reserve currency were enjoyed by Wall Street bankers for many years, but the euro threatened to divert international financial business and banking profits from New York to Frankfurt and Paris. Central bankers across the world could reduce their currency reserve holdings in dollars and diversify into euros. The option to conduct European oil imports in euro currency would reduce economic links between the United States and the Middle East while increasing European influence. Should Great Britain decide to join the common currency, the euro could become powerful enough to divert a significant share of financial transactions from New York to European banks.

The global role of the U.S. dollar had also been weakened by domestic factors as "the Bretton Woods system was being killed by the U.S. government deficit," which was "being financed almost in its entirety by foreign investments in the United States, mostly in government securities like short-term treasury notes and medium-term bonds." The resulting deficit in the U.S. balance of payments made the United States "dependent on massive injections of short-term and panic-prone money from abroad."[22]

Even without matching the world currency role of the U.S. dollar, the introduction of the euro had a significant impact on the distribution of global economic power. Should the euro succeed as regional European currency with a limited but substantial role as second world currency, the effect would be to reduce U.S. economic power even further compared to its absolute supremacy at the time of the Bretton Woods conference. In currency terms, the unipolar moment was in 1944. Since then, the international balance of economic power has changed dramatically.

COMPETITIVENESS IN SELECTED INDUSTRIES

The following examples illustrate that U.S. enterprises no longer enjoyed the comprehensive lead of the 1950s. While U.S. firms remained world leaders in selected fields, Japanese enterprises have taken the lead in important high-tech industries, while European competitors have strengthened their positions in a broad range of industries. In 1990, Joseph S. Nye could still argue that "the United States retained the leading position in world exports in aircraft, industrial chemicals, agricultural chemicals, engines and turbines, and office and computing machines. It ranked a close second in electrical machinery, plastics, and drugs."[23] However, the competitive position of particular U.S. industries has declined further since.

The U.S. steel industry needed government protection from more competitive producers in Asia and Europe. The European steel industry also had to shrink and rationalize in the face of competition from newly industrialized countries. Nevertheless, EU steel producers adapted better than their U.S. counterparts, who tried to survive with the help of "a prohibitive tariff" imposed "on imports of steel from Europe and Japan in 2001" by the Bush administration. This protectionist measure "only accelerated the long-term decline of the traditional mid-western steel producers." Although large steel users such as the U.S. automobile industry were forced to buy more expensive U.S.-produced steel, they "set about cutting their use of steel," resulting in lower demand as an unintended side effect of protectionist tariffs.[24]

From the 1920s to the 1960s, the U.S. car industry dominated the world, but this domination has been dramatically reduced. The most successful new competitor was the Japanese car industry. The relative rise of Europe's carmakers compared to their U.S. competitors was less spectacular than the success of Toyota and Honda. Nevertheless, the total production of German, French, and other EU carmakers surpassed U.S. production in the 1990s. In the 1920s, General Motors (GM), Ford, and Chrysler had made inroads into European markets to become firmly established major producers. However, since the 1970s, European carmakers entered the U.S. market, albeit not with the same success as Japanese carmakers. The historical domination of GM, Ford, and Chrysler has given place to a tripolar competition between Japan (Toyota and Honda), the United States (GM and Ford), and Europe (Volkswagen, DaimlerChrysler, BMW, Renault, and Peugeot-Citroen).

For many years, Boeing and other U.S. companies dominated civilian and military aircraft production. However, over the past two decades a European competitor emerged with the rise of Airbus. Of the U.S. producers, only Boeing survived as major producer of civilian aircraft, whereas others were reduced to niche markets or specialized in military aircraft. On the other hand, Airbus extended its market share steadily and drew even with Boeing in the first years of the twenty-first century.

In the oil industry, U.S. companies retained their dominant position. Among European competitors, BP and Royal Dutch/Shell remained the strongest, whereas continental European oil companies remained bit players. While the United States had oil sources at home and controlled much of the world's oil supply, EU countries suffered from an energy deficit and depended on a multitude of sources. Nevertheless, European firms were capable of taking initiatives clashing with U.S. interests. For example, France's Total, together with Malaysia's Petronas and Russia's Gazprom, negotiated in September 1997 the development of a gas field in Iran, although the United States threatened retaliation against third-country companies acting contrary to the Iran-Libya Sanctions Act (ILSA). Again in February 2004, Total and Petronas signed another agreement with Iran to produce liquefied natural gas. Under ILSA, the United States threatened actions against foreign companies dealing with the governments of Iran or Libya, including the seizure of their assets held in the United States.[25]

The electronic industry of the EU was hardly a match for U.S. and Japanese world leaders. Nevertheless, European electronics and information technology companies such as Siemens, Philips, Thales, Nokia, and SAP could compete on a global scale, although there was no European Microsoft or IBM.

The U.S. defense budget was by far the biggest in the world. It sustained an enormous defense industry, including the biggest three (Lockheed Martin, Boeing, and Raytheon) and another three of the top 10 armament producers (Northrop Grumman in fifth, General Dynamics in sixth, and Honeywell in tenth position). The EU has achieved some cross-border consolidation, creating four prime contractors occupying the fourth (British Aerospace Systems), seventh (European Aeronautic Defence and Space Company), eighth (Thales), and ninth (Finmeccanica) positions among the world's top 10.[26] Out of the top 100 armament producers worldwide, 51 were European and 40 U.S. companies.[27] American defense contractors were clearly bigger and less numerous than their European counterparts, yet the figures also indicate that, globally, European defense industries were a relevant competitor. While the U.S. defense industry remained beyond challenge, the leading EU countries nevertheless consolidated their EDITB, thus gaining some autonomy and winning a share of the global arms export market.

TRANSATLANTIC PARTNERSHIP: FROM SECURITY DEPENDENCE TO ECONOMIC INTERDEPENDENCE

The economic recovery of Europe after World War II was welcomed and encouraged by the United States, even when it began to turn the EEC/EC/EU into a serious economic competitor. The system competition with the Soviet Union required an economically viable Western Europe, and the superior economic strength of the United States made increasing competition by Europe unproblematic, at least initially. While the EEC/EC/EU developed Europe's economy, European security was left to the NATO alliance, in other words, to U.S. leadership. Europe could be called a military protectorate, enjoying the protection of the U.S. nuclear umbrella against the perceived Soviet threat but also enduring the tutelage of its big friend ultimately in charge of Western European security.

Since the 1940s, the military alliance and U.S. involvement in European security had been the centerpiece of the transatlantic relationship. However, with the EU beginning to claim a security role in 1991 and U.S. priorities shifting to East Asia and the Greater Middle East, the remaining foundation of the transatlantic relationship was economic interdependence. The economic emancipation of Europe has resulted in regular trade conflicts between the EU and the United States, acted out in bilateral disputes across the Atlantic or in international institutions such as GATT and WTO. Both sides often threatened one another with trade sanctions and retaliations in the chicken war, the banana war, and other conflicts. Nevertheless, these disputes were only superficial compared to underlying common interests. Both the United States and the EU were interested in the secure supply of raw materials from the Third World, in the stability of their export markets, and in the security and profitability of their investments abroad. The EU and the United States were also one another's most important trade partners and sources of foreign direct investment. This transatlantic economic interdependence formed a solid foundation for future relations, even if the United States was to relinquish its involvement and leadership in European security.

As the EU grew into a serious economic competitor, the United States had more reasons to demand greater military burden sharing to relieve U.S. fiscal problems. Yet this also threatened to increase European demands for autonomy, which explained the inconsistency of U.S. demands for burden sharing. After the Cold War, the transatlantic dispute over burden sharing and control continued in a different context. Countries of the EU had the economic potential either to share NATO's burden of defense expenditure or to finance autonomous European capabilities. The United States found it harder to encourage more burden sharing while retaining a leading role in NATO. And the Europeans had the choice either to demand a greater role within the transatlantic alliance or to repatriate responsibility for European security altogether, thus ending the post-1945 military protectorate.

Transatlantic relations have not yet fully accommodated the changes in the relative economic power of the United States and Europe. Compared to the late 1940s, when the structure of the transatlantic relationship was shaped, the economic power and the political unity of the EU have increased significantly. And the end of the Soviet Union in 1991 also changed the European security environment profoundly. These two changes together propelled the uneven emancipation of Europe from the U.S. military protectorate into a new stage in 1991. Economic emancipation began to have a spillover effect, advancing Europe's security emancipation.

Transatlantic economic interdependence is to be considered in conjunction with the rebalancing of the economic power of the United States and Europe since 1945. "Transatlantic commerce approaches \$2.5 trillion per year and employs directly or indirectly some twelve million workers in Europe and the United States." While European integration created an economic bloc equal to the U.S. economy, the stream of trade and investment across the Atlantic has also created an economic interdependence to be taken into account by foreign and security policymakers. The task force report *Renewing the Atlantic Partnership* pointed out that "the U.S. and European economies depend heavily on one another." Although there were "frequent disputes over tariffs and subsidies through the years," the report notes that the transatlantic crisis before and during the 2003 war in Iraq "had little discernible effect on patterns of European-American trade and investment."[28] Economic interdependence continued regardless of diplomatic tensions.

One long-term effect of World War II has clearly been overcome, as the economic weakness of post-1945 Europe has been replaced by an integrated EU economy. This has already resulted in a rebalancing of the economic roles of the transatlantic partners and is bound to result in a transformation of

Europe's security dependency into a balanced security partnership. The massive transatlantic economic interdependence should ensure that the close and asymmetrical relationship of the Cold War period will be replaced not by a standoff between rival blocs but by a partnership, more balanced but as close as before.

CHAPTER 3

How Long Do Alliances Last? Explaining NATO's Longevity

The centerpiece of the transatlantic relationship was the North Atlantic Treaty Organization (NATO), the most important link in the global network of alliances formed by the United States after 1945. During the Cold War, the shared perception of one overriding threat gave NATO members a unifying purpose. Its integrated military command structure created closer cohesion compared to other alliances usually based on no more than a treaty and, perhaps, joint military exercises. The long duration of the Cold War further consolidated NATO's structures and the habitual roles of participants. However, after its success in winning the Cold War by exhausting the Soviet Union, the question arose whether NATO would continue for long after 1991.

So far, NATO has outlasted predictions that it would not survive the end of the Cold War. Its very success in bringing the Soviet Union to its knees had also completed NATO's primary purpose and robbed it of its main reason for being. Yet NATO's survival, already in its second decade after the end of the Soviet Union, confounded realist theories making alliance formation dependent on the existence of an external threat. On the other hand, claims that NATO was to remain the "bedrock of European security" underestimated the change transforming the alliance since 1991.

NATO's primary purpose did not disappear completely from the alliance's task list. The Strategic Concept of 1991 mentioned a residual threat posed by the Soviet Union/Russia, with "conventional forces larger than those of any other European state" and a "nuclear arsenal comparable only with that of the United States."[1] Nevertheless, in the post-1991 security environment, the alliance had to find "second-order purposes" after it had "lost its first-order purpose."[2] These new tasks included crisis management in the periphery of NATO–Europe (Bosnia and Kosovo), spreading stability by expansion of NATO membership into Central and Eastern Europe (CEE) and crisis management out of area, beyond Europe's periphery. There were also the continuing tasks of providing an institutional frame for transactions between member states and of stabilizing relations between NATO members. Especially the task of making Germany's neighbors feel secure had taken on new urgency after the unification of East and West Germany in 1990.

Besides these secondary purposes, the institutional inertia of its organizational structure also helped NATO survive the end of the Soviet threat. NATO was an institution not only in the sense of neoliberal international relations theory but also in the sense of a sociological analysis of institutions with their structures and roles, creating stable dispositions in participating individuals.[3]

Realist alliance theories focus on external threats to national security as reasons for alliance formation, but they often neglect that alliances also give structure to internal relations. Against outside threats, alliances form a politico-military combination. Internally, they form a security community guaranteeing nonaggression among members. They also institutionalize the roles of members contributing in different ways to the alliance as leaders and followers. NATO's first secretary-general, Lord Ismay, summarized the rationale of the alliance in a useful formula: "to keep the Russians out, to keep the Germans down, and to keep the Americans in." Thus, NATO had, from its beginning, internal purposes besides the external task of deterring any Soviet invasion of Western Europe.

After the Cold War, the loss of NATO's primary purpose started a search for other tasks and a discussion of the nature and durability of alliances in general. As the most powerful alliance in the world and as the only surviving multilateral alliance of the Cold War period, NATO was such a prominent case that it could serve as a test for different explanations of alliance formation and continuity.

ALLIANCES AS RESPONSE TO THREATS

Realists argue that alliances are a response to the balance or imbalance of power, leading either to counterbalancing (finding security in alliances against stronger powers) or to "bandwagoning" (finding security in allegiance to stronger powers). From this perspective, alliances last as long as the external threat that shaped the alliance initially. This approach predicted a short future for NATO unless the alliance found a renewed rationale in threats of a similar magnitude.[4]

In this logic, the end of the Soviet Union would bring about not only the dissolution of the Warsaw Pact but also the end of NATO. Accordingly, John Mearsheimer expected the return of great power rivalry in Europe, with Britain, France, Germany, Italy, and Russia reenacting nineteenth-century balance-of-power games.[5] Yet more than a decade later, European powers still preferred membership in NATO and the European Union (EU) to any renationalization of security.

A better chance of survival for NATO was implied by Stephen M. Walt's "balance of threat" theory. While Morgenthau's classical realism derived alliance formation directly from the balance of power, Walt argued that states "ally to balance against threats rather than against power alone" and that the level of threat perceived was "affected by geographic proximity, offensive capabilities, and perceived intentions" of adversary states.[6] American actions affected the perceptions of allies, and "efforts to demonstrate U.S. credibility through the frequent use of force are more likely to cause others to fear U.S. ambitions," and "the less threatening the United States appears, the more popular it is likely to be."[7] Although Walt's argument was developed in the Cold War environment, applying it to the post-1991 situations would suggest that NATO's internal imbalance between the United States and less powerful European partners need not result in counterbalancing as long as U.S. pre-eminence was not perceived as a threat.

The realist expectations of a fast breakup of NATO after 1991, followed by a renationalization of security, were obviously wrong. Realist approaches failed to understand that NATO was not an alliance concluded merely for one campaign or one war, unlike the short-lived alliances described by historians since Thucydides. During the Pelopponesian War, alliances between ancient Greek city-states could change within weeks or days, depending on short-term threat situations or regime change, whenever the faction friendly to Sparta ousted the faction friendly to Athens from city government or vice versa. This changeability of alliances was also applicable during the European Middle Ages. Realist thinking was also influenced by the examples from the nineteenth century when Metternich, Bismarck, and other leaders managed the European balance of power in ever-changing alliances. However, NATO's structure was more durable than ancient Greek alliances or great power arrangements in the nineteenth century.

BENEFITS OF INSTITUTIONALIZED COOPERATION BUT ALSO ALLOCATION OF ASYMMETRICAL ROLES

Liberal-institutionalist thinkers suggest that alliances might last longer than the need to balance an external threat. International institutions achieve benefits for participant states, such as lower transaction costs, sharing of information, and enforceable rules, making membership rewarding regardless of the existence of external threats. This approach implied that NATO had a future beyond the end of the Soviet Union. However, it also followed that NATO did not have to remain a military alliance (against external threats) but could change into a "security community,"[8] that is, an international organization facilitating peaceful relations between participants.

The liberal-institutionalist approach can explain some of the longevity of NATO, serving as a convenient forum for transatlantic interaction and as a security community creating an internal space of cooperation and excluding armed conflicts between participants. As provider of stability, NATO could extend its membership to create a larger space of stability. Of course, this security community would be different from the military alliance of the Cold War period.

However, such liberal-institutionalist approaches neglect the asymmetrical nature of relations within alliances, with great powers exercising leadership and junior allies acting as followers. Internally, alliances not only function as a security community establishing a zone of nonaggression; they also institutionalize different roles for members in an internal division of labor. While the existence of alliances is shaped by the balance of power and the balance of threats in the entire international system, the distribution of roles within an alliance is shaped by the internal distribution of power among alliance members.

SOCIOLOGY OF INSTITUTIONAL INERTIA

The sociology of institutions offers a stronger concept of institutional stability than liberal-institutionalist theories of international relations. The latter understands institutions as a regime institutionalizing interaction between states. On the other hand, the sociological approach regards institutions as a regulated pattern of interaction with structures, rules, roles, and stable internalized dispositions of participating individuals. This approach to institutions was especially relevant in the case of the transatlantic alliance because it was more than an international regime; it was a massive organization shaping thousands of careers. In the early 1950s, NATO decided "to set up a standing military organization as well as military headquarters . . . and structures for policy co-ordination, an Allied command structure, joint planning procedures as well as joint exercises."[9] Once established, an institution produces habits and attitudes in participants identifying not only with its original purpose but also with its survival while searching for new purposes. At the highest political level, an entrenched institution such as NATO had the capacity to search for a new function in the security architecture of the twenty-first century instead of disbanding.

The institutional structure entrenched over four decades explained some of NATO's longevity. The transatlantic alliance was not just a treaty with pledges by nation-states to support one another, but NATO was, after the end of the Warsaw Pact, the only alliance with an integrated command structure even in times of peace. NATO had headquarters in Brussels as well as regional commands. Member states had allocated forces to the alliance to be permanently under NATO command and participating in regular exercises.

This structural stability was consolidated at the individual level through "the extensive day-to-day cooperation taking place within the relatively large bureaucracy of the Alliance, in Brussels as well as at SHAPE [Supreme Headquarters of Allied Powers in Europe]. . . . It can be safely assumed that it also to an extent moulds the civil servants and military officers serving in NATO and influences them when they return to their home countries."[10] Participant officers and bureaucrats developed habits solidified by years of cooperation and subordination. NATO offered career patterns for senior officers, leading them to identify with the alliance as much as with their respective national governments. The alliance was an entrenched institution, with its civilian committees, military staff structures, facilities, habits of cooperation, military exercises, and individual careers. Personnel delegated from member states were socialized and developed a corporate identity as NATO personnel willing to influence defense policy in the member states.

During the decades of the Cold War, while it served as deterrent against an external threat and as pacifier for internal relations, NATO acquired the institutional stability to survive the loss of its primary purpose by sheer institutional inertia, gaining the time to search for new purposes. The numerous decision makers and officials habituated to NATO were more inclined to search a purpose for an existing structure than to dissolve a structure after the completion of its main purpose.

THE VALUE COMMUNITY AND ITS LIMITS

Shared values and identities were consolidated by long-term cooperation in the NATO framework and in turn contributed to its post-1991 survival. In a constructivist approach to international relations, culture and identity are central concepts, and they can also help explain the longevity of NATO. Indeed, throughout the Cold War, NATO and the Warsaw Pact were held together not just by calculations of the relative power of the United States and the Soviet Union resulting in realist decisions for counterbalancing or bandwagoning by junior powers. NATO was united by common values and preferences in opposition to the communist experiments of the Soviet Union and China, not simply by a pragmatic response to a given balance of power. The entire network of U.S.-led alliances was also a community of values in opposition to the communist bloc. Compared to other Cold War alliances, NATO was a closer community, as it could also rely on a cultural and historical identity shared between the transatlantic partners. This transatlantic community of values was still relevant in the context of Huntington's "clash of civilizations" thesis, which attempted to predict future lines of conflict but also implied future alliance patterns. Huntington's logic suggests that the civilization shared between Europe and North America might sustain the alliance beyond the end of anticommunist cooperation. While Japan and the United States merely shared anticommunist values, the United States and Europe shared the anticommunist orientation as well as their "Western" civilization. This argument has to be questioned, however, because the civilizational unity of the West may not be as solid as Huntington hoped. The discussions about the transatlantic "value gap"[11] since the late 1990s indicated that differences between different versions of the "West" could weaken the transatlantic value community.

The alliance's common culture and identity were indeed shared very unevenly among members. Culturally, the United States and the anglophile Atlanticists of Europe shared a transatlantic identity more deeply than the Gaullists and Europeanists for whom U.S. cultural influence was somewhat alien. This differentiation of alliance cohesion became more relevant after 1991. During the Cold War, the values shared by all NATO members, in contrast to the Soviet Union, were more salient. Against the Soviet Union, the "West" was a normative reality. However, after the end of the Soviet Union, shared anticommunist preferences receded into the background, while previously irrelevant differences became more prominent.

NATO AS U.S. LEADERSHIP INSTITUTIONALIZED

American leadership in the West was institutionalized at the moment of greatest U.S. supremacy at the end of World War II. By founding international institutions, the hegemon exercised self-restraint, sacrificing some freedom of unilateral action. On the other hand, U.S. hegemony gained greater acceptance, legitimacy, and permanence by binding secondary powers into stable structures. Analyzing the post-1945 situation, G. John Ikenberry argued convincingly that this institutionalist approach enhanced U.S. leadership in the West: "If the United States had not endeavoured to build the array of regional and global institutions that it did in the 1940s, it is difficult to imagine that American power would have had the scope, depth, or longevity that in fact it has had."[12] Implied by Ikenberry's argument was the suggestion that President George W. Bush was squandering the leading role of the United States established by Presidents Roosevelt and Truman half a century earlier. While the Bush administration intended to enhance primacy by freeing the United States of institutional restraints, the short-term benefits of unilateralism were, according to Ikenberry, small compared to the long-term damage to U.S. leadership.

The United States had promoted the foundation of the United Nations, the NATO alliance, and other structures not for some altruistic reasons to the detriment of U.S. power but in order to stabilize the supremacy of the mid-1940s in a cost-effective way. A little self-restraint could buy acceptance of U.S. hegemony by junior allies. Offering allies voice opportunities was a small price willingly paid by a confident hegemon, enjoying unprecedented economic and military supremacy in comparison to old rivals such as the exhausted British Empire or France, Japan, and Germany. This was the foundation of U.S. hegemony in the West not understood by neoconservative unilateralists in the Bush administration. Their naive enjoyment of the freedom of unilateral action was squandering the foundations of stable institutionalized hegemony.

NATO structures, at the time of foundation, reflected the internal balance of power among alliance members, which was distinctively asymmetrical. The alliance was not only a defensive agreement against an external threat and a security community stabilizing internal space. It was, at the same time, part of an enduring arrangement for U.S. hegemony within the West. Institutions do not only reduce the transaction costs for nation-states by providing a forum for communication and a stable pattern of relations and roles; they also stabilize asymmetrical relations between hegemon and followers. NATO and other post-1945 alliances "in effect acknowledge the status of Western Europe, Japan and South Korea as American protectorates,"[13] in the words of Zbigniew Brzezinski, President Carter's national security adviser.

Even after the end of the Soviet threat, NATO still had the function of structuring internal relations, by creating a security community among members and institutionalizing U.S. leadership. The security community was enlarged when the alliance expanded into CEE. NATO continued to stabilize Western Europe: according to D. Yost, the alliance and continued U.S. engagement were still required to render Germany unproblematic for its European neighbors. The other aspect of NATO's internal function was implicitly acknowledged in Ikenberry's argument: American leadership in the mid-1940s was successfully exercised and stabilized through the foundation of institutions, including NATO.

French analysts were most sensitive to the asymmetrical nature of relations within the transatlantic alliance. "Because the United States has long been one of the world's main military powers, its alliances have often taken the shape of a positive security guarantee and are thus unequal: one side (in this case the United States) protects the other." Where American commentators might see the United States as exporter of security and altruistic provider of a common good, Bruno Tertrais draws attention to the "great benefit to the United States" in the form of "influence in the respective foreign policies of allied countries" and the availability of "bases for power projection."[14]

MILITARY PROTECTORATE OVER FORMER RIVALS

After World War II, U.S. troops stayed in Europe. Compared to the end of World War I, the situation differed in two respects: first, the bipolar confrontation between the Soviet Union and the United States shaping the years from 1947 to 1991, and, second, the opportunity for the United States to relegate the former superpower Britain as well as several challengers for great power roles to the second rank.

The benign character of U.S. hegemony was emphasized by G. John Ikenberry pointing to the self-restraint exercised by the leader of the West after 1945. American leadership was welcome not only because it offered protection against Soviet communism but also because it was exercised through an "institutional bargain" in a rule-bound, institutionalized manner. Other authors highlighted more clearly the subordination involved in the transatlantic partnership. Brzezinski, for example, compared NATO to historical empires and NATO allies to "vassals" and "barbarians" who were to be kept divided, subordinate, and dependent by the hegemon.[15]

The post-1945 balance of power within transatlantic relations was institutionalized in the NATO alliance. The subordination of former great powers to the second rank in the informal empire of the United States and the replacement of their colonial empires by U.S. hegemony were outcomes of World War II usually overshadowed by more visible outcomes, such as the defeat of the Axis powers (Hitler Germany, Mussolini Italy, and militarist Japan), the rise of new superpowers (the United States and the Soviet Union), and the end of colonial empires. The Cold War and decolonization overshadowed traditional great-power rivalry. Nevertheless, while it had been pushed into the background by the unchallenged supremacy of the United States within the West, by Cold War bipolarity, and by decolonization, great-power rivalry had always continued in the background and reappeared after 1991, albeit not in the manner predicted by John Mearsheimer in 1990. He expected a return of rivalries within Europe and the need to bring about a balance of power to keep future confrontations between Germany, France, Britain, Russia, and other European powers under control.[16] Yet post-1991 reality was different. European integration had put an end to intra-European great-power conflicts. Instead, the European bloc as a whole stated the intention of becoming a geopolitical actor.

This situation defined the options the United States had regarding post-1991 Europe. First, the United States could continue to relate to Europe through NATO, maintaining the asymmetrical relation in a rule-bound institutionalized hegemony. Second, the United States could adopt unilateralism, freeing itself from the restraint of institutional rules and the need to consult allies but also squandering a foundation of U.S. hegemony since the middle of the twentieth century. And third, the United States could accept that the post-1945 military protectorate was coming to an end. Instead of regretting this loss of transatlantic hegemony, the United States could welcome a new, more symmetrical relationship with the European bloc.

UNILATERALISM OR LEADING THROUGH INSTITUTIONS? ARE ALLIANCES OUTDATED?

Alliances last as long as the hegemonic power sees benefits in leading through multilateral institutions. A superpower in a unipolar international system could hope to be better off without cumbersome alliances. The unilateralist freedom to use power without restraint by institutional rules can be tempting, but it risks the advantages of regulated cooperation and legitimacy by consensus. NATO was "the single remaining multilateral alliance of the network created by U.S. diplomacy in the 1950s."[17] Yet the fate of other alliances seems to indicate that "permanent multilateral alliances appear increasingly to belong to the past."[18] The Southeast Asia Treaty Organization ended in June 1977; in May 1979, the Central Treaty Organization came to an end after Iran, Iraq, and Pakistan had left earlier, leaving the last members, Turkey and the United Kingdom, to close down the alliance. As alliances ceased to exist, the United States was also becoming more able to act unilaterally, and NATO was also becoming less relevant to the security of the United States. "The ratio of costs to benefits has changed to such an extent that conservative commentators have called for a radical reshuffling of U.S. commitments and bases abroad."[19] These doubts about alliances could be regarded as expressions of confident supremacy in a unipolar era, when the only superpower was capable of unilateral action and felt hampered by the need to consult allies. However, such doubts about alliances could also be a sign of diminishing supremacy in a transition to multipolarity, when formerly complying allies no longer provide willing and unquestioning followership.

President George W. Bush's choice to bypass alliances in favor of unilateral action, in contrast to President Roosevelt's leadership through institutions and alliances, might be regarded as appropriate for the only superpower in a unipolar era. However, it is more plausible to find greater confidence in comprehensive U.S. economic and military supremacy expressed in President Roosevelt's leadership through alliances and institutions, assured of willing compliance of allies and not dependent on improvised coalitions. Half a century later, the unilateralism of the Bush administration was a symptom of reduced supremacy, limited to the military realm, while the U.S. economy was affected by the competition of Europe, Japan, China, and others.

In contrast to opinions regarding alliances as outdated and rather useless, others argued that the transatlantic alliance was still essential. Either NATO should be maintained as vehicle of U.S. leadership, with its customary asymmetrical roles, or, if the EU was becoming a strong and unified actor, the relationship should become more symmetrical. In either case, an effort to renew the alliance was required. *"Renewing the Atlantic Partnership"* was the title of a report published by the influential Council on Foreign Relations in 2004.[20] The task force included traditional Atlanticists seeking to retain U.S. leadership in a continued alliance, such as Henry Kissinger, but also advocates of more symmetrical U.S.–EU relations, such as Charles A. Kupchan. In spite of differences, they found common ground in their implied critique of neoconservative unilateralism and neglect of Europe. According to the Council on Foreign Relations task force, U.S. national interest required an effort to renew the transatlantic alliance.

CHALLENGES TO NATO'S LONGEVITY AFTER 1991

Realist thinking about alliances expected NATO not to survive the end of the Soviet threat unless a new threat could be found to unite the alliance. The sociology of institutions suggested that organizational structures and habitual roles of participants allowed an alliance to continue through institutional inertia, especially one with a solid structure such as NATO. Constructivists could point to shared values and a NATO identity resulting from decades of cooperation. Finally, liberal institutionalists could emphasize the benefits of institutions in reducing international anarchy and making relations between states more manageable. In addition, there was the interest of the United States in exercising leadership through NATO by continuing the asymmetrical relations with Europe established in 1949. These arguments, taken together, explain why NATO did not instantly disband the moment the Soviet Union disintegrated.

Yet Europe's security environment had changed thoroughly in 1991. While NATO's Strategic Concept of 1991 still identified a residual threat from the successor of the defunct Soviet Union, it also acknowledged that Europe was safer now than ever before. This was bound to affect NATO. The military alliance had to find new purposes. For example, according to U.S. Senator Richard Lugar, it had to go "out of area or out of business," to find a new role in crisis management beyond the territory of member states or else face its demise.

Institutional inertia was capable of buying NATO several years of continued existence, but without a clear external threat, it could not survive as a military alliance. During the Cold War, NATO provided protection against an external threat; it was an intergovernmental forum according to liberal institutionalism; it was consolidated by anticommunist values and a shared Western identity. After the nature of threats had changed in 1991, common values and shared identities were not sufficient to create alliance cohesion in the face of multifaceted and multidirectional threats. And the liberal-institutionalist perspective suggested that if NATO survived, it would do so not as a military alliance against external threats but as a security community regulating internal relations. Realist approaches expected NATO not to survive at all unless it found renewed justification in an external threat of a magnitude similar to the Soviet threat.

As U.S. security interests shifted away from Europe to other regions, the Clinton administration argued for "a broadening, if not globalization of NATO's duties" in "an attempt of the United States to transform the Alliance into an instrument of power projection." However, "the U.S.' European allies are principally interested in having the U.S. Army at their front door."[21] Atlanticists still expected the United States to look after Europe, whereas Europeanists began to imagine European responsibility for regional security.

In the post-1991 security environment, "NATO is slowly transforming from a collective self-defense pact, whose primary task was balancing the Soviet Union, to a mechanism of cooperative security. . . . The inherent dilemma is obvious: An alliance that has transformed into a political organization is of little military interest to the Americans; on the other hand, were NATO to become an organization engaged first and foremost in the fight against world wide terrorism, the Europeans would soon fatigue both militarily and politically."[22]

But NATO also had to respond to the changed internal balance of power. In 1949, NATO brought together an economically and militarily superior United States with a group of grateful medium-sized and small powers in a military protectorate. Half a century later, Europeans had formed an economic bloc of a magnitude similar to the United States. And Europe no longer faced a major threat requiring U.S. military presence. After 1991, when NATO had lost its purpose to keep the Soviets out, its function as vehicle of U.S. leadership in Europe was also less legitimate.

Since 1991, the Soviet threat was absent. The economic superiority of the United States was greatly reduced compared to 1950. On the other hand, there were still the military supremacy of the United States, the structure of NATO entrenching past role allocations, and the habits and perceptions among allies shaped by the preceding 50 years. In this situation, the United States had the option of continuing to use NATO as vehicle of U.S. leadership in Europe at the risk of alienating allies much more capable of looking after their own security than in 1949. The other option for the United States would be to accept Europe as equal partner and to replace "NATO first" by "Europe first," that is, to relate to Europe as a bloc, not as a collection of junior allies in NATO.

A renewal of the transatlantic alliance, together with an end of unilateralism, was suggested by the report of a task force of the Council on Foreign Relations in 2004. It argued that Europe was still the indispensable ally, while the United States was still the indispensable nation for European security. NATO could have a future by taking on a more global role. For this purpose, the transatlantic partners should abstain from polemics exacerbating differences and "lower the rhetorical temperature"[23] and concentrate instead on healing the transatlantic rift and giving NATO a new role.

Institutional inertia allowed NATO's structure to survive the completion of its main task and the loss of its primary purpose. As the pressure to find a raison d'être in the post-1991 security environment continued, NATO found temporary tasks justifying its continued existence while also transforming itself from a collective defense organization into a larger and looser security community. Yet European economic integration had also created the potential for the EU to take on responsibility for security in Europe and to replace NATO in its earlier central function.

CHAPTER 4

Limited New Lease on Life: NATO's Tasks after 1991

The new tasks adopted by the North Atlantic Treaty Organization (NATO) could not do for the transatlantic alliance what the existence of the Soviet Union had done until 1991. NATO's primary purpose had provided a lasting rationale for its existence and for the asymmetrical relations within the alliance. However, the collapse of the Soviet Union and NATO's very success in the Cold War cast doubt on its future. Unless it could find new purposes, its years were numbered.

Since 1991, NATO's new tasks have given the alliance a new lease of life, but each of these secondary purposes also transformed and weakened it. The inclusion of new members in Central and Eastern Europe (CEE) extended NATO as a security community but also diluted it as a military alliance. Intervention in Bosnia and Kosovo demonstrated the indispensability of the United States but it also made European powers more determined to become capable of autonomous crisis management. And while NATO's reorientation from territorial defense to power projection made the alliance more capable to respond to post-1991 security risks, the diversity of new threats also increased disunity in NATO.

NATO's post-1991 secondary purposes posed challenges to alliance cohesion. If European members did not adapt their forces to NATO's new tasks, the capabilities gap between the transatlantic partners could develop into a mission gap if forces ceased to be interoperable. In the 2001 campaign in Afghanistan, "the question already raised in Kosovo of whether the Europeans would again be able to fight alongside the high-tech Americans became more acute than ever."[1] On the other hand, Europeans could upgrade defense capabilities sufficiently to take on responsibility for their own security.

In this case, U.S. engagement in Europe would no longer be indispensable. Each of the answers to NATO's loss of primary purpose posed new questions. The most likely outcome was its transformation from a collective defense alliance into a looser security community.

The transatlantic alliance had been the center of Western European security architecture during the Cold War, and "though NATO may have lost its first-order purpose, it has served many second-order purposes very well"[2] after 1991. However, while the new tasks extended the alliance's life span, they also advanced the quest of the European Union (EU) for a security role and multiplied sources of disunity between the United States and European NATO members.

NATO'S CONTINUING OLD TASKS

NATO's original purposes still had some residual relevance. The alliance had been founded "to keep the Russians out, to keep the Germans down, and to keep the Americans in." A decade after the end of the Soviet Union, some commentators still expected NATO "to provide a defensive and collective security system against Russia and Yugoslavia."[3] NATO's Strategic Concept of 1991 identified a residual threat from the Soviet Union or from Russia as the heir of Soviet nuclear forces. And after German unification had added a quarter to the Federal Republic's population in 1990, Germany's neighbors could once more appreciate U.S. presence as insurance against German ambitions. Yet the reasons for NATO's third original purpose, "to keep the Americans in," had grown weaker compared to 1949. Russia was not the Soviet Union, although the nuclear arms were still there. And Germany, even after unification, was smaller than it had been in 1914 and 1939; it was also deeply integrated in the EU. Thus, with a weakened Russia and a very Europeanized Germany, the original reasons for continued U.S. involvement in Europe via NATO were less convincing. Finally, the interest of the United States in a leadership role in Europe weakened as priorities shifted to the Middle East and East Asia.

NATO'S NEW TASKS

Extending a Zone of Stability: Expansion into CEE

NATO found a new task in the stabilization of CEE. As these countries were no longer separated from Western Europe by the Iron Curtain, the former Warsaw Pact members expected the EU to support their economic development, but they looked to the United States and NATO for security. Recognition as part of the West and acceptance by its leading power, the United States, was of enormous symbolic significance for CEE governments. NATO and the United States were welcomed as liberators from Soviet control. Historically, especially Poland had experienced aggression and domination by Russia and Germany. These deeply embedded memories made NATO membership and U.S. presence imperative for CEE leaders. The willingness of CEE countries to join was greater than the initial willingness of NATO to admit them. Through halfway houses such as the Partnership for Peace and the North Atlantic Cooperation Council, CEE countries were brought closer to NATO. The new members were admitted in two waves, so far. The Czech Republic, Hungary, and Poland joined on March 12, 1999; Estonia, Latvia, Lithuania, Slovakia, Slovenia, Bulgaria, and Romania followed in April 2004, increasing NATO membership from 19 to 26 countries.

Germany was especially interested, because of its location at the former line of division between NATO and the Warsaw Pact, in preventing instability among its immediate neighbors to the east of united Germany's new borders. Thus, the German government advocated, in the early 1990s, expansion of NATO into CEE. This issue was first taken up by Defense Minister Volker Rühe, whereas Foreign Minister Hans-Dietrich Genscher argued for developing the Organization for Security and Cooperation (OSCE) as a framework of East–West cooperation. Yet Genscher's approach was sidelined as Chancellor Helmut Kohl backed Rühe's proposal.[4] By advocating parallel expansion of NATO and the EU, Germany was once more able to combine and balance Atlanticism and EU integration. While German politicians took the first initiative regarding NATO expansion into CEE, the United States eventually took the lead. President Clinton announced in July 1994 that Poland, the Czech Republic, and Hungary were to join NATO in 1999.[5]

A significant negative effect of NATO's expansion was the alienation of Russia. The first wave of expansion brought Russian cities within easier striking range of NATO missiles and planes. The second wave included the former Soviet republics of Lithuania, Latvia, and Estonia, bringing NATO within a few kilometers of St Petersburg. While the alliance's expansion was accompanied by diplomatic measures to make it more acceptable for Russia, it was still perceived as a threat by Russian generals, nationalist politicians, and many voters. It has motivated Russian strategists to find ways of weakening NATO and to seek opportunities for antihegemonic counterbalancing. Russia's siding with France and Germany regarding the war in Iraq made sense as an attempt to counter NATO expansion and to encourage divisions within the alliance.

To minimize the damage to relations with Russia caused by NATO expansion, Russia was brought closer to NATO with the Founding Act on Mutual Relations, Cooperation and Security between NATO and the Russian Federation of May 1997. This agreement stated that "NATO and Russia do not consider each other as adversaries" and established the NATO-Russia Permanent Joint Council, making Russia a participant in most NATO deliberations.[6] This form of cooperation succeeded in making NATO expansion more palatable to Russia, although it did not prevent serious disagreements with Russia during NATO's military conflict with Serbia in 1999.

Parallel expansion of NATO and the EU could be unproblematic as long as the traditional division of labor between them continued. With NATO providing the security framework, the EU could concentrate on economic integration and the pursuit of prosperity and welfare objectives as it had done since the European Defense Community failed in 1954. For CEE countries, NATO membership came faster than EU membership. Compared to the cumbersome process of preparing for the EU, joining the transatlantic alliance offered fast symbolic rewards as well as lasting benefits, including civilian control over the military, a prerequisite for NATO membership. Membership in the EU, on the other hand, required more elaborate preparation to fulfill the Copenhagen Criteria adopted by the EU in 1993. Since then, CEE governments and EU bureaucrats cooperated to enable future members to adopt the "acquis communautaire."[7] Admission to a single-purpose military alliance was less complex than participating in multipurpose economic and political integration affecting the daily lives of all citizens.

In the short and medium term, NATO expansion consolidated U.S. influence in Europe through an impressive network of military advisers working with CEE forces and defense departments. The U.S. defense industry has gained customers likely to buy American rather than European. American strategy has also gained new locations for military facilities as well as participants in U.S.-led coalitions of the willing, contributing troops to the Iraq campaign, for example. NATO membership of CEE countries has become a vehicle of U.S. influence used to counter EU influence. Thus, NATO's expansion into CEE also contributed to tensions between the United States and the EU, although both developments were initially conceived as complementary.

In the short term, new NATO members in CEE were looking to NATO and the United States for security, while the EU managed economic integration. In the long term, however, stronger influence was likely to be exercised by membership in the EU, by the everyday experience of economic and political integration.[8] The longer new members participated in EU economic integration, the more plausible the EU was to become as provider of security, eventually replacing NATO. American disengagement from Europe was also likely to affect attitudes in CEE countries, although some U.S. troops withdrawn from Western Europe were relocated to CEE. In the long run, the reorientation of U.S. strategy away from Europe would leave CEE countries with little choice but to accept the EU as main provider of regional security.

NATO found new legitimacy in this successful expansion of a zone of stability in CEE. Nevertheless, the very success of NATO expansion also diminished its relevance. NATO traditionalists argued that the new members were adding not to NATO's military capacity but only to possible entanglements. Expansion raised the question, "Is NATO a military alliance performing the function of collective defense or is it a collective security organization seeking to expand a zone of security within Europe?"[9]

This outcome irritated defenders of NATO's traditional role. "The Clinton administration is gradually converting NATO from a collective defense organization . . . into a collective security organization . . . that allows little flexibility on the part of the nation's policymakers. . . . , the decision to transform and expand NATO will be seen as a critical error." The countries of CEE were joining NATO for invalid reasons: "Aspiring NATO members are seeking membership in the Cold War NATO. But that NATO no longer exists."[10] Especially Poland was concerned about NATO's diminishing territorial defense function and weakening anti-Russian posture, but Polish efforts to forge close links with the United States and to extend NATO's old primary function could not stop U.S. disengagement and NATO's transformation.

In its promotion of NATO expansion, "the United States appears to place the enlargement of NATO before its effectiveness. This reinforces the impression that whilst the United States might be *with* NATO it is hardly any longer *of* NATO." If the alliance becomes "'political NATO,'" the United States will have transformed it into "a means of creating and disciplining European political support for unilateral American action."[11]

NATO expansion extended U.S. influence and gave the alliance a temporary rationale. The alliance has also been strengthened by the Atlanticist orientation of new members. On the other hand, expansion contributed to the transformation of the military alliance into a security community. In the long run, the tortoise of EU integration should overtake the hare of NATO membership in the race for relevance, especially as U.S. troops were redeployed away from Europe, while the everyday experience of economic integration strengthened the EU's credibility as provider of security.

Stabilizing Post-Soviet Space by Association with NATO

NATO and the EU contributed to stability during postcommunist transformation by extending membership to their immediate neighbors in CEE. Farther to the east, however, membership was not on offer for most successor states of the Soviet Union, but other forms of association were developed. Arrangements such as the Partnership for Peace program or the North Atlantic Cooperation Council served either as halfway houses for prospective NATO members or as loose associations with NATO for those destined never to become members. Through these measures, all former Soviet republics were associated with NATO in a large and loose security community. These links encouraged pro-Western orientations among new leaders and helped contain the crisis potential in post-Soviet space, in contrast to the violent disintegration of Yugoslavia.

While the Soviet Union had been the enemy providing the rationale for NATO's existence, Russia, the military heir of the Soviet Union, was considered a residual threat but also a potential partner in economic and security cooperation. Russia was brought closer to the alliance through its participation in the NATO-Russia Permanent Joint Council, established in May 1997.[12] This institutionalized mode of consultation made NATO less threatening to Moscow and its expansion into CEE more palatable, reducing the potential of a nationalist backlash against pro-Western Russian leaders.

NATO's success in contributing to stability in post-Soviet space was also beneficial for the EU by transforming a zone of potential instability into a region where the EU could establish economic links. Yet beyond this shared general interest in stability, the interests of the EU and the United States diverged in relation to Russia, the Caucasus, and Central Asia. For Russia, the United States was a competitor challenging Russian influence in Central Asia and the Caucasus. The EU, on the other hand, was Russia's most important trade partner and a potential ally in an effort to counter U.S. hegemony.

In the early 1990s, the United States had been reluctant to expand NATO because extending security guarantees to CEE countries added significant conflict potential without greatly enhancing the military capabilities of the alliance. Over time, however, the United States agreed to the admission of 10 new members. This suggested that the United States accepted or welcomed the transformation of NATO. The eventual membership of Ukraine would advance this process further, and Russian membership would complete it. The more NATO expanded, the less it was a military alliance against external threats by state actors and the more it was becoming a security community securing peace within.

Crisis Management at Europe's Periphery: Bosnia and Kosovo

The alliance's first out-of-area mission took place in ex-Yugoslavia, at the periphery of NATO–Europe. Interventions in Bosnia and Kosovo showed that NATO was capable of action. On the other hand, they also made divisions within NATO visible. The United States vacillated between the impulse to stay out of irrelevant European crises and the need to demonstrate that U.S. leadership was still indispensable. Leading EU powers displayed a lack of political cooperation and unity, deficient military capabilities, and continued dependence on the United States as guarantor of European security. This guarantee was, however, undermined by the realization that the United States was, first, hesitant to get involved and, second, reluctant to consult allies regarding the conduct of the intervention.

The first serious challenge to NATO occurred when Yugoslavia's disintegration crises reached Bosnia. Earlier, ethnically rather homogeneous Slovenia and Croatia had separated from the Serb-dominated Yugoslav federation with only limited violence. However, to replicate the formation of a mono-ethnic mini-state was impossible for Bosnia-Herzegovina, where the population consisted of three substantial ethnic-religious groups. Bosnia could either function as a multicultural society or break up into three political entities separating Bosnian Serbs, Bosnian Croats, and Bosnian Muslims, but it could not be dominated by one group. The eruption of nationalism in other parts of Yugoslavia deepened divisions in Bosnia, resulting in a civil war, including massacres and ethnic cleansing. While Bosnian Muslim and Croat forces were not innocent of human rights violations, the massacre of Srebrenica committed by armed forces of the Bosnian Republika Srpska provoked international intervention.

The cohesion of the transatlantic alliance was severely tested when the refusal of the Clinton administration to provide U.S. ground troops left the peacekeepers of the United Nations Protection Force (UNPROFOR), most of them British and French, in a perilous situation. The U.S. Senate's vote in July 1995 to lift the arms embargo against Bosnian Muslims threatened to destroy UNPROFOR's impartiality and provoke Serb attacks. Without U.S. ground troops sharing the risk, the strategy of lifting the arms embargo and threatening air strikes implied serious risks for British and French UNPROFOR troops. At this moment, if the United States had "left allied forces to fight their own way out against both Serbs and the deserted Bosniaks . . . the whole American security guarantee and process of NATO consultation would be exposed as a sham."[13] Finally, the United States pledged ground troops if necessary.

American involvement eventually induced the warring parties to a compromise in the Dayton Agreement of 1995. The territories under the respective control of Serbs, Croats, and Muslims were held together by a tenuous political construction, bringing together the Croat-Muslim federation and the Republika Srpska under the umbrella of a joint government for Bosnia-Herzegovina. The stabilization of this precarious balance depended on the Implementation Force, succeeded after one year by the Stabilization Force. Here NATO became involved in a multinational operation requiring ground troops to keep peace in Bosnia for years to come.

The next focus of Yugoslavia's disintegration crises was Serbia's Kosovo province. Ethnic Albanians, clearly the majority of Kosovo's population, demanded independence, whereas Serbia wanted to retain the province. As fighting between the insurgent separatists of the Kosovo Liberation Army (KLA) and regular Serbian government forces escalated, NATO intervened on the side of the KLA. The cruelties of the Bosnian civil war had sensitized the international public, and repressive actions by Serb forces were interpreted in the West as the beginning Serbian plans to drive hundred thousands of ethnic Albanians out of Kosovo. Effectively, as armed actions by the KLA provoked Serb government retaliation, the separatist guerilla organization succeeded in enlisting NATO, de facto, as its air force.

American intervention in Kosovo came late, as in Bosnia, and when it happened it was conducted on U.S. terms with limited consultation of NATO allies. When the Clinton administration finally decided to get involved through NATO, the allies were hardly consulted about the course of negotiations with Serbia and the conduct of the war after negotiations in Rambouillet had broken down. Once more reluctant to risk the lives of ground troops, the United States opted for high-altitude bombing as the preferred method for the campaign against Serbia's government. While this approach made use of unique U.S. capabilities, it hardly achieved the stated objective of the war. Instead of protecting Kosovo Albanians from expulsion, the six-week bombing campaign of NATO multiplied the numbers of displaced persons leaving the province.

The intervention in Kosovo and the war against Serbia in 1999 were the first combat mission of NATO in its entire history since 1949. For analysts with Atlanticist leanings, it showed the indispensability of the United States as guarantor of security in Europe. "NATO has been looking for a reason for its continued existence. The humanitarian intervention in Kosovo may become that raison d'etre."[14] NATO and U.S. leadership were still indispensable because European NATO members on their own were not even capable of pacifying the Balkans. The Kosovo crisis demonstrated that European powers did not have the unity of political will to implement any Common Foreign and Security Policy (CFSP) as intended by the Maastricht Treaty. Nor did they have the required military capabilities. The conduct of the war relied heavily on U.S. bombers and satellite intelligence. If the Kosovo experience demonstrated the indispensability of U.S. involvement in Europe, the allies should enhance the cohesion of the transatlantic alliance by not allowing the capabilities gap between the transatlantic partners to develop into a mission gap.

However, the political and military events in Kosovo 1998–99 also raised doubts whether the U.S. could be relied on in future European crises. On the surface, "the events of the 1990s suggest that the United States will remain Europe's chief protector and peacemaker long into this new century. . . . NATO's intervention in Yugoslavia demonstrated that, in President Clinton's words, America is 'the indispensable nation,' and that American power and purpose are alive and well in Europe. Beneath the surface, however, a different picture is emerging."[15] In spite of the leading role of the United States in the war against Serbia, "America's behavior in Kosovo was indicative of a broader retrenchment in U.S. foreign policy that will become more pronounced in the years ahead. . . . As America's unipolar moment comes to an end, so too will its willingness to be the global guarantor of last resort."[16] Thus, the Kosovo crisis of the late 1990s confirmed what the Bosnian crisis of the early 1990s had revealed: EU members were too disunited to prevent crises, the United States was capable but reluctant to intervene, and, finally, the cumbersome task of stabilization was left to the Europeans.

The Capabilities Gap: Acceptable in 1950s, Divisive in 1990s

The conduct of the Kosovo campaign highlighted the capabilities gap between the United States and European NATO members. As the United States had a near monopoly of relevant armament, the decisions about the conduct of high-altitude bombing were taken by U.S. generals with little consultation of others. The most important European weaknesses were a lack of strategic airlift capacity, bombers, and satellite intelligence besides numerous other items identified in NATO's Defense Capabilities Initiative

(DCI) of 1999.[17] This capabilities gap was regarded as a serious threat to NATO's cohesion, and saving the alliance would require greater armament efforts by European allies. Yet this argument ignored that the transatlantic rift had been caused not by the capabilities gap, which had existed for 50 years, but by the fact that after the end of the Soviet threat, the roles of the transatlantic partners could not remain the same.

The capabilities gap of the 1950s did not threaten the existence of the alliance but defined the roles of the allies, although David S. Yost claimed that "capability gaps have been a constant irritant throughout NATO's history."[18] The conventional forces of NATO–Europe supplemented the superior capabilities of the nuclear superpower United States in the territorial defense of Western Europe. This capabilities gap provided Europe with a strong protector and the United States with a leadership role in the transatlantic relationship. Britain learned to accept this allocation of roles after the Suez crisis of 1956. The British and French empires were coming to an end; the United States was the undisputed leader of the West. Among British leaders, the realization of weakness led to identification with the superior transatlantic ally, and dependency was reinterpreted as "special relationship."

The capabilities gap of the 1950s also ensured that the Gaullist challenge to U.S. leadership remained unsuccessful. With the French-German Elysée Treaty of 1963, President Charles de Gaulle and Chancellor Konrad Adenauer founded the Franco-German core of future European power. Yet in recognition of the real transatlantic balance of power, an Atlanticist majority in German parliament added a preamble to the treaty asserting the priority of the transatlantic alliance.[19] In the Cold War security environment, the capabilities gap ensured European reliance on U.S. leadership in European security.

For the United States, this early capabilities gap was not a serious problem; it underpinned its leadership role in the West. Over the years, U.S. leaders repeatedly called for "burden sharing," that is, for greater contributions to NATO's armament expenditure, especially as European economies had grown stronger. Yet the United States was never very insistent on burden sharing in spite of occasional complaints about Europeans enjoying a free ride while the United States financed their security. The 1990s capability gap, on the other hand, became a threat to NATO's existence in the post-1991 security environment, after the end of the Soviet threat and with the EU developing as geostrategic actor.

Contradictory Conclusions from 1990s Capabilities Gap

For Atlanticists, the main conclusion was that, in the 1990s as in the 1950s, Europeans could not act without the United States and should therefore rely, as before, on the transatlantic partner. "America's unique credibility in deterrence remains indispensable for the preservation of stability in Europe. And so does the U.S. role as primus inter pares, for the same reasons that required American engagement when NATO was founded half a century ago."[20] Therefore, an effort by European NATO members was needed to upgrade their military capabilities in order to become more useful partners in NATO. Without this upgrade, the capabilities gap could become a mission gap rendering NATO useless. However, the opposite conclusion was now more feasible than in 1956. After the Suez crisis, France opted for the long road to military autonomy without, however, being able to end Europe's security dependence on the United States. Half a century later, the option for an autonomous European capability was still difficult but much more realistic than in the late 1950s. The Gaullist option of achieving security autonomy for France alone was still impossible, but the Europeanist option of giving the EU an autonomous security role appeared feasible.

For Atlanticists, the Kosovo crisis confirmed the indispensability of the United States as guarantor of European security. An upgraded European contribution along the lines of NATO's DCI was needed to restore the interoperability of NATO forces. For Europeanists, on the other hand, the capabilities gap demonstrated that it was time to become more serious about the CFSP adopted at the Maastricht Intergovernmental Conference (IGC) of 1991. From this perspective, upgrading of European capabilities was also necessary, but it would eventually lead to EU autonomy.

The conclusion that the United States was indispensable for European security did not necessary follow from the experience in Yugoslavia. First, U.S. reluctance to get involved in the Balkans indicated the potential of U.S. disinterest and disengagement. Second, once the United States decided to intervene, it took the lead and acted without seriously consulting allies. Third, European leaders had to face a capabilities gap threatening a mission gap. These factors made a future conceivable in which U.S. priorities outside Europe might render NATO irrelevant. "It is no coincidence that in the aftermath of Kosovo, the European Union redoubled its efforts to forge a collective defense policy and a military force capable of operating independently of the United States."[21]

For the United States, one possible conclusion from the Kosovo experience was to find a constructive solution to strengthen the transatlantic alliance. In this sense, the DCI gave European allies clear guidelines to strengthen NATO's European pillar. However, another possible conclusion for the United States was to dismiss Europe as weak and meddlesome. "Whereas many in Europe saw the Kosovo air campaign as excessively dominated by the United States and American generals, most Americans . . . saw just the opposite: excessive European meddling."[22] After Kosovo, the United States was reluctant to conduct any more war by committee. This was the conclusion drawn by the unilateralists in the incoming Bush administration in 2001. Instead of formal alliances in general and the restraints imposed by consulting NATO allies in particular, the Bush administration preferred ad hoc coalitions of the willing.

From here on, European leaders embarked on a course of strengthening European capabilities with ambiguous outcomes. Enhancing capabilities could strengthen NATO, but it could also pave the road to autonomous European capabilities outside NATO. European leaders agreed to NATO's DCI, but they also adopted the recommendations of the 1998 St Malo agreement between France and the United Kingdom that the EU should develop autonomous military capabilities.

Crisis Management beyond Europe: Going Out of Area in the War on Terrorism

Having lost its territorial defense purpose in Europe, NATO could adopt a role as crisis manager beyond Europe. This was regarded as the only solution to NATO's loss of purpose by U.S. Senator Richard Lugar, who suggested that NATO had to go out of area to avoid going out of business. However, going out of area could also be a terminal threat to the alliance's cohesion, according to Christoph Bertram's assessment of the post-1991 threat environment. "The new threats are different: They are divisive, not unifying; they are cumulative rather than immediate; and they are coalition-breaking, not coalition-forming. In the past, the big danger again and again jolted NATO's sixteen nations into common assessment and common action. The new, lesser dangers produce sixteen different assessments and sixteen different reasons for inaction."[23] The interventions at NATO's periphery, in Yugoslavia, as well as the crises in Afghanistan and Iraq confirmed Bertram's assessment rather than the hopes of Senator Lugar. NATO's Strategic Concept of 1991 had suggested that the alliance could turn its attention to the multifaceted and multidirectional threats coming from other regions since security in Europe had vastly improved. However, NATO traditionalists argued that going out of area was just as damaging to the core business of NATO as expanding into CEE. "Senator Richard Lugar (Republican, Indiana) has argued that if NATO does not go out of area, it will go out of business. . . . In its determination to expand scope and missions, NATO has set itself on a course that may lead to its collapse. Senator Lugar is incorrect. The phrase should read: 'If NATO goes out of area, it will go out of business.'"[24]

In this intractable dilemma, NATO could go out of business either way. A NATO limited to European regional security was of diminishing interest to the United States. On the other hand, the more NATO was expected to tackle out-of-area missions, the more the differences of interest between the United States and Europe were highlighted. Because of the diversity of the post-1991 "multifaceted" and "multidirectional"[25] threats, it would be inherently difficult to agree on a course of action in out-of-area crises.

In the 1990s, the United States demanded a wider geographic range for NATO missions, including intervention in regions outside the scope of the Washington Treaty, whereas European members argued for a more limited range. By contrast, when the alliance was founded half a century earlier, the United States had insisted on restricting the area of potential operations in order to avoid entanglement in the colonial conflicts of European powers. In turn, Europeans were wary of extending alliance obligations into supporting U.S. involvement in Vietnam in the 1960s. In discussions about the 1999 Strategic Concept, the United States argued for the widest definition of NATO's radius of action, while Europeans wanted to limit to territorial defense of member countries or, at most, to interventions at Europe's periphery. These disagreements continued in spite of the compromise formulation adopted for the Strategic Concept.[26]

The intervention in Afghanistan in late 2001 illustrated some of the difficulties NATO was likely to encounter in any out-of-area action. The multifaceted nature of post–Cold War threats made it very likely that NATO members in Europe or North America would be affected in very different ways. While NATO unanimously declared solidarity with the United States after the terrorist attacks of September 11, 2001, action in Afghanistan did not involve the alliance in anything more than "backfilling"[27] for the absence of U.S. capacities in Europe and the North Atlantic. Instead of drawing on the alliance, the United States formed a coalition of the willing. While official NATO discourse adopted out-of-area action as new rationale, U.S. practice countermanded this rhetoric and bypassed the alliance.

Regarding the "war on terrorism," soon differences appeared between NATO partners. The threat perception of the Bush administration linked the terrorist threat to several "rogue states," justifying the extensive use of military means against terrorist organizations and all states in an alleged "axis of evil." Europeans, on the other hand, preferred a more selective approach targeting only terrorist organizations and states harboring them. In addition, they emphasized nonmilitary means to tackle the root causes of terrorism.[28] These transatlantic differences became more relevant in 2002 and 2003 when the Bush administration persuaded the U.S. public that attacking Iraq contributed to fighting terrorism, whereas most Europeans did not see the connection between a religious fundamentalist Saudi terrorist such as Osama bin Laden and a secularist, nationalist Iraqi leader such as Saddam Hussein.

The Iraq War of 2003 created even deeper divisions within NATO. France and Germany sided with Russia in blocking resolutions in the UN Security Council legitimizing U.S. action in Iraq. The U.S.-led coalition of the willing included NATO members, but the alliance as such was not involved. President George W. Bush preferred unilateral action if a UN mandate was not available, whereas many Europeans wanted to wait until a stronger case for intervention could receive UN endorsement. The U.S. government saw sufficient justification for preemptive action, whereas many Europeans argued that UN inspectors should be given more time to confirm the absence or presence of weapons of mass destruction in Iraq. They also rejected regime change as a reason for preemptive war.

There was, for the first time ever, cooperation by France, Germany, and Russia in an open attempt to block or delay U.S. action. There was also, for the first time since U.S. engagement in Europe, a majority of European popular opinion opposed to U.S. policies even before the beginning of a war. European governments joining the coalition of the willing had to face reluctant electorates. In spite of these electoral costs, "preserving the Atlantic link was one of the key motivations inducing Britain, Spain, Italy, and most Central European countries to side with the Bush administration."[29]

Out-of-area action also required a capability of power projection, which European NATO partners, with the exception of France and the United Kingdom, did not have. During the Cold War, this weakness was unproblematic because European forces were meant to fight in a conventional war in the center of Europe. However, after the Cold War, their very preparedness for territorial defense left them without the capability of power projection needed in out-of-area missions. The more NATO focused on out-of-area actions, the more the capabilities gap became relevant. Germany was the prime example of this problem. More than other NATO members, the Federal Republic had geared its forces for territorial defense, and the biggest European NATO member was ill prepared for post-1991 requirements rendering the adaptation of armed forces more cumbersome in Germany than in other NATO countries.

These experiences with out-of-area missions confirmed that NATO cohesion had been easier to maintain before 1991, when a clearly defined unidirectional threat required unified territorial defense and deterrence. The more distant and diverse the threats were after 1991, the more difficult it was becoming to find a common response by NATO members. The transatlantic rift over Iraq was serious but not beyond repair. In 2004, Chancellor Schröder visited Washington, and in early 2005, President Bush began his second term with a visit to European capitals. Differences were overcome to some extent, but it remained significant that the level of disagreement seen in 2002 and early 2003 had been possible.

NATO'S EMERGING FUTURE

NATO's new tasks ensured its survival, but they were also transforming the alliance. While the alliance was pursuing its new secondary purposes, the closely integrated collective defense organization of the Cold War gradually ceased to exist. The following sections outline the likely future of NATO resulting from the alliance's post-1991 transformation.

Renationalization of Security in Europe Unlikely

From its beginnings, NATO not only served "to keep the Russians out" but also functioned to prevent a return of older nation-state rivalries or a renewed threat of German domination. NATO as a security community stabilized peaceful relations among its members, with Europeans as the main beneficiaries. European integration was easier in the safe knowledge that the United States acted as an overwhelming balancer against German or any other hegemonic ambitions. Security in Western Europe was achieved through membership in the multilateral transatlantic alliance, not through arms races between European nations trying to balance one another.

The fear of a renationalization of security in Europe arose in 1990, when the end of the Cold War allowed East and West Germany to unify. A revival of European nation-state rivalries seemed possible, as outlined in John Mearsheimer's "back to the future" scenario.[30] British Prime Minister Margaret Thatcher expected German unification to destabilize Europe. Although French President François Mitterrand shared some of Thatcher's concerns, "his emphasis was on the need to deepen European integration and West Germany's ties to the European Community."[31] Thatcher's Euro-skepticism did not allow her to see European integration as the best insurance against renationalization. Mitterrand, on the other hand, quickly moved beyond nationalist reflexes, whereas British foreign policy remained paralyzed, responding to German unification with increased Euro-skepticism and continued reliance on the "special relationship" with the United States. France and Germany renewed their role as the twin engine of European integration. The joint initiatives of President Mitterrand and Chancellor Kohl added impetus to ongoing discussion about deeper integration with their letter of April 19, 1990, suggesting to their partners accelerated moves toward Economic and Monetary Union as well as European Political Union (EPU), which EU leaders adopted at the Maastricht IGC.[32]

The successful introduction of the common currency in 1999 and its consolidation since then have tied Germany's economic weight irreversibly into the EU. The EPU, that is, the development of common policies in Justice and Home Affairs as well as foreign and security policy (CFSP), progressed more slowly than monetary union. Nevertheless, since 1991, modest but substantial steps toward CFSP and European Security and Defense Policy (ESDP) have been taken. Renationalization of security, as feared in 1990, has not happened. Instead, Germany became more European, EU integration deepened, and the potential of nationalist conflict in CEE was dampened by the prospect of membership in EU and NATO. The need for U.S. involvement as balancer in Europe has greatly diminished. However, total U.S. disengagement and a sudden departure would still unsettle European sensibilities. While Germany and France no longer feared one another, British and Polish feelings still required the transatlantic reassurance against hypothetical German hegemonic ambitions for some time to come.

Renationalization of security was also conceivable in CEE after the dissolution of the Warsaw Pact in 1991. The dissolution of Yugoslavia illustrated the potential of nationalism and ethnopolitical tensions leading to violent conflicts under the stress of postcommunist transformation. Yet, except in Yugoslavia, potential conflicts never turned violent. Czechoslovakia was dissolved peacefully into the Czech Republic and Slovakia in 1992. Countries aspiring to NATO membership were bound to abstain from territorial disputes with neighbors. Candidates for membership in the EU had to guarantee minority rights domestically and to forgo irredentist claims regarding minorities outside their borders. In CEE as in Western Europe, NATO and the EU helped prevent renationalization of security. The only exception was the violent breakup of Yugoslavia, and even the successor states of Yugoslavia had the long-term prospect of stability through EU membership.

The potential of renationalization justified continued U.S. involvement in Europe and NATO's survival immediately after 1991. However, the diminished threat of renationalization also made possible a future U.S. role as "offshore balancer,"[33] no longer with a massive military presence but linked to Europe through a NATO functioning as security community.

Diminished Need for Collective Defense

NATO traditionalists defended, above all, two characteristics of the NATO alliance: U.S. leadership in European security and NATO's central task of collective defense of its members. "The Alliance's future depends above all on the United States. Without a continuing U.S. engagement, NATO will have no credibility, cohesion, or future."[34] David S. Yost argued that "the Alliance's collective defense mission and the supporting institutions, including the integrated military structure and defense planning systems, must be retained, because they constitute the basis for the Alliance's cohesion and its several valuable internal functions … including the promotion of stability in relations among the major Western powers and the avoidance of a renationalization of defense policies."[35] Without identifying an imminent threat, Yost claimed that "an erosion of collective defense as the central and primary purpose of the Alliance could lead to two damaging consequences: renationalization of defense policies and a simultaneous breakdown of the basis for stability in Europe."[36] Thus, the "collective defense function" was necessary "as a hedge against the unforeseen in Russia" and for the "containment of potential mistrust and rivalry among the European member states"[37] (in other words, to contain united Germany).

This vision of NATO's future was predicated on the need for collective defense against a future Russian threat and the need to balance a potentially hostile Germany. However, without a clear external threat of invasion, the maintenance of collective defense structures would be an extremely expensive way of preventing the reemergence of national rivalries in Europe. The military structures inherited from the Cold War task of collective territorial defense were costly and of limited use in the post-1991 security environment with its new threats demanding small, highly mobile, professional forces for power projection. And the nature of U.S. involvement in Europe was changing, as the bulk of U.S. forces had been withdrawn since the end of the Cold War. The exclusive reliance on a collective defense role would relegate NATO to the limited role of reinsurance for a very unlikely case. After the end of the Soviet threat, collective defense against invasion could no longer be the foundation of a transatlantic security partnership.

Diminishing Need for U.S. Leadership

The asymmetrical transatlantic relationship had been acceptable to most Europeans because the benefits vastly outweighed the disadvantages. It also reflected the balance of power among allies in 1949, when NATO was founded. American leadership was welcome because of a combination of the Soviet threat, the memories of recent German aggression, and the vast economic and military superiority of the United States compared to European allies exhausted by World War II. However, 40 years later, the Soviet threat ceased to exist, six decades have passed since the defeat of German aggression, and Germany has become a rather peaceful member of the EU. Finally, the economic weight of the integrated EU has become a match to the U.S. economy.

The one remaining justification for U.S. leadership was unchallenged military superiority. And even in this respect, U.S. responsibility for European security was diminishing not because European forces were likely to equal the global role of U.S. forces but because the EU was developing the capability to manage all likely regional crises while the United States was decamping from Europe to focus on the Middle East, Central Asia, and East Asia.

Half a century after its foundation, NATO's military structures still reflected the internal balance of power of 1949. Yet Europe's economic weight and the potential geopolitical role of the EU suggested that NATO's internal structures be rebalanced. If role allocation in the alliance continued to reflect the situation of 1949 without accommodating the results of half a century of change, an autonomous EU security policy would become more attractive than reliance on NATO. In Bosnia and Kosovo, the United States showed it was capable of taking the lead once determined to do so, while European powers lacked a united approach to crisis management. However, the United States was also reluctant to get involved in European crises not affecting vital U.S. interests. As the EU developed its CFSP, a new transatlantic partnership was replacing the post-1945 allocation of roles.

NATO Not Replaced but Transformed

In the early 1990s, it was conceivable that NATO would be replaced as framework for European security, either by the OSCE or by the West European Union (WEU). In a changed security environment, alternatives to NATO as key security institution were discussed. German Foreign Minister Hans-Dietrich Genscher favored an upgrading of the OSCE into a pan-European security community.[38] While NATO was identified with one side of the Cold War, the OSCE had the advantage of including countries in Eastern and Western Europe. Another candidate was the WEU, founded in 1954, kept in a dormant state for three decades but revived in the 1980s because of a French initiative. "In 1990–91 countries such as France and Germany had either expected or hoped that the WEU, as an integral part of the EU's CFSP, would replace NATO as the primary security organization." However, "this view diminished in the mid 1990s and does not appear as a credible alternative in the late 1990s."[39] Neither the OSCE nor the WEU posed a serious challenge to NATO's role. The OSCE, only weakly supported by its large membership, lacked organizational strength. And an increased role for the WEU was opposed by the United States, with the Bush administration insisting that any European Security and Defense Identity had to accept the primacy of NATO in security matters.

In the late 1990s, the old division of labor still seemed intact: "NATO has emerged as the key security institution governing and maintaining order in the European geostrategic space; the EU has emerged as the key institution governing and maintaining order in the European geoeconomic space."[40] And a security role for the EU had not developed beyond declarations on paper. "The emergence of a security order anchored by the European Union (EU) and the North Atlantic Treaty Organization (NATO) has not yet replaced the one which evolved after the end of World War II."[41]

NATO had survived the doubts of the early 1990. Eastern Europe and the successor states of the Soviet Union were either included in NATO, as membership of the alliance grew to 26 by 2004, or drawn closer to NATO through bilateral Partnership for Peace (PfP) agreements. Thus, the NATO-based network matched the reach of the OSCE. Yet this very enlargement changed the nature of the alliance. While it had not been replaced by the OSCE, NATO was slowly becoming a security community more like the OSCE. This transformation was helped along by the EU's new role in crisis management as CFSP and ESDP developed. NATO had survived and had a future, but its transformation was well under way.

Selective Commitment: Combined Joint Task Forces and the Coalitions of the Willing

The transformation of NATO included a loosening of previously tight military integration, occurring already in the first half of the 1990s, as well as a "Europeanization" of the alliance. Bertram observed a trend for issues discussed in NATO to become more limited to regional European affairs, thus lacking wider relevance after the end of the Cold War. Membership of CEE countries would increase this European focus, making the alliance less interesting for the United States.[42] Another aspect of Europeanization was the French attempt to redistribute command positions in NATO, in particular, to replace the American CINCSOUTH [Commander in Chief Southern Europe], in charge of AFSOUTH [Allied Forces Southern Europe] in Naples, by a European officer. This led to a "stand-off … between the United States and France"[43] as the United States insisted on retaining the CINCSOUTH position, especially because AFSOUTH included the U.S. Sixth Fleet in the Mediterranean Sea. The United States welcomed Europeanization only as long as a distinct ESDI within NATO promised better burden sharing and accommodated Europe's role claims without greatly affecting U.S. leadership.

More serious than the Europeanization of NATO was the loosening of military integration. NATO had in the early 1950s created a cohesive military structure ready for a conflict scenario with an identifiable opponent in a predictable geographical setting. In the post-1991 security environment, however, threats were more diverse, while none was an existential threat to all allies. It had become conceivable that a crisis would concern only some but not all NATO members. A structural response by the alliance was the adoption of the concept of Combined Joint Task Forces (CJTF), that is, WEU-led European NATO members acting with approval but without participation by the United States. Out-of-area interventions did not require the integrated military structure distinguishing NATO from other alliances. Instead, depending on changing constellations of threats and national interests, crisis management required flexible coalitions. This could be a U.S.-led coalition of the willing, a NATO-approved CJTF of Europeans, or even an EU force acting outside NATO.

There was some symmetry in this development: if Europeans wanted to loosen alliance structures by developing detachable CJTFs, they could not be surprised that the diversity of threats also led the United States to form coalitions of the willing. Of course, there was still the asymmetry that a U.S.-led coalition of the willing could act without asking NATO for approval. Any WEU-led CJTF, on the other hand, could act only after NATO had decided not to act in a particular crisis. Furthermore, the CJTF remained dependent on the use of NATO assets provided by the United States.

Nevertheless, the approval of the CJTF concept by President Clinton, at NATO's 1994 summit in Brussels, signaled a loosening of the alliance's unity of purpose and tight military integration. American commitment to European security was still there in general, but for each particular crisis, it had become optional. That U.S. commitment had become more selective was illustrated by the CJTF concept and by the initial U.S. reluctance to get involved in Bosnia and Kosovo. The United States now had the option to stay out of European crises and to act without involving NATO as a whole in crises in other regions.

The changes of the early to mid-1990s could be interpreted as "internal adaptation to allow NATO to face the challenges of the twenty-first century."[44] Having lost its historical primary purpose with the end of the Soviet threat, NATO could acquire a "role as a coalition facilitator, most notably by developing the Combined Joint Task Forces (CJTF) concept." Thus, NATO could become a "training ground for coalitions formed either within, or outside of, the Alliance framework."[45]

However, this transformation of the military alliance into a toolbox also reduced NATO's relevance. The CJTF concept was an ambiguous measure capable of enhancing NATO's viability while also increasing European security autonomy. While France regarded "the CJTF as a mechanism that allows Europeans to act militarily outside American control," Britain saw it "as a device for sustaining the relevance of NATO's integrated military structure to new tasks in a complex world, while avoiding the creation of wasteful rival structures."[46] In any case, NATO's new structural flexibility meant that U.S. involvement in European crises had become optional.

Unintended Outcomes of Atlanticist Efforts

Even the efforts of European Atlanticists to strengthen NATO cohesion had the paradox effect of advancing European autonomy. The alliance was threatened by European military weakness as the capabilities gap between the transatlantic partners threatened to become a mission gap. Yet any upgrading of EU capabilities could lead to ambiguous outcomes. For Atlanticists, there was the need to strengthen European military capabilities in order to become more credible NATO partners. On the other hand, for the European critics of U.S. hyperpower, any strengthening of European military capabilities could bring closer the end of the U.S. military protectorate. In order to strengthen the alliance, Europeans had to coordinate their efforts, pool their defense dollars, and merge defense industries. Yet such methods of achieving a credible European pillar within NATO also contributed to an autonomous European security policy. Thus, NATO's cohesion was threatened by European strength as much as by European weakness.

The Atlanticist objective of making Europe a good NATO partner could be achieved only by strengthening Europe. Yet this was also making the transatlantic alliance less relevant. This ambiguity became apparent in the St. Malo agreement of 1998, when the United Kingdom and France suggested to their fellow EU members that they needed an autonomous military capability. For very different reasons, France and the United Kingdom agreed on the same course of action. For France, an autonomous EU capability was needed in order to create *Europe puissance* and to develop an ESDP intended to grow beyond NATO. For the United Kingdom, on the other hand, Europe could become a credible partner in the transatlantic alliance only by becoming stronger.

While the experience of European weakness in the 1940s and 1950s had resulted in an acceptance of security dependence, the experience of Kosovo in 1998–99 resulted in a greater determination to create an autonomous capability for the EU. Before 1991, the prevailing response to European weakness was willing subordination to and cooperation with the benevolent hegemon. Yet since 1991, the main response to the capabilities gap was an effort to develop an autonomous EU security policy.

The conflicting intentions of Atlanticists and Europeanists regarding the purpose of European defense cooperation suggested ambiguous outcomes. However, the gradual detachment of the United States from European security tended to favor an eventual Europeanist solution to this ambiguity. The more the United States replaced military presence in Europe with a role as offshore balancer providing background assurance, the more Europeans were forced to look after their own security. The Atlanticists in Europe began to learn that the United States would continue to contribute to stability in Europe as a preeminent member of the transatlantic security community but no longer as part of a collective defense organization. In most cases of crisis management in Europe, the Europeans would be on their own.

Embedding NATO in a Broader Transatlantic Agenda

For half a century, the military alliance had been the centerpiece of the transatlantic relationship. While transatlantic economic interaction and the value community of cultural interaction and shared identities contributed to cohesion, the most institutionalized and strongest link was NATO. Yet after the end of the Soviet threat, the transatlantic military alliance had "become too narrow to carry the trans-Atlantic roof. Instead, Bertram argued, NATO would "have to be complemented by additional U.S.-European institutions, both to ensure its own survival and to ensure a resilient trans-Atlantic relationship for the future."[47]

Since the end of the Cold War, attempts have been made to institutionalize nonmilitary aspects of the transatlantic relationship. The New Atlanticism of the Bush administration introduced regular meetings between the United States and the EU besides the established bilateral relations and the NATO framework. Under President Clinton, a New Transatlantic Agenda, including a New Transatlantic Marketplace (NTM), was adopted in December 1995. However, when "EU trade commissioner Leon Brittan attempted in March 1998 to get the NTM off the ground, . . . it was defeated by the member states . . . at an EU foreign ministers' meeting on 27 April 1998."[48] Economic integration within Europe was given priority over transatlantic free trade.

Supplementing the military alliance by a Transatlantic Free Trade Area was suggested by Henry A. Kissinger, with a supervising Atlantic Steering Group providing political coordination of the transatlantic agenda.[49] Yet, the outcome of such ideas was limited. The strongest transatlantic link was still the military alliance, to be retained as overarching reinsurance but replaced in practical crisis management by U.S.-led coalitions of the willing or the EU's own rapid response forces. Economic interdependence across the Atlantic was very deep since trade and foreign direct investment between the United States and Europe surpassed economic relations between any other regions; however, this interdependence was a relation between two economic blocs. Integration within the EU had gone too far for any attempt to make this economic bloc part of a U.S.-dominated Transatlantic Free Trade Association. American leadership in European security could no longer be leveraged into leadership of a transatlantic economic bloc. On the other hand, European economic integration was gradually being translated into an autonomous security role for the EU.

NATO as a single-purpose military organization was disadvantaged compared to the EU, which was capable of adding more and more tasks. The EU was growing into a multipurpose organization capable of deep integration. This had been the logic of the "spillover effect" beginning with basic economic integration in the EEC's customs union, leading to comprehensive economic integration with the Single European Market of 1992 and monetary union of 1999, followed by steps toward common foreign, security and defense policies since 1991. On the other hand, NATO was not capable of adopting nonmilitary purposes in spite of suggestions for a transatlantic community. Kissinger's New Transatlantic Agenda was still a single-purpose, U.S.-led military alliance supplemented by economic and cultural interaction. Yet in contrast to the Cold War period when the security link was central, since 1991 economic and political links were becoming central to the transatlantic relationship, while the security link was becoming looser.[50] The economic interaction between North America and Europe was more intensive than either of them had with any other region, although integration within the EU's Single Market was even more intensive than transatlantic trade and investment. Transatlantic economic interdependence was so important for both sides that a regime of political, economic, and security consultation was desirable.

CONCLUSION: NATO'S TRANSFORMATION

Since NATO lost its primary purpose in 1991, the alliance has found new tasks, but each of these has also given momentum to an autonomous EU security policy. Expansion of NATO membership extended a zone of stability into CEE, but it also transformed the military alliance into a large and loose security community that might as well one day include Russia. NATO's function as guarantee against external threats could not be sustained because it would bind the United States into an array of risk situations increasing with the extension of NATO membership. Intervention in Bosnia and Kosovo demonstrated the capabilities of NATO, but it also illustrated diminished U.S. interest in European crisis management. Out-of-area interventions further afield were of greater interest to the United States than to Europeans. The new post-1991 tasks gave NATO a new lease of life, but they also propelled the alliance on a path of transformation. The old tasks of NATO were of greatly reduced relevance. Russia's conventional forces were not a threat to Europe, and Germany's unification had resulted not in renationalization of foreign policy but in deeper European integration. If "keeping the Russians out" and the "Germans down" was no longer so important, then "keeping the Americans in" had also become less urgent.

The slow transformation of NATO since 1991 accelerated under the impact of the Kosovo experience of 1998–99 when the EU embarked on its own ESDP. Instead of a military alliance against a well-defined external threat, NATO was becoming a large security community stabilizing internal space. Out-of-area interventions were not giving NATO a new rationale, contrary to Senator Lugar's expectation. The experience of Bosnia, Kosovo, Afghanistan, and Iraq supported Bertram's arguments: the greater the diversity and distance of out-of-area threats, the more political disunity and loosening of military integration. The diversity of threats and crises could involve the United States alone or with a coalition of the willing (including NATO members or others). Or it could involve European countries, acting either through NATO as CJTFs or autonomously as EU Rapid Response Forces. Crisis management by NATO forces acting under NATO auspices would be the exception.

One conceivable future was "a refoundation of the Alliance in the fight against terrorism," but "this scenario hardly had a chance of realization."[51] Nevertheless, French analyst Frédéric Bozo expected not a Euro-American divorce but rather a new security partnership. On the one hand, Europeans had to prove themselves as allies relevant for global security tasks by making a military contribution to the fight against terrorism and "acknowledging that American primacy in these matters would be incontestable for a long time. On the other, the Americans had to remain involved in European security while also encouraging a devolution of the principal responsibility for European stability toward a Union called to become the major security actor on the Old Continent."[52] For the relations between Europe and the United States, the alliance would offer "a framework at once too rigid and too narrow for the redefinition of the strategic link between Europe and America." And beyond Europe, "the Alliance, obviously without disappearing neither legally nor institutionally, will have increasingly the tendency to melt into a much larger ensemble with contours . . . approximating the G8."[53]

"NATO is becoming more of a European security organization, less of an alliance." It has become more European because of enlargement in CEE and interventions in the Balkans. Although "the security priorities of its leading members were shifting away from Europe," the United States "should not expect too much from NATO itself, as a formal alliance, outside Europe."[54] The transformation of NATO into a broad security community also pointed to the end of the post-1945 U.S. military protectorate. In Western Europe, U.S. influence through the alliance was diminishing. In CEE, NATO remained a vehicle of U.S. influence to a much greater extent, but even there the Atlanticist orientation of CEE governments had to contend with the everyday experience of deep European integration.

The reduction of the U.S. military presence in Europe was the clearest indicator of the changing nature of U.S. involvement in Europe. The role of the United States as directly involved leader of a collective defense organization was diminishing; instead, the United States was becoming an offshore balancer and an important member of a security community including North America, the old NATO partners in Western Europe, the new NATO members in CEE, as well as Russia and the other successor states of the Soviet Union, either through the PfP or, eventually, through an even larger NATO including Russia.

The two objectives of serving as framework for European security and as support for U.S. global strategy "may well prove irreconcilable." Yet the "value of extending security across the whole of Europe" justified the expansion of NATO. "Such a broad security gain is worth the sacrifice of a degree of military coherence,"[55] resulting from NATO's transformation into a large security community.

After the loss of its primary purpose, the alliance has taken on "multiple tasks" that "will keep NATO in business for many years to come."[56] Yet it will not be the military alliance under U.S. leadership shaped by the conditions of the late 1940s. Instead, NATO will have adjusted to the post-1991 security environment and the new, more symmetrical role allocation of the transatlantic partners.

CHAPTER 5

The Europeanization of European Security

The development of a Common Foreign and Security Policy (CFSP) was firmly put on the agenda of European integration by the Maastricht Intergovernmental Conference (IGC) in December 1991. European integration was taking a step beyond economic integration into the field of foreign, security, and defense policy, previously a preserve of national governments reluctant to hand over this core of national sovereignty to the European Union (EU). It had been less problematic to cede national control over external trade when the European Economic Community (EEC) became a customs union (1957–68), and it had been acceptable to let the EU regulate much of domestic economic life in order to achieve the European Single Market (1986–92). Even giving up national currencies for the sake of European Monetary Union (by 1999) was less daunting than the prospect of ceding defense tasks to EU institutions. Yet since 1949, European NATO members had already allocated decision making over security and defense policy to the transatlantic alliance by participating in its closely integrated military structure. Thus, the EU's intended CFSP raised questions not only about its compatibility with national prerogatives but also with NATO's role as framework for European security since 1949.

The needs of European integration placed the CFSP on the agenda after the end of the Cold War. From the beginning, Franco-German reconciliation had been a motor of economic integration, in order to find security in ever-closer cooperation, instead of fighting wars as in 1870–71, 1914–18, and 1939–45. When the end of the Cold War had made German unification possible in 1990, Franco-German relations were, for a moment, at risk of relapsing into historical nation-state rivalries. To prevent this relapse, President

Mitterrand and Chancellor Kohl opted for deepening European integration even further, urging fellow European leaders to prepare for monetary union and to take steps beyond economic integration toward a common foreign and security policy.[1]

The post–Cold War security environment made it possible to reconsider Europe's security architecture. Before 1991, the threat situation made alternatives to North Atlantic Treaty Organization (NATO) and U.S. security leadership almost inconceivable in spite of latent tensions in the transatlantic alliance. However, after 1991, the multitude of new threats did not include any existential threats to NATO members comparable to Soviet conventional invasions or mutual assured destruction in a nuclear war. While NATO remained the most important security structure, hypothetical alternatives, such as a greater role for Organization for Security and Cooperation in Europe or the West European Union (WEU), could be explored and tested with impunity. The nature of U.S. involvement in Europe could also be reconsidered at the end of the Cold War.

Gradually, the United States reduced costly European commitments, and the EU started growing into a security role, commensurate with its economic weight. For most of the 1990s, NATO–Europe worked toward a European Security and Defense Identity (ESDI), that is, a European pillar within the transatlantic alliance. The turn toward a more autonomous European Security and Defense Policy (ESDP) was taken by the EU only in the late 1990s. Many preparatory steps had been taken since 1991, and if this line of development was to continue, the EU could replace NATO as the institution responsible for European security. An autonomous security and defense policy would constitute the second half of Europe's emancipation from post-1945 weakness. Based on the EU's economic strength, the ESDP would end the post-1945 military protectorate in Western Europe, transforming the asymmetrical roles of the transatlantic allies into a partnership of equals.

In the emerging division of labor, the NATO alliance could continue as security community providing a forum for peaceful relations among its members while the EU assumed a role as crisis manager in Europe. NATO's function of collective territorial defense was changing into a role as background reassurance for unlikely situations. For more likely events, transatlantic cooperation in crisis management was becoming optional, to be handled either by U.S.-led coalitions of the willing, by European Combined Joint Task Forces (CJTF) in a NATO context, or by the EU's Rapid Response Force. The responsibility for European security was becoming Europeanized, with NATO and the United States acting as reinsurance.

NATO'S LATENT PROBLEMS: DIFFERENTIAL SECURITY AND FEAR OF DECOUPLING, 1949–89

The growth of the EU's security role after 1991 can be traced back to the problem of differential security in NATO during the Cold War. Even while

NATO was united in its primary purpose of deterrence against the Soviet Union, there were latent tensions in the alliance, never strong enough to threaten its cohesion but substantial enough to affect decision making and to help explain developments after 1991.

As NATO's strategies adapted to changing phases in the nuclear confrontation, the problem of differential security persisted because of the geography of the alliance, placing NATO–Europe right at the line of confrontation but leaving the United States and Canada safe from conventional invasion on the other side of the Atlantic. In case of war, the outcome would have been worse for NATO–Europe than for NATO–North America. Furthermore, its advantageous location at great distance from the expected theater of war gave the United States the hypothetical option of insulating itself from the effects of war. NATO–Europe's concerns about possible decoupling by the United States surfaced now and then, although reliance on the U.S. deterrent prevailed generally. Before 1991, these tensions over differential security were containable because of the unifying effect of the Soviet threat. However, in the post-1991 security environment of "multifaceted" and "multidirectional"[2] threats, differences in threat perceptions between the United States and Europe increased.

Differential security was inherent in NATO's earliest strategy of "massive retaliation," under which the United States threatened the Soviet Union with nuclear retaliation against any conventional attack on Western Europe. As the Soviet Union did not have the means to deliver a nuclear strike against U.S. territory, massive retaliation was expected to punish and repel a Soviet attack in Europe. However, instead of withdrawing, the Soviet Union could also have responded by advancing further into Western Europe because the small U.S. nuclear arsenal of the early 1950s could inflict only limited damage. Massive retaliation meant that the United States would be safe, except for U.S. troops in Europe, whereas European NATO members would possibly remain occupied even after a U.S. nuclear strike against the Soviet Union.

NATO adopted a strategy of "flexible response" after the Cuban missile crisis of 1962 had shown that U.S. territory could be threatened by forward deployment of Soviet medium-range missiles or by intercontinental ballistic missiles (ICBMs) capable of delivering nuclear bombs across oceans. Under flexible response, NATO planned a graded reply to a Soviet invasion of Western Europe, always capable of stopping on the escalation ladder short of an all-out nuclear exchange. Flexible response ensured that the United States would not be automatically exposed to the risk of a nuclear strike. However, because of this flexibility of U.S. decision making, NATO allies feared that the United States could opt to avoid the risk of Soviet nuclear strikes on its territory by abandoning Europe. European leaders insisted on the presence of U.S. troops to make sure a Soviet attack would not result in decoupling by the United States. As the two nuclear superpowers faced the risk of mutual assured destruction, the U.S. nuclear guarantee for Europe seemed unworkable. Yet when the United States demanded greater conventional armament by NATO–Europe in order to reduce reliance on nuclear deterrence, Europeans were reluctant to carry the costs. American leaders were never sure what their European allies feared more: a guarantee of automatic nuclear retaliation against any Soviet invasion, with devastating effects for Europe, or a flexible response by the United States, implying the risk that the nuclear guarantee was not necessarily applicable. Fortunately, nuclear deterrence was never tested, and the Cold War remained cold.

Latent fears of differential security were activated in the early 1980s by the deployment of medium range ballistic missiles and cruise missiles (Intermediate Nuclear Forces, or INF). European leaders had encouraged the United States to deploy Pershing II and cruise missiles in Europe since exclusive reliance on ICBMs threatening the superpowers' own territory would have made the United States reluctant to use the instruments of nuclear deterrence. Thus, INF deployment was meant to make U.S. guarantees more credible by lowering the nuclear threshold. Paradoxically, deployment of the INF in the early 1980s activated another aspect of differential security: it increased the risk of a regional nuclear war limited to Eastern and Western Europe. An exchange of these medium-range missiles would have devastated Europe and the western parts of the Soviet Union. On the other hand, the U.S. homeland would remain safe as long as the exchange did not involve long-range missiles (ICBMs).

European fears of decoupling were also stirred in the early 1980s by President Reagan's planned Strategic Defense Initiative (SDI). These antimissile defenses were to protect the United States from Soviet missiles, but they would also leave Europeans in a situation of high risk while the United States sheltered safely behind the SDI shield. This was the moment when the French government suggested that the WEU should be reactivated to form the core of a future autonomous European defense structure. In 1984, WEU members agreed to its revival, yet the "decision by foreign affairs ministers of June 12, 1984 to activate the WEU was, characteristically, not followed by any action."[3] In the 1990s, the reactivated WEU became an institutional vehicle for European security autonomy. The growth of the EU's security role can thus be traced to the pre-1991 problems of differential security, although the mid-1980s crisis in the alliance over INF deployment and SDI plans receded when Presidents Reagan and Gorbachev agreed in 1987 to withdraw medium-range missiles from Europe.

All NATO strategies implied differential security. For Europeans, there was always a greater risk of devastation or the fear of U.S. decoupling from European security. The problem of differential security never grew virulent, and the transatlantic division of labor remained stable until the end of the Cold War while the alliance was held together by a shared threat perception. Nevertheless, "the recurring fear that nuclear weapons might 'decouple' the United States from its European allies reveals that the problem was taken seriously on both sides of the Atlantic."[4]

NATO'S DETACHABLE COMPONENTS: FROM ESDI TO CJTF

Since 1991, a distinctive ESDI developed within the alliance, whereas outside NATO the EU began to claim a wider role in foreign and security policy. The ambiguity of these developments became apparent in the roles intended for the WEU. The French motivation in reactivating the WEU in 1984 was to build an autonomous *Europe puissance*, but for the Atlanticists in Britain and Germany, the WEU was to be the vehicle for the ESDI, the European pillar within NATO. The ESDI was welcomed by the United States as a contribution to NATO objectives,[5] and the primary responsibility of the forces allocated to the WEU was to remain the collective defense of NATO according to the Washington Treaty. Yet even the development of an ESDI within NATO contributed to EU autonomy by transforming individual NATO members into a European caucus.

More European autonomy became conceivable by 1994, when the alliance accepted the concept of CJTF at the NATO summit of Brussels (January 10–11, 1994).[6] The CJTF concept allowed European powers to utilize NATO assets for operations of the WEU without U.S. participation. These CJTFs were detachable but not detached from NATO structures, allowing separate actions by groups of European powers. The United States remained involved insofar as their approval for missions and for the use of NATO assets was needed, but it also showed that the United States was not interested in intervening in all possible future European crises. And while European CJTFs were not permanently detached from NATO, their temporary detachability made further decoupling conceivable.

The CJTF concept indicated a loosening of NATO's tight military integration. During the Cold War, the alliance had been united by a shared threat perception, the U.S. military presence in Europe, and an integrated military structure ready for a common response to aggression. In the new security environment, however, the CJTF concept loosened mutual commitment and military integration. "The unraveling of military integration is taking place; it is even explicitly accepted. . . . Now, Combined Joint Task Forces are to be set up and made available for subgroups within the Alliance willing to use them; 'coalitions of the willing' are envisaged as the most likely model for the future, . . . The integration of military planning and staff work, a major factor in NATO's past accomplishments . . . has been loosened. No longer are all the nations represented in NATO staffs willing to take part in all operations. . . . Flexibility in coalitions, in procedures, and in integration will become normal for NATO. It will also extend to what few in the Alliance yet admit: flexibility in commitment."[7] NATO was still united as the primary forum of consultation, but WEU forces had become detachable in case the United States decided to stay out of any particular European crisis.

During the Cold War, NATO allies had relied on mutual security guarantees and collective territorial defense in spite of the problem of differential security and latent fears of decoupling. In contrast to this pre-1991 assumption of a united response to threats, with the CJTF concept it had become official NATO strategy that U.S. involvement in European crises was optional and that separate missions conducted by Europeans were possible.

INSTITUTIONAL PREREQUISITES OF AN AUTONOMOUS ESDP

In the ambiguous development of U.S.–EU security relations, the steps to relative autonomy within NATO were interconnected with steps toward a EU security role besides NATO. For several years, the EU prepared political and institutional prerequisites that were not sufficient in themselves to turn the "military dwarf" into a strategic actor. Nevertheless, such institutional arrangements were important steps toward *Europe puissance*, taken together with the development of the European Defense Industrial and Technological Base (EDITB) and the formation of actual EU military forces.

Reactivating the WEU

In 1984, other members of the WEU followed French suggestions, still rejected in the 1970s, to reactivate this dormant military alliance of Western European nations. Thirty years earlier, it had for the last time served a major purpose when West Germany's admission to the WEU paved the way for its NATO membership in 1955. Initially, WEU reactivation involved no more than periodical meetings of ministers. In 1990, however, the end of the Cold War opened the way for a reconsideration of its role.

In the lead-up to the Maastricht IGC of 1991 which expressed the intention to develop a CFSP for the EU and to bring the WEU closer to the EU, there was "a clash between the Bush administration, which wanted the WEU to be an integral part of NATO, and the Mitterrand government, that adopted the Gaullist view of a Europe able to defend itself and, hence, saw the WEU as the military arm of the EC. The Maastricht Treaty devised the non-solution of ambiguous wording, which probably suited Germany."[8] This ambiguous suspension of the WEU between NATO and EU continued for several years.

Common Foreign and Security Policy for the EU

In 1991, the Maastricht IGC included the CFSP in the Treaty on European Union. This began to change the transatlantic division of labor in which the EU had been responsible for Europe's economy while leaving defense matters to NATO and the United States With the adoption of the CFSP in principle, the course was set to end European security dependence. Yet, initially, the CFSP was no more than a statement of intentions with few practical implications.

WEU's Petersberg Tasks Adopted by the EU

The WEU claimed a role in crisis management when its Council of Ministers adopted the "Petersberg Tasks" (June 19, 1992), including humanitarian and rescue missions, peacekeeping, and peacemaking. Territorial defense, on the other hand, remained NATO's exclusive prerogative. With the incorporation of the Petersberg Tasks into the Amsterdam Treaty of 1997,[9] the EU assumed the WEU's claim to a crisis management role. Attempts by France (and Germany) to give the EU or the WEU an even greater role in defense matters, at the expense of NATO, met with resistance by Atlanticist EU members. "Britain, as well as Denmark, Ireland and Sweden, opposes attempts to include the WEU in the EU or to give the EU any military responsibility." Britain also wanted "to prevent the WEU from acquiring an independent command structure or an integrated military command."[10] However, over time, the Atlanticist countries made greater concessions to Europeanist proposals.

Formalizing the EU's Security Role

The St Malo agreement (1998) between France and the United Kingdom started a new phase of European security policy by demanding a "capacity for autonomous action" for the EU. The experience of European weakness during the Kosovo crisis of 1998–99 strengthened the willingness of EU members to implement the St Malo recommendations. Subsequently, "the German presidency worked on transforming this bilateral initiative into a European reality and changing the European defense *identity* into a European security and defense *policy*."[11] In June 1999, the Cologne summit of EU leaders appointed Javier Solana as high representative for CFSP and created a Political and Security Committee, a European Military Committee, and a European Military Staff. In December 1999, the Helsinki summit adopted the "Headline Goal" to establish a European Rapid Response Force of 60,000 soldiers consisting of earmarked national contingents. In 2001, the Laeken summit declared that the Headline Goal had been achieved.

The proposed EU Constitution, drafted by the Convention on the Future of Europe in 2002–03 and adopted by the EU summit in mid-2004, included provisions to strengthen the institutional framework for CFSP and ESDP by establishing an EU foreign minister and by codifying European mutual defense obligations.[12] The draft constitution went beyond the Petersberg Tasks of crisis management and made a claim for an EU role in collective defense, thus encroaching on NATO's prerogatives in spite of assertions of the alliance's primacy. If adopted through ratification in all 25 member countries, the EU Constitution could be a capstone document in the development of a security role. Although ratification of the draft EU constitution was unlikely after its rejection by the electorate in France and the Netherlands in mid-2005,[13] the text was indicative of the intended future security role of the EU.

From NATO–WEU to NATO–EU Cooperation

The overlapping but not corresponding membership of NATO, the WEU, and the EU formed a very basic obstacle to any clarification of the security roles of these organizations. While the WEU lay dormant and the EU was preoccupied with economic integration, it mattered little that some EU members were not WEU members, some EU members were not NATO members, and some European NATO members were not EU members. However, as soon as the WEU was being drawn closer to the EU, Norway and Turkey feared that any reduction of NATO's role might leave these two non-EU countries on the margin. Within the EU, the strategic culture of France or Britain differed clearly from the neutralist traditions of Austria, Finland, Ireland, and Sweden. These differences affected the EU's emerging security role.

The cooperation between NATO and the WEU was given a framework in negotiations in Brussels in January 1994 and in Berlin in June 1996, concretizing the development of the ESDI in the form of WEU missions supported by NATO's planning and command capacities. The 1999 NATO summit in Washington agreed to the so-called Berlin Plus package, which gave the EU access to NATO assets, and "developed the role of the Deputy Supreme Allied Commander Europe in order to support European command options."[14] Here it was assumed that the EU and no longer the WEU would be conducting missions under the CJTF concept. This clarification of relations between NATO and the WEU/EU was complicated by Turkish concerns. As Turkey was a member of NATO but not of the WEU or the EU, it feared that any upgrading of the EU's role and corresponding reduction of NATO's role would leave Turkey on the margins of decision making about European security.

The consultation modalities between the EU and NATO were redefined in 2000, especially concerning European NATO members outside the EU. Confirmed at the Nice Summit of late 2000, "these provisions reaffirm the EU's control over ESDP while assuring the participation of European NATO members that are not part of the EU."[15] The Nice provisions on Berlin Plus were finally approved after the more accommodating government of Prime Minister Tayyip Erdogan had come to power in Turkey. In December 2002, a new framework was adopted for cooperation between the EU and NATO in crisis management. This agreement confirmed recognition of the EU's new security role by NATO and the United States.

Agreements between NATO and the WEU included the condition that the WEU should not duplicate NATO assets. This included the understanding that NATO's staff and planning capacities should not receive competition from a WEU/EU military staff. Therefore, Britain had rejected earlier French proposals to establish WEU headquarters. Yet in September 2003, Britain, France, and Germany agreed that the EU should set up a unit of operational planners to make possible autonomous EU missions. And in May 2004, Britain, France, and Germany agreed to set up a planning cell for EU forces (although not EU headquarters). This constituted a significant modification of the earlier British resistance against EU command structures outside NATO, but it still respected, at least formally, the rule not to establish a military staff in competition with NATO. The EU had the beginnings of a military planning capacity, while NATO had retained its preeminent status as the only institution with headquarters and a military staff.

These small steps and compromises amounted to significant change compared to 1990, when the United States had clearly rejected any security role for the WEU or the EU separate from NATO. Twelve years later, the Berlin Plus agreements acknowledged the existence of the EU as a separate strategic actor and cooperation partner. NATO had retained its status as primary security framework, but the transatlantic alliance had also acknowledged that the EU had acquired a crisis management role previously claimed by the WEU.

European Security Strategy of 2003

In December 2003, EU leaders endorsed a first European Security Strategy (ESS), defining the EU as a global actor ready to share responsibility for global security, aiming for "a secure Europe in a better world."[16] The ESS intended to extend the security zone around the EU to include not only the Balkans but also the Mediterranean as well as Ukraine and Moldova. Another objective of the ESS was to establish effective multilateralism based on the United Nations. Finally, the ESS outlines a response to the threats of terrorism and proliferation of weapons of mass destruction with a variety of instruments not limited to military force. Like the WEU's Petersberg Tasks of 1992, the EU's ESS was an ambitious claim for a greater security role for which the EU had the potential but not yet all the actual capabilities.

INDUSTRIAL AND TECHNOLOGICAL PREREQUISITES FOR THE ESDP

The EDITB began to grow out of national defense industries, in parallel to the creation of political and institutional prerequisites for a European security policy. Mergers in the United States resulted in the world's three biggest prime contractors (Lockheed-Martin, Boeing, and Raytheon). European defense enterprises in selected industries also merged within and across national boundaries. As a result of consolidation in the 1990s, British Aerospace Systems (BAe), European Aeronautic Defence and Space Company (EADS), Thales, and Finmeccanica occupied the fourth, seventh, eighth, and ninth positions among the world's top 10 defense enterprises, with U.S. companies Northrop Grumman (fifth), General Dynamics (sixth), and Honeywell (tenth) completing the top 10.[17] This consolidation of the EDITB achieved economies of scale and helped avoid technological dependence. A comprehensive defense industry was no longer possible at the national level; even the economies of France, Germany, or Britain were too small to manage the most expensive armament projects. However, at the European level, a globally relevant defense industry was achievable.

The pressure to seek economies of scale came from three sides: first, the increasing cost of the most advanced systems; second, the concentration of U.S. defense industries, fostered by the Clinton administration in the late 1990s and resulting in prime contractors exceeding the size of the leading European companies; and third, the decline in European defense spending in the 1990s. As defense budgets declined, shorter production runs made each item of equipment more costly. Acceptable costs per item were no longer achievable for national defense industries; these could be achieved only by either buying American or producing for an all-European market.

While the four leading European companies did not match the size of the largest U.S. defense contractors, they were nevertheless relevant global actors in defense electronics and aerospace, the most consolidated sectors of the defense industry. In the industries with the most expensive projects (aeronautics, space, missiles, and electronics), mergers had crossed national boundaries to create European prime contractors. In other industries, the costs of development and production were lower, and therefore consolidation had so far occurred predominantly within national boundaries. "In land armaments and shipbuilding, the situation is different. . . . Trans-European consolidation has failed in these sectors, leaving European companies in a rather weak position vis-à-vis their US counterparts."[18]

Besides the economic need for rationalization, there were also political motives for the consolidation of the EDITB. For European governments, especially for the six major armament-producing countries, economic ambitions converged with the interest in an autonomous security policy. In civilian industries, it had long been accepted that European industries could compete with the United States and Japan only if they operated in a large domestic market and learned to compete in a global market. However, in defense industries, this development had been delayed by the jealous maintenance of national defense equipment markets. It was only in the 1990s that this issue was tackled from several sides at once when it became obvious that separate national defense industries would succumb to global competition.

Armament cooperation had been taking place in Europe since the 1960s at the level of particular projects and once-off agreements between national producers. In the 1990s, the most important projects included the A400M transport aircraft (involving Germany, Belgium, Spain, France, Luxembourg, the United Kingdom, Portugal, and Turkey), the Eurofighter new-generation combat aircraft (Germany, Spain, Italy, and the United Kingdom), the HELIOS optical observation system (France, Italy, Spain, and Belgium), and the TIGER new-generation combat helicopters (Germany and France).[19] Some of these projects addressed crucial shortcomings in European capabilities. The biggest single project was the A400M, intended to give European forces the airlift capacity required in long-distance interventions. And if European powers wanted to conduct their own missions without U.S. support, they could not rely on GPS, the U.S.-controlled global positioning system, but had to develop Galileo, Europe's own global positioning system.

These European projects could reduce the transatlantic capabilities gap threatening NATO's cohesion, but these projects also weakened U.S. leadership in the alliance. The A400M project strengthened the Airbus consortium, the major competitor of Boeing. The Galileo global positioning system would make EU countries independent of U.S. satellite intelligence; furthermore, after its planned launch in 2008, the Galileo system threatened to compete with the commercial applications of the older American global positioning system. Therefore, when President Jacques Chirac and Chancellor Helmut Kohl agreed in December 1995 on Germany joining French-led production of the Helios II optical reconnaissance satellite and on France joining German-led production of the Horus military satellite, "this Franco-German cooperation was achieved in the face of intense high-level pressure from all relevant U.S. agencies and was an area in which Bonn had been entirely in Washington's hands. The Americans clearly have not appreciated the German quest for a link with Paris in such a key area."[20] While German participation in the Helios and Horus projects had been canceled later by Chancellor Kohl, his successor, Gerhard Schröder, reversed the decision. In June 2000, the French–German summit in Mainz decided to produce "an independent satellite observation system. France will contribute its optical satellite, the *Helios* II, while Germany will contribute the all-weather radar satellite (SAR-LUPE)."[21]

Such projects were necessary, from a French perspective, in order to resist U.S. attempts to use technology to shape "the Atlantic Alliance as a unified strategic zone under American leadership. In Prague, technological progress replaced the former Soviet threat as a vehicle to push military integration within the Atlantic are to a magnitude never seen even during the Cold War period."[22] The Defense Capabilities Initiative, adopted by NATO at the 2002 summit in Prague, was not only an attempt to modernize the alliance but also an attempt by the United States to lock European allies into long-term technological dependency. Technological and industrial leadership in defense industries could cement U.S. hegemony long after the end of the Soviet threat and after the end of U.S. supremacy in civilian industries. "That is to say if the Europeans unconditionally follow the U.S. leadership they will occupy 'niches' in the U.S. military 'system of systems.' Accordingly, they will become completely dependent on the U.S. for their defense."[23]

Yves Boyer questions whether this would "be compatible with the place and the role which the EU wishes to play on the international stage if it remains only capable of providing forces, mainly on the ground, depending on intelligence and flows of data processed by U.S. forces. This would be a situation close to what was the status of foreign troops serving in British and French armies during the colonial period." To reach "the goal of strategic autonomy," Europeans have to acquire decisive technologies. "The domain of intelligence satellites is a case in point, . . . In the area of navigation systems, the development of the Galileo satellite system will enable European forces to carry out a new range of tasks in the future. . . . Step by step a truly autonomous European defense policy is thus about to take shape."[24]

Besides expected economic benefits of Galileo to European aviation and shipping, there were political and security reasons for the development of Galileo: to reduce "the risks associated with signal loss from GPS at critical stages of an operation" of EU forces and to give "Europeans greater weight during negotiations with the United States."[25]

Such agreements on specific projects reduced costs somewhat compared to fully national production, but rationalization effects were limited by ad hoc organizational structures for each project. The principle of *juste retour* also required that each participating nation received a proportional share of the work for each project with little regard for greater efficiency. Further rationalization, beyond shared once-off projects, could be achieved only by unifying the defense equipment market and the procurement process.

MAKING BETTER USE OF EUROPEAN DEFENSE BUDGETS

Defense budgets were reduced on both sides of the Atlantic during the 1990s as governments in North America and NATO–Europe were reaping the "peace dividend" after the end of the Cold War. Europe had become a safer place with the withdrawal of Soviet troops from CEE. In the Conventional Armed Forces in Europe Treaty (November 1990), NATO and the Warsaw Pact countries agreed to reduce troops and equipment levels between the Atlantic and the Ural Mountains; in the Strategic Arms Reduction Treaty II (January 1993), the United States and Russia agreed to dismantle or mothball thousands of nuclear warheads. Yet by the late 1990s, the question reappeared whether NATO–Europe was spending enough on defense. Reduction of armament spending came under attack in the late 1990s, when U.S. neoconservatives of the Project for the New American Century accused the Clinton administration of "living off the capital" and "failing to sustain American influence around the world."[26] Under President George W. Bush, defense budgets were raised again, especially after the terrorist attacks of September 11, 2001, whereas European defense expenditure stabilized, not falling further but not following the rise of U.S. budgets.

Compared to the United States, European defense budgets were small, but compared to everyone else, Europeans spent large amounts in spite of the civilian power image of the EU. The United Kingdom ($37 billion in 1999), France ($38 billion), and Germany ($31 billion) each had defense budgets almost of the same order of magnitude as China ($40 billion), Japan ($40 billion), or Russia ($57 billion). Taken together, the total sum of all EU members' defense budgets was even more impressive, although they achieved surprisingly little for this expenditure. In 1999, EU members allocated a combined total of $166 billion to defense, or almost 60 percent of the U.S. defense budget of $283 billion. While the 15 EU members had 1.7 million men under arms in 1999, compared to 1.4 million for the United States,[27] only a very small percentage of these was available for power projection or long-distance intervention. This had been very visible in the Gulf War of 1990–91. European forces were still geared for the Cold War purpose of territorial defense. Reorienting them task to the post-1991 tasks of power projection would take years of restructuring and vast expenditure.

While the Bush administration increased U.S. defense spending from 2001 on, European budgets remained stable and, consequently, fell behind in comparison with the United States. On the other hand, an improving exchange rate of the euro against the U.S. dollar made European defense expenditure appear more substantial. For 2003, Britain ($43 billion), France ($46 billion), and Germany ($35 billion) had defense budgets roughly similar to China ($56 billion), Japan ($43 billion), and Russia ($65 billion). The EU total for 2003 (15 members) amounted to $199 billion, or almost 50 percent of the U.S. defense budget of $405 billion.[28]

Another cause of inefficiency of European defense spending besides outdated force structures was the existence of separate national defense budgets, a problem compounded by the increase of EU membership from 15 to 25 in May 2004. As long as national defense departments planned for separate all-round national armed forces, there would be fragmentation and duplication compared to the hypothetical economies of scale achievable in an integrated European defense effort. To put it positively, there was the promise of massive economies of scale if EU members could coordinate their defense planning, procurement, and production. Even without increasing national defense budgets, just by making better use of the present total of about $200 billion defense expenditure, the EU could become a global power, well behind the United States with a budget rising beyond $400 billion in the plans of the Bush administration but far ahead of China, Japan, or Russia. Coordinated defense planning could enable the EU to respond to any foreseeable threat from state actors and non–state actors on the periphery of Europe and to play a role in crisis management beyond Europe.

Rationalizing European defense expenditure by spending the same total more purposefully could achieve the capability to address the Petersberg Tasks and any residual needs for territorial defense. Expenditure could not be expected to increase for several reasons. In the post-1991 security environment, increases would be electorally unacceptable; the welfare function of the state was much more entrenched in Europe than in the United States; last but not least, the fiscal discipline imposed during the introduction of the common euro currency limited the level of government debt incurred by participant nations. Furthermore, the growth of Germany's economy has been sluggish because of the ongoing burden of rebuilding the East German regions after their economic collapse following unification. Thus, without raising taxes, cutting welfare, or raising government debt, with limited economic growth, defense planners had to make do with current levels of expenditure, trying to achieve more by using stable budgets more efficiently.

Parallel to the consolidation of armament production in the EDITB, the demand for equipment could also be rationalized by forming an integrated European Defense Equipment Market (EDEM). This would eventually expect member countries to accept EU-wide tendering without privileging national suppliers. For civilian goods and services, the European Single Market had been completed between 1986 and 1992, removing nontariff barriers to trade, after tariffs had been removed between 1957 and 1968 during the formation of the EEC customs union. For military goods, on the other hand, national markets had remained relatively closed for security reasons. However, without an integrated European defense equipment market, there was "the danger that Western Europe will fall further behind the US in the race of weapons technology, and possibly information and communications technology generally."[29] The imperatives of economic competitiveness demanded the integration of defense planning and production.

There was considerable potential for "getting a bigger bang for the Euro"[30] without increasing total expenditure through the following measures:

1. The transition of European forces to post–Cold War structures involved reductions of personnel (the end of conscription in France and the reduced significance of conscription in Germany). This could free up money for innovation and research.

2. Coordination of procurement could lead to economies of scale in production and reduce duplication and fragmentation.

3. The formation of EU forces, together with coordinated specialization of national forces, could contribute to more purposeful use of total defense expenditure.

4. The formation of an integrated EDEM and a more integrated EDITB could achieve more efficiency.

Such measures "could stretch current European budgets to pay for much more of the necessary high-tech weaponry, . . . even without raising taxes." French security expert François Heisbourg's "proposed remedies were to nudge Germany and Italy to adopt professional armed forces, to improve Europe's institutional ability to respond swiftly to crises and to converge disparate national defense policies toward active intervention; to acquire the requisite satellite surveillance, military electronics, heavy airlift, more versatile aircraft, and precision-guided weapons; to consolidate European defense industry and establish two or three large producers that would be competitive worldwide; to spend more on equipment and merge national weapons acquisition programs into a pan-European procurement agency that could correct the existing wasteful duplication through economies of scale; and to internationalize bids."[31]

This interdependence of European defense efforts could become acceptable even for a traditionally Atlanticist and NATO-oriented country such as the Netherlands. Smaller and medium-sized powers realized that they could not sustain all-round forces. The Netherlands was accepting the need to specialize and to rely on EU neighbors providing the force components that the Netherlands could not afford in the future.[32]

Several attempts to coordinate European defense planning had been made but without decisive results. The Western European Armaments Group functioned since December 1992, attached to the WEU, its membership increasing from 13 to 19 countries. Meetings of defense ministers and bureaucrats served to foster cross-border cooperation. In November 1996, France, Germany, Italy, and the United Kingdom decided to create the Organization for Joint Armament Cooperation. This organization facilitated the management of transnational armament projects. Six European countries with substantial armament industries (France, Germany, Italy, Spain, Sweden, and the United Kingdom) signed a letter of intent in July 1998 "aimed at facilitating cross-border restructuring of defense industries" and accepting that this implied "possible abandonment of national industrial capabilities and mutual dependence."[33] Finally, with the establishment of the European Defense Agency in 2004, an attempt was made to unify these methods of rationalizing procurement.

Even without increasing total defense spending of EU members, considerable improvements were possible. The economic prerequisites for integrated defense procurement had developed over time. European integration had developed beyond a customs union into an integrated market for civilian industries. Among defense industries, the aerospace and electronics sectors had seen cross-national mergers, while other sectors would be encouraged to consolidate across national boundaries if EU governments were to progress toward a unified EDEM. An increase in EU defense spending to match the military capabilities of the United States was neither desirable nor politically possible in spite of the aggregate of all EU economies matching the U.S. gross domestic product. However, without increasing defense expenditure, the rationalization of procurement and production alone would enable Europeans to sustain a globally relevant defense industry and to fulfill the Petersberg tasks.

ARMED FORCES FOR THE EU

The decision to establish European Rapid Response Forces (ERRFs) taken by EU leaders at their Helsinki summit in December 1999 was meant to give the EU the autonomous military capabilities suggested by the British–French St Malo agreement of 1998. These forces could complement the institutional and industrial-technological prerequisites for a common security policy developed earlier. Transnational cooperation between European forces had already taken place in various forms. NATO forces, including U.S. troops, had conducted regular joint exercises in Germany, the most likely theater of war in a Warsaw Pact–NATO confrontation. And national troops allocated to NATO, including the entire *Bundeswehr* (Germany's armed forces), had been subordinated to allied headquarters, with a U.S. general serving as Supreme Allied Commander Europe. Working within the transnational structures of NATO made cooperation in a multilateral context habitual for European forces.

In addition to the broader NATO structure, several transnational military units had been formed by two or more European NATO members between the 1970s and the 1990s. The British-Dutch Amphibious Force was started in 1973. The French-German Brigade of 1989 underlined Franco-German cooperation as the core of European integration. The Eurocorps of 1992 included troops from Germany, Belgium, Spain, Luxembourg, and France to a total of 60,000. The German-Dutch Corps of 1993, with personnel of 35,000, contributed to postconflict stabilization in Afghanistan since early 2002 and took on command of the International Stability Assistance Force in February 2003.

The WEU began to acquire operational capabilities on May 19, 1993, when Belgian, French, and German representatives declared to the WEU's Council of Ministers that their Eurocorps was to be regarded as part of the military units allocated to the WEU. This decision as well as the subsequent "double-hatting" of units from the Rapid Reaction Corps of NATO as WEU units could have enabled the WEU to form CJTFs for NATO-approved missions. However, any development of WEU capabilities ended in 1999. "Since it had become apparent that the WEU could not produce the desired capacity, EU members decided at the Cologne summit in June 1999 to make the EU proper the locus of security decision-making."[34]

Finally, in 1999, the decision was made to form armed forces under EU command, complementing the institutional and industrial prerequisites established earlier. At the Helsinki summit, EU leaders agreed to set up the ERRF by 2003. This force of 60,000 was to be deployable at short notice, within a radius of 4,000 kilometers from Brussels. At the Capability Improvement Conference of November 19, 2001, member states identified shortfalls and agreed on a European Capability Action Plan. After the EU's Laeken summit (December 2001), the "Presidency Conclusions" stated that the union was "now capable of conducting some crisis-management operations." In May 2003, the General Affairs and External Relations Council stated that the EU now had "operational capability across the full range of Petersberg tasks, limited and constrained [only] by recognized shortfalls."[35] The EU had achieved the Helsinki Headline Goal of 1999, at least nominally, by earmarking national forces as part of the ERRF.

The idea to form rapidly deployable EU "battle groups" was launched by Britain and France at their bilateral summits in Le Tourquet (February 2003) and London (November 2003) and adopted by EU defense ministers in April 2004. The battle groups were to consist of 1,500 soldiers, deployable to crisis regions within 15 days, for missions of 30 to 120 days' duration. Their most likely role was to intervene in failed or failing states, in line with chapter 7 of the UN Charter. This definition of tasks made African failed or failing states the most likely place of intervention. In May 2005, EU defense ministers confirmed their commitment to form such battle groups. "France and Britain have already placed on standby battle groups composed entirely of their own troops, and Italy has pledged to do the same." Other EU members as well as non-EU Norway intend to participate in multinational battle groups.[36]

Headquarters or Just a "Planning Cell"?

The proposal by France, Germany, Belgium, and Luxembourg of April 29, 2003, to establish headquarters for the EU's ERRF at Tervuren in Belgium was regarded in Washington "as an attempt to create an alternative to NATO, and thus to weaken the alliance." The proposed EU military headquarters would have advanced the EU's autonomous security role, but without their own planning capacity, EU forces would have remained an appendix of NATO. At the height of the transatlantic controversies before the Iraq War, the Tervuren proposal added to tensions and was unsuccessful, especially because of British objections. However, in September 2003, a meeting of the British, French, and German leaders arrived at a compromise. The EU would strengthen its links with NATO by deploying a group of operational planners to the Supreme Headquarters of Allied Powers in Europe, NATO's planning headquarters. This would ensure NATO–EU cooperation regarding "'Berlin-plus' missions, when the EU borrows NATO assets." At the same time, the EU itself acquired "a new unit of operational planners for the EU's military staff" that "will help with the planning of EU military missions."[37]

The depth of feelings about this seemingly small issue was apparent not only in the response by U.S. Secretary of Defense Rumsfeld but also in comments by the French daily *Le Monde*. It claimed that the United States intended to shape the EU into a large free trade area unable to make its own strategic decisions, "an immense Europe but without political leadership." This was bound to fail, *Le Monde* claimed, because the "French-German-British will to achieve an autonomous strategic capability" and the efforts of the EU to develop the CFSP European were an antidote against an alliance in which "America continues to exercise a preponderant influence."[38]

Without this planning cell, EU forces would have depended completely on NATO planning. "For EU-led operations using NATO-assets and capabilities, the EU summit in Nice stated that operational planning would be carried out by NATO. . . . In practice, this means that the EU would formally lead the operation, but that NATO would handle all the planning and command arrangements. . . . US influence would be substantial as long as US and NATO assets were used, and EU autonomy would be nil."[39] Yet between the Nice summit of December 2000 and the decision of May 2004 to establish the planning cell, EU security autonomy had become somewhat more acceptable.

THE EU AS MILITARY AND NONMILITARY CRISIS MANAGER

In 2003, the EU deployed police and military personnel abroad for the first time. The European Union Police Mission in Bosnia-Herzegovina, launched on January 1, 2003, to replace the UN International Police Task Force, was the EU's first civilian crisis management operation under the ESDP. The first military operation of the EU was the *Concordia* mission in Macedonia, launched on March 31, 2003, replacing NATO's *Operation Allied Harmony*. The *Concordia* mission was drawing on NATO assets under the NATO–EU Berlin Plus agreement of December 2002. *Concordia* was followed by an EU police mission called *Proxima*, launched on 15 December 2003 and involving 200 police officers. The EU's first military operation outside Europe was the *Artemis* mission under a UN mandate (Security Council Resolution 1484, May 30, 2003). Launched on June 12, 2003, and ending on September 1, 2003, *Artemis* intended to stabilize security in the Ituri region of the Democratic Republic of Congo.[40]

In spite of the small number of personnel involved (about 1,000 in EUPM, about 350 in *Concordia*, and about 1,800 in *Artemis*), these missions demonstrated the political will and the capability to act as the EU. The EU could be called on by the UN Security Council for interventions under chapter 7 of the UN Charter, and it was capable of fulfilling most of the Petersberg Tasks set out in 1992. These missions also indicated the regions where the EU was interested in and capable of intervening. In southeastern Europe, the EU was replacing NATO as stabilizer. In the short term, police and military missions supported political and economic stabilization under the Stabilization Pacts between the EU and several successor states of Yugoslavia. In the long term, EU membership promised to make military missions in southeastern Europe superfluous. The EU was also assuming a crisis management role in Africa, continuing and modifying a tradition of French and British interventions.

Besides setting up its battle groups, the EU also established nonmilitary crisis management mechanisms. The EU summit at Feira in June 2000 decided to develop "four aspects of civilian crisis management: police, rule of law, civil administration and civil protection." For this purpose, EU members would "provide up to 5,000 police officers for international missions by 2003, with 1,000 available at 30 days' notice."[41]

AMBIGUOUS U.S. RESPONSES TO ESDP AND EDITB

Burden Sharing and EU Autonomy

American responses to the emerging ESDI/ESDP indicated that increased European defense efforts were welcome only if they contributed to burden sharing without creating European autonomy. The ESDI should remain "subservient to NATO encouraging the European partners of NATO into greater burden sharing, providing an additional base for US global policing . . . and avoiding becoming a 'European caucus' which would challenge American leadership."[42] American commentators also noticed this ambiguity. "To many Europeans, the implicit meaning of such comments was that the European nations should do more and pay more to carry out policies of a US-dominated NATO. They were also aware that a major portion of America's political and policy elite was openly unenthusiastic about ESDI, fearing that it would automatically become a competitor to NATO and dilute Washington's influence in the overall transatlantic relationship."[43]

It was even suggested that U.S. leaders did not seriously want greater European burden sharing in NATO: "American policymakers are also disingenuous when they demand that they want to see a strong ESDI develop. That result would, in reality, be Washington's worst nightmare. Even if European leaders did not seek to make a robust ESDI a competitor to NATO, the dynamics of international politics would ultimately lead to that result."[44] This ambiguity toward the ESDP confirmed the conclusion of Geir Lundestad's study that, over the preceding 50 years, the United States had generally supported European integration, "but this support has always been conditioned [*sic*] on Europe being fitted into a wider Atlantic framework. . . . So once the Atlantic framework is seriously questioned, it seems likely that US support for European integration will falter rather quickly."[45]

Instead of continuing this balancing act between retaining leadership and asking for burden sharing, "Washington should accept the fact that a functional ESDI would gradually displace NATO as Europe's primary security organization. . . . Washington's preeminence began in the context of a Western Europe that was devastated and demoralized by World War II. . . . It is hard to believe that more than half a century later, a prosperous, capable and confident European Union will forever defer to the United States."[46] Yet instead of looking forward to a new transatlantic division of labor, Clinton's secretary of state, Madeleine Albright, warned Europeans against the "three Ds": to decouple Europe from the United States, to duplicate expenditure and capabilities, and to discriminate against members of NATO who were not members of the EU, such as Turkey.[47]

Nevertheless, the United States learned to live with the progress beyond an ESDI limited to CJTFs within NATO toward an ESDP including the formation of EU forces outside NATO. Significant concessions to EU autonomy were made in the Berlin Plus agreement of December 2002. This agreement allowed the EU to use NATO assets for future missions; it was implemented for the first time in the *Concordia* mission when about 350 soldiers were sent to Macedonia in March 2003. In the Berlin Plus agreement, NATO acknowledged that EU forces existed outside the transatlantic alliance, not only as ESDI within NATO.

Ambiguous U.S. attitudes resulted in slow acceptance of EU autonomy and slow disengagement from Europe. American policy, on the one hand, reasserted leadership and showed continued involvement in NATO, but, on the other, there was the Bush administration's demonstrative disinterest in NATO, sidelining the alliance in favor of ad hoc coalitions of the willing. In a contradictory approach, the United States used influence on NATO's new members in Central and Eastern Europe to counter the EU's autonomous

ESDP. Yet reducing the U.S. military presence in Europe made the ESDP inevitable.

U.S. Trojan Horse against Defense-Industrial "Fortress Europe"

The EU's claims for an autonomous security role depended on a viable EDITB. Should Europe's defense industries fail to consolidate into enterprises of competitive size and technological competence, any political claims to autonomy would be weakened by technological dependency. American influence could rely on the size of the U.S. defense budget, the volume of the U.S. defense market, and the strength of the largest defense-industry enterprises. The military supremacy of the United States also implied economic preeminence in the defense industry, which could help perpetuate U.S. leadership in European security.

American concerns were illustrated in a RAND study, "The Future of the European Defense Industry," sponsored by the Pentagon's Office of the Deputy Undersecretary of Defense, Industrial Policy. The stated objectives of the report included "enhanced competition and interoperability with coalition partners" to "be achieved through transatlantic collaboration with reliable firms in countries that have policies with objectives similar to the policies of the United States." In this respect, "developments in the European defense and aerospace industry" were "of particular importance."[48]

However, besides the stated objectives, there was also the unstated concern about EU security autonomy. The three scenarios discussed in the study left out a possible fourth scenario that could transform the EU into a relevant strategic actor. Scenario A envisaged developments driven by market forces expected to link two European prime contractors closely with four U.S. mega primes, thus binding Europeans into an overwhelming U.S. defense market. This scenario followed the free trader logic preferred by nations enjoying industrial supremacy. The U.S. defense industry could best act out its advantages in a free trade environment, especially while European competitors were divided into national defense industries. De facto, the free market scenario was a subtle continuation of U.S. hegemony allocating to European defense industries a permanent junior role. Scenario B assumed that Europeans would continue to "muddle through" at the present level of consolidation of industries but without integrated defense planning and procurement. Without coordinated EU industry policy, the four European prime contractors could be transformed into two or three outliers of the U.S. defense market. In Scenario C, "deconsolidation" would turn EU defense industries into profitable niche players. This would perpetuate their technological and economic dependence on U.S. prime contractors even more clearly than scenarios A and B.[49]

Another possible course of events was ignored by the study. If EU governments coordinated their procurement and if consolidation of defense industries went beyond the level achieved in the late 1990s, Europeans could actually retain autonomy and strengthen their EDITB by integrating procurement and defense planning. In that case, transatlantic cooperation would not result in EU players being swallowed up by the larger U.S. defense market. The inherent imbalance between one gigantic Pentagon budget and 25 separate national budgets in the EU could be reduced by two factors: the political will of EU governments and the strength of civilian EU industries. If European governments supported further consolidation of defense industries and coordinated their defense planning and procurement, a competitive EDITB could be sustained. Otherwise, each of the three scenarios of the RAND study implied subordination to U.S. defense industries.

Taking into account political developments since the EU had adopted the CFSP in Maastricht in 1991, the least likely outcome was the free market scenario A. As European governments faced the stark choice either to accept the decline of national defense industries into irrelevance or to seek the economies of scale available by integration of production and procurement at the EU level, they were likely to do the latter. Scenario C of the RAND study, involving deconsolidation, was also a very unlikely outcome as long as EU governments were willing to buy defense equipment from EADS, Thales, BAe, and Finmeccanica.

The most likely outcome was a mixture of the muddling-through scenario B and the consolidation scenario not envisaged by the RAND study. Over the past 50 years, much of European integration looked like muddling through. Nevertheless, the multitude of small, practical steps had usually resulted in EU consolidation. The most likely outcome was therefore a gradual and imperfect consolidation of the EDITB, neither to be absorbed by the larger U.S. defense market nor to become an isolationist "Fortress Europe." Key projects such as the Airbus A400M, the Eurofighter, and the Galileo, Helios, and Horus satellite projects were contributing to EDITB consolidation. On the other hand, transatlantic interdependence was remaining substantial, for example, in the Medium Extended Air Defense System (MEADS) project, shared by the United States, Germany, and Italy. From a German perspective, the MEADS project had "alliance-political significance" as an indicator that "the German as well as the American government . . . endeavored to improve bilateral relations"[50] in spite of tensions over the 2003 Iraq War. Furthermore, the MEADS agreement also signaled greater willingness to transfer U.S. technology to the German and Italian partners. The most likely outcome, in defense industries as in the entire transatlantic relationship, was a more balanced partnership of two autonomous and interdependent partners. The sheer size of the Pentagon's budget consolidated the primacy of U.S. defense industries; however, an integrated EDEM and the political will to achieve security autonomy for the EU should, nevertheless, sustain a viable EDITB.

The United States took practical steps to prevent increased defense-industrial protectionism. Inviting European companies to participate in the development and production of the Joint Strike Fighter (JSF), in partnership with Lockheed Martin, was meant to counter the development "of a 'Fortress Europe' that would lock out American weaponry." Therefore, the Pentagon and its defense contractors "had to devise an industrial strategy for capturing the European market at this critical time. That strategy was to offer foreign partners something of a Trojan horse, as JSF would enter European (among other) arsenals through co-development and co-production of the plane with local governments and firms."[51] The United Kingdom became a "full collaborative partner," whereas Denmark, the Netherlands, and Norway became "associate partners."[52] Including European partners achieved longer production runs and economies of scale, but it also served the strategic purpose of binding European producers and governments into transatlantic arrangements shaped by U.S. technological and industrial leadership.

In the early years of NATO, the US had dominated European defense markets but "between 1953 and 1964, . . . US defense exports to NATO-Europe fell from \$15bn to \$3.3bn."[53] While the increasing costs of military technology required economies of scale which even the huge US defense market could not provide and therefore demanded increased exports, access to the European market was getting more difficult in the 1990s due to the consolidation of European defense contractors and initiatives of European governments to coordinate procurement. "The challenge, then, was to devise a political and economic strategy for locking in at least some European governments so that their dependence on American weaponry would continue for many years to come. The solution was found in co-development and co-production of the most advanced aircraft that the United States had ever built."[54]

The development of defense industries mirrored the change in the transatlantic security relation. The asymmetrical relation of the late 1940s was replaced by a more balanced relationship. Europe's EDITB was substantial enough to be sustainable if backed by strong civilian industries and cooperation between European governments. Yet transatlantic cooperation was also substantial enough to prevent total decoupling of an industrial Fortress Europe from the United States.

GERMANY, THE BIG LAGGARD: SLOWING DOWN NATO MODERNIZATION AND ESDP

German unification was one of the reasons for the survival of NATO after the Cold War and for the deepening of EU integration in the 1990s. The fact that German foreign policy was being "normalized" very slowly and that German armed forces were being restructured and modernized even more slowly made it possible for NATO and the emerging security role of the EU to coexist and to develop in an evolutionary way, allowing transformation with little disruption. West Germany had been Atlanticist as well as Europeanist for four decades, seeking integration in the transatlantic alliance as well as European integration and reconciliation with France, whereas Euro-skeptic

Britain had emphasized the transatlantic "special relationship," and NATO-skeptic France had prioritized *Europe puissance*. After unification, the enlarged Federal Republic of Germany (FRG) did not renationalize its foreign policy but continued its involvement in the transatlantic alliance and the EU.

In the short run, German unification provided a rationale for NATO as a multilateral structure embedding German armed forces and for U.S. involvement as balancer reassuring Germany's neighbors. German unification also gave momentum to deeper EU integration. In the long run, however, the more Germany will be Europeanized and the more the EU takes on responsibility for European security, the less NATO and U.S. military presence will be required. This transition will, however, take place very gradually.

The slow pace of the reform of the *Bundeswehr* is hindering the development of both an effective European pillar within NATO and a viable ESDP for the EU. "Without a significant German contribution, ESDP will remain at the level of 'Petersberg minus.' The success of the ESDP will rest primarily on the ability of the UK, France and Germany to pull their respective weights."[55] On the positive side, the slow pace of adjusting German foreign and defense policy to post–Cold War requirements made it easier for the United States, NATO, and the EU to adjust their respective roles regarding European security.

Normalizing Foreign Policy: Between Civilian Power and New Interventionism

From 1949 to 1989, West Germany had acquired the habits of a "civilian power" for the same reasons as post-1945 Japan.[56] The FRG's foreign policy was shaped by restrictions imposed after World War II by the victorious four powers and by the conditions under which it was admitted to membership of WEU (1954) and NATO (1955). The FRG placed all its forces under NATO command; could not engage in wars of aggression or produce nuclear, biological, or chemical weapons; and could engage only in military activities outlined by the NATO treaty. The FRG not only adapted to these restrictions but also positively adopted them as firm habits of multilateralism and civilian power. After the catastrophic failure of Germany's aggressive posture of 1914 and 1939, the FRG did very well with this emphasis on civilian power and multilateral integration of its military potential. Self-restraint became habitual in the foreign policy elite and was widely supported in public opinion.

These conditions made it impossible for Germany to follow calls for participation in the Gulf War of 1990–91. Over the next decade, government policy and public opinion changed gradually to allow the first deployment of combat troops abroad, justified as humanitarian intervention, in Kosovo in 1999. This gradual normalization of German foreign policy was helped along by the Constitutional Court's 1994 reinterpretation of the constitutional ban on wars of aggression in the Basic Law of 1949. Under this new interpretation, the FRG was allowed to participate not only in alliances for territorial defense but also in multilateral military actions farther afield.[57]

Normalization after 1990 involved the lifting of these restrictions over several years, allowing Germany to act more like a normal assertive nation-state, no longer hindered by memories of World Wars I and II. However, this assertiveness was still balanced by the realization that German national interests, even after unification, were best realized in the multilateral context of EU integration and thus depended on the goodwill of all other EU members. Normalization included the gradual extension of the acceptable limits of the missions of German armed forces, but it did not lead to a renationalization of security policy. The civilian power preference for nonmilitary means remained entrenched in German foreign policy, and the preference for multilateral approaches continued in the commitment to EU integration and to the transatlantic relationship.

Reforming German Armed Forces since 1990

The restructuring of Germany's armed forces was taking place in the context of three major developments: the unification of Germany in 1990 followed by the normalization of German foreign policy, the reorientation of NATO since 1991, and the development of a European CFSP. First, German unification implied the end of the East German NVA and the transformation of the West German *Bundeswehr*. Until 1989, the *Bundeswehr* numbered about 490,000 soldiers, whereas the East German NVA had about 170,000. This total of 660,000 was brought down to 330,000 very quickly by dissolving most of the units of the NVA and by reducing the duration of national service in the *Bundeswehr*. Second, NATO's Strategic Concept, adopted at the Rome summit in November 1991, demanded a reorientation of armed forces from collective defense toward interventions out of area. Third, the Europeanization of European security began with the adoption of the CFSP in the EU's Maastricht Treaty in 1991 and the adoption of the Petersberg Tasks by the WEU in 1992. The practical consequences of German unification for the *Bundeswehr* were drawn rather quickly, whereas both NATO modernization and ESDP development were pursued over the next two decades in an ambiguous mixture of complementarity and conflict.

Both ESDP and NATO were affected by the slow pace of restructuring German armed forces. "*Bundeswehr* reform to date has prioritized German domestic concerns—particularly financing, conscription and threat assessment—over European and NATO preferences."[58] A thoroughly reformed *Bundeswehr* was required for NATO's European pillar but also for the EU's autonomous ESDP. "ESDP will not be a serious policy unless Germany moves more quickly and dramatically toward creating the kinds of forces required for the European Rapid Reaction Force to have real teeth. . . . The stakes are high, and ultimately the credibility of both NATO and the emerging European Security and Defense Policy are on the line."[59] If the EU's biggest economy could not modernize its forces, the transatlantic capabilities gap would threaten NATO interoperability. And if the FRG did not carry its share, the ESDP could not function either.

Successful *Bundeswehr* modernization could also sway reluctant European countries to accept a global mission for NATO beyond the defense of Europe. "The UK and France already have made or are making the shift towards smaller, professional militaries capable of a broader spectrum of missions, . . . Germany's ability to join this trend could create a critical mass politically in terms of defining a new European mainstream." A reformed *Bundeswehr* could bring Germany and Europe closer to U.S. perspectives on global security, overcoming an exclusive focus on European regional security: "Its attempt to become a more normal European power will facilitate the emergence of a more global European strategic outlook as well as a willingness and ability to act in concert with the United States."[60]

Bundeswehr reform was crucial for transatlantic relations and for the international role of the FRG. "If it attempts to muddle through, it . . . will run the risk of creating a crisis with its European and Atlantic allies. . . . The U.S. stakes in the outcome of the German reform are too high for American officials to remain silent. This is not just a German domestic debate but one with far reaching implications for the future of the trans-Atlantic relationship and, ultimately, the future American role in Europe."[61]

Germany, the Big Laggard

At the end of the Cold War, the security environment changed more profoundly for Germany than for France, the United Kingdom, or the United States. "Germany's defense posture has been geared to territorial defense. . . . Therefore, the shift towards a more mobile and flexible set of forces to meet new demands posed a greater challenge to Germany than to many other European allies."[62] During the Cold War, the West German *Bundeswehr* had been trained for territorial defense in a war at the central front between NATO and the Warsaw Pact. When NATO's priorities changed in 1990, the *Bundeswehr* was not capable of out-of-area power projection. The conspicuous absence of the *Bundeswehr* from the Gulf War was caused not only by the preoccupation with German unification at the time but also by its lack of preparation for long-distance intervention.

Other important NATO members, such as the United States, the United Kingdom, and France, adapted faster than Germany. American forces were, because of their global role, geared for a variety of purposes, ranging from nuclear war to (possible) territorial defense in Europe, (actual) interventions in Korea and Vietnam, and low-intensity conflicts elsewhere. British forces were prepared for long-distance intervention in cooperation with U.S. troops more than any other NATO partner. In 1991, British forces numbered only about 200,000, less than half of West Germany's Cold War conscript forces, but these professional soldiers were capable of participating in interventions abroad, including the Gulf War of 1990–91, the Kosovo campaign of 1999, and the Iraq War of 2003.

In the mid-1990s, France embarked on a determined course of restructuring its forces, achieving results much faster than Germany. French forces included a large number of conscripts, more than British but fewer than German forces. France had sustained a colonial tradition of interventionism but was less capable of power projection than the armed forces of the United Kingdom. Whereas the United Kingdom was able to contribute 35,000 to the Gulf War, France could make available only 9,000 out of a total of 280,000. President Chirac "announced in February 1996 that France would professionalize and slim down its armed forces … to an estimated 136,000 men by the year 2002."[63]

While France phased out conscription and carried out major aspects of the transformation envisaged by NATO's Strategic Concept of 1991, Germany was the laggard among the major European NATO partners. During the Cold War, power projection into distant theaters of war had not been among the task of the *Bundeswehr*; mobility was limited to extended territorial defense. Therefore, the adaptation of German forces to the post-1991 security environment was more difficult and time consuming.

Conceptualizing *Bundeswehr* Reform

While the foreign and security policy of the FRG was still in the early stages of normalization, military planners already conceptualized the post-1991 security interests of united Germany. NATO's Strategic Concept recommended structural adaptation of armed forces to the new security environment. Forces were to be differentiated, first, into Reaction Forces, including Immediate Reaction Forces (ready within two to seven days) and Rapid Reaction Forces (ready within seven to 30 days); second, the bulk of NATO were to be the Main Defense Forces, more numerous but not fully combat ready; third, the Augmentation Forces were to be mobilized only when required. Accordingly, in the early 1990s, the *Bundeswehr* was divided into "the mobilization-dependent Main Defence Forces" and "the operational Crisis Reaction Forces."[64]

Defense Minister Rudolf Scharping continued the reform of the *Bundeswehr* from 1998 on under the newly elected government of Social Democrats and Greens "by initiating a second, more radical reform that further reduced the *Bundeswehr* and further reoriented it away from territorial defense and towards crisis management and crisis prevention operations outside of Germany."[65] Significant reduction of total military personnel and an expansion of crisis response forces was recommended by three papers on *Bundeswehr* reform published almost concurrently in May 2000.

The Weizsäcker Commission (Kommission für Gemeinsame Sicherheit und Zukunft der Bundeswehr, chaired by former President Richard von Weizsäcker) recommended a reduction of *Bundeswehr* personnel to about 240,000 but an expansion of crisis reaction forces from 60,000 to 140,000.[66] This went further in the reduction of personnel than the other two reports, although it still recommended the retention of conscription and the importance of territorial defense. Parallel to the work of the Weizsäcker Commission, the most senior officer of the *Bundeswehr*, General Inspector Hans-Peter von Kirchbach, prepared a paper recommending an expansion of crisis response forces to 157,000, whereas total *Bundeswehr* personnel were to be reduced to 290,000.[67] More than the Weizsäcker Commission, Kirchbach still emphasized territorial defense, which required conscription and the ability to call up reserves.

A third paper under the name of Defense Minister Scharping was accepted by the cabinet in June 2000. Its main objectives were to shrink the *Bundeswehr* to 280,000 soldiers, to support the EU's Headline Goals of Helsinki 1999 by contributing to the EU Crisis Reaction Force, to consolidate the Main Forces and the Rapid Reaction Forces into a Readiness Force of 150,000, and to upgrade equipment in order to enhance strategic mobility as well as command, control, and communications. In its total numbers and in the share of conscripts, the minister's draft ended somewhere between the Kirchbach paper and the Weizsäcker report. "Like the Weizsäcker and Kirchbach reports, it uses the unpredictability of the future as a justification for conscription. Territorial defense remains a high priority for this reason. . . . On top of this, the 'integration of soldiers in society as citizens' remains a fundamental guiding principle for the *Bundeswehr*."[68]

Retaining Conscription Incompatible with Restructuring

The future of conscription became a contentious issue. As a result of contradictory political pressures from many sides, neither the Kohl government (until 1998) nor the Schröder government (since 1998) followed the example of French President Chirac in ending conscription quickly. In both major political parties, the defenders of conscription prevailed. In the right-of-center Christian Democratic Union/Christian Social Union, traditionalists favored the retention of conscription because the *Bundeswehr* had to be ready for territorial defense, as there was still a residual threat from Russia; conscription would also instill in young men a sense of duty and national pride. On the center-left, Social Democrats supported conscription for historical reasons. In the 1920s, the professional *Wehrmacht* had been a state in the state, more loyal to the emperor deposed in 1918 than to the new republic, and ready to sacrifice the democratic regime of the Weimar Republic, preferring a return to an authoritarian monarchy or even the transition to Hitler's Nazi totalitarianism in 1933. Therefore, Social Democrats insisted on a citizens' army of conscripts embedded in civilian society and democratic political structures. Opposition to conscription, on the other hand, was clearly articulated by the minor parties. The right-of-center Free Democrats, less traditionalist than their Christian Democratic allies, were ready to embrace modernization of the *Bundeswehr*, and the left-of-center Greens also argued for the professionalization of the *Bundeswehr*.[69]

In this contradictory political context, the Schröder government was, de facto, drifting toward ending conscription in spite of the repeatedly stated intention to retain it. Such indecisiveness limited political pain but added to the costs of transformation. "The Schröder government's efforts to maintain conscription and to restructure forces seem to avoid a choice that must be made. . . . It cannot afford to maintain a conscript force and restructure at the same time."[70] The reform attempts under the Kohl government (until 1998) and in the first years of the Schröder government, under Defense Minister Scharping, did not end conscription and could not reduce personnel costs to the extent necessary to finance modernization. "Both conceptually (the prioritization of territorial defence) and practically (the inadequate reform budget), *Bundeswehr* reform is ill-suited to enabling Germany to pull its weight in ESDP to the same degree as the UK and France."[71]

Yet Peter Struck, Scharping's successor as defense minister, signaled a turn away from territorial defense and conscription toward power projection, with his memorable formulation that Germany's security was also being defended in the Hindukush.[72] While not abandoning conscription, he embarked on a course of action that would make it possible to phase out conscription later.

The Kohl government had explicitly rejected following the French model of restructuring, and the Schröder government had continued the priority for territorial defense and retaining conscription in Minister Scharping's proposal, but Minister Struck had "increasingly set priorities in favor of military crisis management."[73] In March 2004, he announced new guidelines preparing German forces for the most likely missions, that is, conflict prevention and crisis management, whereas he regarded the need for "territorial defense in the traditional sense" as "having become less likely." By 2010, the new *Bundeswehr* was to be reduced to "250,000 soldiers as well as 75,000 positions for civilian employees" and structured into reaction forces, stabilization forces, and support forces.[74]

Minister Struck repeatedly stated his intention to retain universal conscription, but his reform plans included measures effectively undermining conscription. As the numbers of professional personnel increased, either the lengths of service for conscripts had to be reduced to accommodate the numbers of potential conscripts or the number of individuals conscripted had to be diminished. Reducing the length of national service raised questions of quality because recruits could not acquire sufficient skills in six months of service (plus three months of exercises that may or may not take place). Reducing the number of recruits, on the other hand, raised questions of equity between the conscripted minority and their peers avoiding the draft. In effect, Minister Struck's methods of retaining conscription weakened its political legitimacy and functional relevance, thus preparing the end of conscription.

Budgetary Restraints Slowing Down
Bundeswehr Reform

The time frame of *Bundeswehr* reform was determined by the transformation from Cold War territorial defense to power projection, the difficulty of "normalizing" German foreign policy, and the political complications of ending conscription. A further delaying factor was the impossibility to increase defense expenditure. For several years after 1991, Germany, like other NATO members, had been reducing defense budgets. Unlike the United States under President Bush, the FRG did not return to increased defense spending. The main obstacles were the continuing costs of German unification and the budget discipline imposed on all countries participating in the common euro currency.

The technological modernization of the *Bundeswehr* was conceptualized clearly when Inspector General Harald Kujat, on March 16, 2001, outlined guidelines for procurement and equipment for the next 15 years. "If implemented in time, it would make Germany's armed forces a reliable partner able to catch up with the Revolution in Military Affairs."[75] However, underfunding could not only slow down modernization but might also make it unworkable. "The point is that Germany has embarked on a reform of the *Bundeswehr* that is guided by a reasonable concept which is lacking money to a degree that the fulfilment of this reform is endangered."[76] Budgetary restrictions and political complications connected with *Bundeswehr* reform suggested that General Kujat's 2001–16 time frame for technological modernization might have to be extended.

Regarding the development of NATO and the EU's security role, the slow pace of *Bundeswehr* reform indicated that the consequences of the end of the Cold War would be clearly visible only after a slow transformation over 25 years. The Soviet Union and its Eastern European sphere of influence disintegrated instantly in 1991. On the other hand, the post-1945 benign hegemony of the United States over Western Europe was ending much more gradually. Nevertheless, the asymmetrical role allocation in the transatlantic relationship was coming to an end.

CLARIFYING AMBIGUITIES BETWEEN NATO AND THE EU

The relations between NATO and the EU's claimed security role remained ambiguous throughout the 1990s and beyond. From its beginnings, the ESDI was meant to create and strengthen the European pillar of the transatlantic alliance, with European burden sharing an integral part of NATO. At the same time, coordinated European defense efforts always had the potential to develop beyond the temporary detachability of the CJTF into an autonomous EU security role. While the ESDI remained suspended in this ambiguity for most of the 1990s, there were several factors gradually modifying NATO's role while enhancing the EU's security role, especially after it turned to the ESDP in 1999.

The Paradox Effect of NATO's New Tasks

While the EU was slowly proceeding beyond institutional prerequisites toward the formation of armed forces and its first military missions, the

NATO alliance searched for a rationale to justify its existence after its decisive victory in the Cold War. NATO's old tasks of "keeping the Russians out, keeping the Germans down, and keeping the Americans in" were of diminishing urgency, as Russia was becoming a strategic partner for the EU while German unification resulted in deeper European integration. NATO's new post-1991 tasks gave the alliance a new lease on life, but each of these secondary purposes reduced NATO's long-term relevance either by transforming it from a military alliance into a security community or by provoking European steps toward an autonomous security policy.

NATO expansion also facilitated the expansion of the EU. In the short run, CEE countries looked to the United States and NATO for security, but in the long run, the EU was expected to become a widely acceptable provider of security, as economic integration was bringing old and new EU members closer together. NATO's intervention in the Bosnian civil war and the Kosovo campaign against Serbia demonstrated that the United States was still the indispensable nation and NATO the primary framework for European security. The Atlanticist conclusion was that Europe could not and should not act without the United States. Yet the opposite conclusion was also possible. European disunity demonstrated the need for a coordinated foreign and security policy, and European weakness showed that an autonomous crisis management capability was required. The capabilities gap motivated Europeans to upgrade their capability as NATO allies but also to strengthen their autonomous ESDP.

The out-of-area tasks suggested by Senator Lugar created problems for NATO, as members could not agree on the alliance's future range of actions since multifaceted and multidirectional threats (Strategic Concept of 1991) had replaced the simpler scenario of the Cold War. Although Senator Lugar argued that going out of area was required to prevent NATO going out of business, the experiences of Afghanistan and Iraq supported Rupp's claim that NATO would go out of business if went out of area.[77]

NATO as a collective defense organization was becoming irrelevant because there was little need for the territorial defense of Europe in the post-1991 security environment. On the other hand, going out of area evoked a diversity of views among NATO members in response to a diversity of threat situations because "the new threats are different: They are divisive, not unifying; they are cumulative rather than immediate; and they are coalition-breaking, not coalition-forming."[78] NATO's old tasks were completed so successfully that Europe no longer needed the alliance for these purposes, and NATO's new tasks had side effects encouraging the development of an autonomous ESDP.

The Paradox Effect of Atlanticist Efforts to Close the Capabilities Gap

Even the efforts of European Atlanticists to strengthen NATO ties had the paradox effect of advancing European autonomy. NATO was threatened by

European military weakness, as the capabilities gap between the transatlantic partners threatened to become a mission gap. Yet any upgrading of EU capabilities could lead to ambiguous outcomes. For Atlanticists, there was the need to strengthen European military capabilities in order to become more credible NATO partners. On the other hand, any strengthening of European military capabilities was also bringing closer the end of the U.S. military protectorate. In order to strengthen NATO, Europeans had to coordinate their efforts, pool their defense dollars, and merge defense industries. Yet such methods of achieving a credible European pillar within NATO also facilitated an autonomous European security policy. Thus, NATO's cohesion was threatened by European strength as much as by European weakness.

British support for the 1998 St Malo agreement was motivated by the desire to have a credible ESDI within NATO, whereas it was commonly assumed that French support for this Franco-British initiative was motivated by the drive for European security autonomy. Atlanticist and Europeanist intentions differed regarding the intended long-term outcome but converged on the same intermediate steps. Whether these steps built an ESDI within NATO or an autonomous ESDP would be decided not so much by British or French intentions as by the desire of the United States to loosen European commitments. In the context of U.S. disengagement, the intentions of European Atlanticists translated in de facto contributions to a stronger, autonomous ESDP.

The Effect of Reducing U.S. Military Presence since 1991

The gradual withdrawal of U.S. forces from Europe meant that Europeans had to prepare for a future without U.S. security guarantees, according to Nicole Gnesotto, director of the Institute for Strategic Studies of the European Union. As "the United States fixes its priorities elsewhere," Europeans have to accept that the ESDP was being transformed "from an option to a strategic obligation."[79] While Europeans adapted their armed forces, ambiguously contributing both to a stronger European pillar within NATO and to emerging EU autonomy, U.S. disengagement from Europe was deciding the outcome. As U.S. security policy prioritized East Asia, Central Asia, and the Greater Middle East, the relation between NATO and the EU's claimed security role was becoming less ambiguous.

In 1990, Joseph S. Nye still rejected the suggestion that the United States withdraw troops from Europe in order to reduce military expenditure and fiscal deficits: "Policies of retrenchment are premature and, ironically, they could produce the very weakening of American power they are supposed to avert."[80] Nevertheless, when Nye was assistant secretary of defense in the Clinton administration, U.S. military presence in Europe was substantially reduced.

As a matter of fact, the United States has been disengaging from Europe since 1991. One indicator was the reduction of U.S. troops in Europe, especially the withdrawal from Germany. This reduced U.S. troops in Europe from more than 300,000 before 1990 to 70,000 in 2004, while plans for further reductions were announced aiming for figures below 30,000 within 5 to 10 years.[81] Another indicator was the nature of U.S. involvement in Kosovo: late, reluctantly, by high-altitude bombing, without ground troops, and without involvement in peacekeeping afterward. After 1991, U.S. involvement in European crisis management had become optional. And there was the clear demotion of Europe in the list of U.S. strategic priorities in the *Quadrennial Defense Review* 2001 of the incoming Bush administration.

President George H. W. Bush had managed very carefully the immediate implications of the end of the Cold War. The United States fulfilled its role as stabilizer and balancer for Western Europe, supervising the unification of Germany and the withdrawal of the Soviet Union from Central and Eastern Europe. Subsequently, under Presidents Clinton (1993–2000) and George W. Bush (since 2001), disengagement was increasingly gaining the upper hand in the conflict between retaining security leadership in and withdrawing from Europe. American disengagement was the decisive fact undermining the intentions of European Atlanticists to retain NATO as the bedrock of European security.

CONCLUSION: NEW DIVISION OF LABOR BETWEEN NATO AND THE EU

A new transatlantic division of labor has been developing for the past 15 years. The earlier division of labor had been shaped by European weakness and comprehensive U.S. supremacy after World War II. While the Cold War lasted, U.S. leadership in European security remained welcome, while European autonomy was limited to the pursuit of economic integration. With the end of the Soviet Union, the security environment in Europe changed. Furthermore, European integration had created the prerequisites for a common foreign and security policy. Since 1991, NATO coexisted with the EU's emerging security role. The EU put into place institutional prerequisites, defense industries merged across borders, and EU forces began to conduct small missions abroad. NATO's role was still predominant, although it was changing from a collective defense alliance to a looser security community. On the other hand, the EU's limited role as strategic actor was growing.

The fundamental shift in the transatlantic division of labor began with the adoption of the CFSP in the Maastricht treaty. While the purpose of NATO became less clearly defined and the United States redirected its attention to other regions, the EU claimed a security role. The principle that Europeans could deal with crises on their own was acknowledged in NATO's adoption of the CJTF concept in 1994. Since then, European powers could use NATO assets for temporary missions, provided that the United States approved of the action without wanting to get involved. In 1999, the ESDP concept carried European autonomy claims beyond an ESDI within NATO or the temporarily detachable CJTF. The development of the ERRF and the battle groups did not give the EU capabilities matching those of the United States. However, it gave the EU the ability to deal with the most likely scenarios involving conflict prevention and crisis management. In the future division of labor between the transatlantic partners, EU forces will be capable of handling all crises except a nuclear war or a conventional war on a large scale.

Gradual disengagement was bringing the post-1945 period of U.S. involvement in Europe to an end. The EU was gradually completing Europe's uneven post-1945 emancipation by supplementing its massive economic power with sufficient military power. European security was gradually becoming European business again not by returning to a concert of competing nation-states but by transforming the EU into a strategic actor. In the development of its security role, the EU was taking small steps, not overtaxing transatlantic consensus. Other retarding factors included the lack of unity in the EU, budgetary constraints, and the sheer magnitude of the task to reorient armed forces from territorial defense to power projection. The development of a security role for the EU was taking time. It began in 1991 with the Maastricht IGC; it reached a relevant threshold with the Headline Goal of Helsinki 1999 and the first EU military missions in 2003. It was bound to remain incomplete for another decade at least, until *Bundeswehr* reform could make German armed forces similar to the professional forces of France and Britain. In this timetable, the gradual disengagement of the United States and the gradual growth of the EU's security role could proceed without disrupting effects, not abolishing NATO but transforming it from a collective defense organization into a security community.

Hans-Christian Hagmann estimated that "by 2010, military reform will have been completed in France, and probably also in Germany. Most European armed forces will be geared towards military crisis management, and expeditionary capabilities will play a central role. . . . By 2010, it is likely that EU states will be able to meet the 2003 Headline Goal in full." This implies a 20-year time frame for the full development of the EU's security role, although the reform of the German *Bundeswehr* will probably take longer than assumed by Hagmann. A time frame of 20 to 25 years will be necessary to experience the full impact of the events of 1989–91 on the transatlantic relationship. The accumulation of small steps in the first decade since 1991 has already changed the European security order. "The ESDP has fundamentally altered the institutional setting, and the shape of the transatlantic link." While the United States prioritizes homeland security and involvement in other regions, Europeans are taking responsibility for their own security. This was leading to "a new transatlantic relationship, where the US and Europe cooperate foremost on a global level, fighting common threats and defending common interests."[82]

CHAPTER 6

Transatlantic Relations under Presidents Bill Clinton and George W. Bush

American policy toward Europe since the end of the Cold War asserted continuing leadership but also took steps toward disengagement. While insisting on the primacy of the North Atlantic Treaty Organization (NATO) as a forum for transatlantic communication and as a provider of European security, the United States also acknowledged the existence of a European bloc requiring direct dialogue with the European Union (EU). The intermittent neglect of Europe, in favor of Asia–Pacific and the Greater Middle East, alternated with the intermittent rediscovery of Europe as most important economic partner and essential ally. In Europe, at the same time, Atlanticists asserted the unchanging primacy of NATO for European security, while Europeanists strengthened the potential for autonomy by building the euro into the second world currency and giving the EU a limited security role. For the day-to-day observer, the limited steps toward EU autonomy looked futile since U.S. primacy appeared unchallenged; however, looking at the whole period since the end of the Cold War, a trend was observable. Whether the United States communicated positively with Europe, as under Bill Clinton, or whether U.S. unilateralists showed open disdain for meddlesome and weak European allies, as during George W. Bush's first term, the transatlantic relationship was changing from U.S. hegemony within a U.S.-led collective defense organization toward a mature partnership acknowledging the EU's economic weight and European responsibility for regional security.

The transatlantic rift had been developing well before the disagreements of President George W. Bush with European leaders Jacques Chirac, Gerhard Schröder, and Vladimir Putin regarding the Iraq War of 2003. When the incoming Bush administration stated in its *Quadrennial Defense*

Review of 2001 that Europe was less important than the Middle East and East Asia for U.S. military planning, the transatlantic rift had already been developing for a decade, since 1991. It was only taking on a new quality during Bush's first term.

George W. Bush was the first U.S. president to encounter a European economic bloc with an incipient ability to implement a common foreign and security policy. For four decades, from the late 1940s to the late 1980s, Western Europeans had welcomed U.S. leadership and protection while the Soviet threat lasted. From 1989 to 1992, President George H. W. Bush successfully managed the end of the Cold War in cooperation with Russian President Mikhail Gorbachev and Western European leaders, making sure that Eastern European transformation and German unification occurred without erupting in major conflicts. While the historical task of supervising the end of the Cold War was being handled, it was neither possible nor urgent to develop a comprehensive U.S. policy toward Europe. Later, under President Clinton, transatlantic relations were still not changing dramatically. For most of the 1990s, the common foreign and security policy of the EU was a piece of paper, and the common currency was still a plan to be introduced after a transition phase from 1991 to 1999.

It was only during the first term of President George W. Bush, a decade after the Cold War had ended, that the consequences of the EU's common currency and common foreign and security policy were becoming uncomfortable for the United States. Instead of welcoming a stronger Europe as a more capable but also more independent ally, the Bush neoconservatives asserted Europe could be bypassed and the NATO alliance reduced to a toolbox for coalitions of the willing assisting the United States in the Middle East. At the beginning of his second term, the newly reelected president visited Europe in early 2005 to mend fences, but it was not clear which of three options the Bush administration would pursue: to neglect and bypass the transatlantic alliance, to try to coax Europeans back into the role of junior allies providing auxiliary forces, or to accept the EU as an emerging equal partner and necessary ally.

1989–1992: GEORGE H. W. BUSH MANAGING THE END OF THE COLD WAR

The bipolar confrontation between the United States and the Soviet Union was the most important issue in U.S. foreign policy throughout the entire political career of George H. W. Bush. As president, he was well prepared to manage the end of the Cold War, but it was too early to develop a vision for post–Cold War relations with Europe beyond the tentative beginnings of "New Atlanticism." When Soviet President Gorbachev signaled the willingness to relinquish the Soviet Union's buffer zone in Eastern Europe and to accept the unification of Germany, President Bush was aware of possible repercussions. For several decades, the division of Germany and Soviet control over a buffer zone in Central and Eastern Europe (CEE) had offered a guarantee against any repeat of German aggression against Russia as in 1914 and 1941. Thus, Gorbachev's offer of withdrawal could have produced a nationalist backlash in the Soviet Union. Conceivably, angry generals could have unseated the Soviet leader before he could jeopardize national security by relinquishing the CEE buffer zone and allowing a strong Germany to reemerge.

President Bush guided the Western response to Gorbachev's surrender in a way minimizing perceptions of threat or humiliation in Moscow. German unification was prepared in an orderly manner through the negotiations leading to the 4+2 Treaty. Soviet withdrawal from CEE was accompanied by Western force reductions under the Conventional Forces in Europe (CFE) Treaty of November 1990. The effects of Soviet withdrawal clearly favored the West; nevertheless, change was conducted in a manner allowing Soviet leaders to save face. President Bush also managed to make German unification acceptable to Western Europeans by continuing U.S. engagement in Europe as balancer against any potential German threat.

While the end of the Cold War was managed competently, a new vision for the future of Europe was not developed in the United States except for first steps toward New Atlanticism. The United States regularized contacts with the EU, giving more recognition to this channel of communication with Europe, besides NATO and bilateral relations with individual countries. However, Secretary of State James Baker clearly stated "that one of our key goals must be to ensure that NATO remains the principal venue for our consultations and the forum for agreements on all security and defense commitments of its members."[1] The United States ensured that NATO was not replaced by the Organization for Security and Cooperation in Europe (OSCE), as suggested by German Foreign Minister Hans-Dietrich Genscher and several CEE leaders. Genscher had envisaged the OSCE as a security framework encompassing Eastern and Western Europe.[2] Instead, corresponding more closely to the balance of power after the collapse of the Warsaw Pact, NATO became the anchor of the security framework for the whole of Europe, with Eastern Europeans attached at the margins through the North Atlantic Consultation Council and the Partnership for Peace program. Several years later, NATO was to expand into CEE, closer to Russia's borders, but at this earlier stage Eastern Europeans were offered no more than a halfway house.

During George Bush's presidency, NATO started its adaptation to the post-1991 security environment. The Strategic Concept adopted by the 1991 summit in Rome still mentioned the territorial defense role of NATO, but the reorientation toward power projection had started. To meet the multifaceted and multidirectional new threats, NATO had to go "out of area." Yet, in spite of the adoption of this new Strategic Concept, most European NATO members lacked either the political will or the military capabilities to participate in the Gulf War of 1990–91. Therefore, the alliance was bypassed and the war conducted by a U.S.-led coalition of the willing.

The renegotiation of roles within the alliance started with very small steps. The Bush administration welcomed a European pillar in NATO for the sake of burden sharing. This European Security and Defense Identity (ESDI), however, was to be firmly embedded in NATO under U.S. leadership. Any ideas that the West European Union (WEU) should grow into the main provider of European security were firmly rebuked by President Bush and by Secretary of State Baker. When questions about the old transatlantic division of labor appeared at the end of the Cold War, the United States firmly asserted its security leadership, leaving only economic policy to Europeans. In this context, the Common Foreign and Security Policy (CFSP) of the EU, adopted as principle by the Maastricht conference of 1991, was narrowly circumscribed by the primacy of the transatlantic framework.

One defining feature of the post-1945 world had ended when the Soviet Union collapsed, bringing the bipolar structure of the international system to an end. However, another defining feature of the post-1945 world was still in place: the noncommunist world was still structured as a unipolar alliance network with the United States in a leadership role. It would take another decade until the alliance network would be visibly affected. At the end of George W. Bush's term, German unification had been managed without upsetting EU cohesion or relations with Russia; the postcommunist transformation of the countries of CEE and the Commonwealth of Independent States had started without violent instability; Yugoslavia was a containable exception. The NATO alliance was looking forward to a future with a new Strategic Concept and a role as anchor of security for all of Europe.

The New Atlanticism of the Bush administration gave more recognition to the EU as dialogue partner, but NATO and bilateral relations were still the preferred channel of communication facilitating U.S. leadership. Yet the EU had also stated its claim for geostrategic autonomy. In Maastricht in 1991, the EU had embarked on monetary union and CFSP, and in 1992, the WEU had claimed a security role of its own, as crisis manager taking on the Petersberg Tasks, contrary to expressed U.S. wishes to retain NATO as sole provider of security. And disengagement from Europe had also started with a reduction of U.S. military presence in Europe under the CFE Treaty.

1993–2000: BILL CLINTON: UNITED STATES HESITANTLY INDISPENSABLE—EUROPE BECOMING DETACHABLE

Transatlantic relations changed gradually during President Clinton's two terms. NATO remained the bedrock of European security, and the United States remained engaged in Europe, and this continuity was not greatly disturbed by a series of smaller changes, the cumulative effect of which was to become visible later. Within the existing pattern of transatlantic relations, elements of European autonomy in security matters emerged, although NATO retained its preeminent role. And the United States decamped from Europe in small steps while retaining its role as guarantor of European security.

The New Transatlantic Agenda was signed at the U.S.–EU summit in Madrid on December 3, 1995. The U.S.–EU relationship was upgraded "to reflect the EU's newly acquired powers under the Maastricht Treaty."[3] And the "Joint US-EU Action Plan" gave some recognition to the possibility that Europe might be growing beyond a merely regional role in stating, "Our partnership is also global."[4]

The Clinton administration went further than its predecessor in the encouragement of burden sharing through a European pillar within NATO. This was concretized in the concept of Combined Joint Task Forces (CJTF), adopted by NATO in late 1994. While adding to NATO's range of instruments, the CJTF concept also contained an element of U.S. disengagement. In contrast to the unconditional U.S. security guarantee during the Cold War, U.S. involvement in future European crises was distinctly optional. European NATO members could form task forces using NATO assets to undertake missions of little interest to the United States. The United States remained the security supervisor since approval by NATO for these missions was still necessary. Yet as these CJTFs were temporarily detachable from NATO structures, they also contained an element of European security autonomy. American security leadership continued, but it was weakened by potential disinterest in future European crises not threatening vital U.S. interests.

During Bill Clinton's two presidential terms, the United States demonstrated that it was still the "indispensable nation" for European security. However, this was done in a way indicating doubts about the need to be engaged in European crises. American decisions to get involved in Bosnia and Kosovo were preceded by reluctance and followed by unilateral actions displaying impatience with allies hardly consulted about the conduct of the war. "Clinton's air-only, ambivalent conduct of the war for Kosovo and the Bush administration's indications that it would like to withdraw U.S. troops from the Balkans make clear that America's days as Europe's chief protector are fast coming to an end."[5] Consequently, the trend toward EU security autonomy accelerated. Motivated by the experience of Bosnia and Kosovo, the EU decided to form its own Rapid Response Forces. Although NATO asserted its role by forming the NATO Response Forces by the end of the Clinton presidency, the EU was now determined to have its own forces.

The rhetoric of concern for transatlantic cohesion was still strong. Secretary of State Madeline Albright warned allies against the three Ds: decoupling, duplication, and discrimination.[6] At the same time, practical steps were taken toward decoupling. American military personnel in Europe were reduced during the 1990s from about 300,000 down to 70,000, with most of them being removed from Germany. For several decades, U.S. military presence had served as a guarantee that the United States was sharing European security risks in spite of the geographic separation causing differential security for Europe and the United States. As most U.S. troops left Europe under Clinton, the threat scenarios for Europe and the United States differed more and more.

In January 1994, the Brussels summit of NATO declared that the alliance was open to new members, thus giving the alliance a role as provider of stability in CEE. During President Clinton's second term, Poland, the Czech Republic, and Hungary joined in 1999, and another seven CEE countries had firm expectations of membership. Thus, NATO succeeded as regional stabilizer in CEE but was also brought closer to its transformation into a looser security community.

The Clinton era prepared the change in transatlantic relations that became more visible in the first term of President George W. Bush. Under Clinton, the United States was still asserting leadership in Europe by confirming its role as indispensable guarantor of European security. However, the interventions in Bosnia and Kosovo were probably the last U.S. missions in Europe. After military intervention by NATO, the EU took on the responsibility for policing and economic stabilization in the Balkans. The primacy of NATO was retained, but the alliance was diluted through expansion and its military integration loosened by adopting the CJTF concept. While the United States demonstrated rather hesitantly that it was still the indispensable nation, the EU took concrete steps toward a security role. The accumulation of little steps during Clinton's two terms created a new quality in transatlantic relations, more clearly visible by 2001, when George W. Bush took office.

2001–04: GEORGE W. BUSH: FIRST-TERM TRANSATLANTIC TENSIONS

An emphatic turn away from Europe characterized the first term (2001–04) of the Bush administration. It treated transatlantic relations in the spirit of R. Kagan's dismissal of Europe as weak and irrelevant, not even important as a central battlefield anymore.[7] More clearly than under Clinton, the United States was now directing its attention to the Greater Middle East and the East Asian Littoral. The *Quadrennial Defense Review* of 2001 expressed this reorientation very clearly. NATO–Europe was, at best, a toolbox for U.S.-led coalitions of the willing. This dismissal of Europe was, nevertheless, accompanied by measures to retain control over Europe by asserting the continued primacy of NATO as a security framework and by using divide-and-rule tactics playing off "New Europe" against "Old Europe."

Cultural signals added to the distance between the Bush administration and many Europeans. Previous U.S. leaders had been closer to Europe in their cultural background, paying more attention to this central front in the Cold War and ascribing more importance to the transatlantic alliance. Bush, on the other hand, seemed remote, with the swagger of a Texan cowboy, the religious vocabulary of a midwestern or southern churchgoer, and a rhetoric defining the conflicts of this world in stark contrasts of good and evil. He became a visible signal for the value gap opening up between the transatlantic partners.

UNILATERALIST SUPERPOWER DOES NOT NEED ALLIANCE IN THE "WAR ON TERROR"

Voices arguing against the strategy of neglecting alienating Europe were ignored as long as the Bush–Cheney–Rumsfeld leadership was confident that the military and economic might of the United States acting alone could solve all problems, including the "war on terrorism" and the democratic restructuring of Iraq and the entire Middle East. In response to the terrorist attacks of September 11, 2001, NATO invoked the alliance case for the first time since its foundation. However, after declarations of solidarity for the United States, very little shared action followed. The Bush administration preferred to conduct the campaign in Afghanistan involving not NATO alliance forming but rather a coalition of the willing. After the experience of Kosovo, the United States opted against another "war by committee" involving too much cumbersome consultation with allies not contributing significant capabilities.

After September 11, 2001, the transatlantic allies differed in threat analysis and strategy. There was little agreement in defining terrorism and its causes; there was less agreement in defining the required response. While Bush wanted to extend the war on terrorism to several countries he included in an "axis of evil," Europeans doubted whether military action should be the primary response and expected the response to be limited to Afghanistan and "to precise terrorist targets."[8]

ASSERTING NATO PRIMACY BUT ADAPTING TO THE EU SECURITY ROLE

The war on terrorism and the intervention in Afghanistan showed that out-of-area interventions were unlikely to provide NATO with a unifying rationale, but the transatlantic alliance was consolidated in other ways. At the Prague summit of 2002, NATO offered membership to another seven countries and enhanced its role as stabilizer in CEE. And the 2002 renewal of the 1999 Defense Capabilities Initiative meant that NATO members still worked on closing the capabilities gap. Regarding the ESDI, the Bush administration continued the approach taken by its predecessor. It rejected moves toward an autonomous EU security role, for example, in rebuking the proposal of EU headquarters in Tervuren. Yet, continuing Clinton's welcome for temporarily detachable CJTFs, the Bush administration went one step further in the Berlin Plus agreement of December 2002.[9] The CJTF concept of 1994 had allowed European NATO members to use NATO assets for WEU-led crisis management without U.S. participation; the Berlin Plus agreement extended this to EU-led missions. Thus, the EU as a separate entity had a security role recognized by NATO, although the Berlin Plus arrangement also made sure that the EU would act in close cooperation with NATO.

DISAGREEMENTS OVER TERRORISM AND IRAQ

The Prague summit had given NATO new energy, and the Berlin Plus agreement had found a new compromise between NATO and the EU's security role. However, another out-of-area crisis intensified differences in the transatlantic relationship. When the United States wanted to extend the war on terrorism to include a war on Iraq, many Europeans disagreed with Bush's claims that Iraq was connected with al-Qaeda. France, Germany, and Russia rejected the idea that invading Iraq and enforcing regime change by military means was justified. German Chancellor Schröder won the 2002 election by promising the electorate that Germany would not get involved in a war in Iraq. This was the first time in the history of the Federal Republic of Germany that electoral opinion rewarded a political leader for disagreeing with the United States. For the first time ever, France, Germany, and Russia cooperated in opposing U.S. intentions in the United Nations. The war in Iraq was conducted without involving NATO. The United States acted unilaterally and assembled a small "coalition of the willing," receiving support from Britain and several CEE countries, symbolically in the Letter of Eight and Letter of Ten[10] and practically through troop contingents mainly from Britain and Poland. In spite of this support by several European governments, the United States had alienated other European governments as well as the majority of European public opinion.

CONTINUITY FROM CLINTON TO BUSH

Differences between Europe and the United States were more visible during the first term of the Bush administration than during the Clinton presidency. The United States acted as if the benefits of the transatlantic alliance were too small compared to the restraints imposed by alliance structures and the need to consult allies unwilling and unable to use military means in the war on terrorism. Yet there was substantial continuity of transatlantic trends between Clinton and Bush, a continuity of change driven more by structural factors than by differences in the diplomatic style of the two presidents.

Philip Gordon, foreign affairs official during the Clinton administration, suggested that the transatlantic rift had been aggravated by President Bush's style and policy choices. Under a President Al Gore, assuming a slightly different outcome of the elections of 2000, transatlantic relations might not have worsened as they did in Bush's first term. Gordon argues that Bush's victory in 2000 should not obscure the fact that half the U.S. electorate was much closer to European sentiments than the elected president and his neoconservative advisers. "Certainly, the Texan George W. Bush and the deeply conservative cabinet members who surround him . . . have little in common with most of their European counterparts. . . . It is less clear, however, that Bush's election really represented a fundamental shift in American values. . . . After all, Bush's opponent in the last election, Al Gore, won some 540,000 votes more than

Bush did, and Gore did so on a platform that was much closer on most issues to the European norm."[11]

Gordon also insisted that "the United States still needs its European allies not primarily for their military contributions. . . . Rather, even an all-powerful America will need Europe's political support, military bases, cooperation in international organizations, peacekeepers and police, money, diplomatic help with others, and general good will. . . . Not to do the minimum necessary to ensure that Europeans remain positively disposed to American aims—or worse, to actually provoke Europe into playing a kind of 'balancing' role—would be to squander the potential advantages of a position of strength."[12] A more consultative approach could hold the alliance together under a more benign U.S. hegemony. "The lesson of these episodes is not that Europe is unwilling to use force or has nothing to contribute, but that when the United States shows leadership it is able to bring allies along—even to the fight."[13]

However, Gordon's emphasis on the cultural and strategic distance of Bush from Europe underestimated the continuity between Clinton and Bush. Under both presidents, the United States insisted on NATO's primacy in European security but also continued its transformation from a collective defense organization into a security community by expanding the alliance into CEE. The EU continued to build its security role without, however, challenging NATO's primacy openly. The United States, on the other hand, was making concessions to detachable European crisis management while objecting to an autonomous EU security role. American ambiguity toward the European Security and Defense Policy continued. "Clinton understood that a stronger and more self-confident Europe could in the end work to America's advantage. There were, however, limits to the Clinton team's ability to tolerate a stronger Europe. When the EU in 2000 embarked on efforts to build an independent defense capability, the administration proved unable to let go of old habits. Bush's advisers have been equally tentative about Europe's defense aspirations—even as they have made known their intention to downsize America's strategic commitment to Europe. Control over security matters is, after all, the decisive factor in setting the pecking order and determining who is in command."[14]

And out-of-area interventions continued to strain NATO cohesion, more so regarding Afghanistan 2001 and Iraq 2003 than earlier during the Bosnian and Kosovo crises of the 1990s. American interest in European crises was even weaker under Bush than under Clinton. Where Clinton had hesitated to get involved in combat missions, Bush was keen to extricate the United States from peacekeeping in the Balkans. And, vice versa, European interest in distant crises was less in 2001 and 2003 than in 1990, at the time of the first Gulf War. A significant exception to this was the willingness of CEE countries to support the United States in Iraq in 2003. However, their interest in U.S.-led, out-of-area power projection had probably peaked in 2003.[15]

Disengagement from Europe continued the trend of the Clinton period. In 2003–04, under Bush, plans for further troop reductions were announced.

More than half of the 70,000 U.S. soldiers remaining in Germany were to be withdrawn,[16] with only some of them to be redeployed in the new NATO members in CEE. As the threat scenario had changed in 1991, the United States had few reasons left to deploy troops in Europe. The EU, on the other hand, moved closer toward a geostrategic role by consolidating the euro currency introduced in 1999, by completing the European Rapid Response Forces, and by undertaking the first EU crisis management missions abroad.

The differences between the United States and Europe were exacerbated during Bush's first term by clashes in personal style and by the unilateralism of the Bush administration, exercising continued U.S. hegemony more crudely and turning away emphatically from irrelevant Europe. The differences were also accentuated because there was no Bosnian or Kosovo crisis calling for U.S. involvement in Europe; instead, the events of September 11, 2001, directed U.S. attention toward the war on terrorism and the Greater Middle East. Personalities and events accentuated the transatlantic tensions, but there was also substantial continuity between presidents. Regardless of Clinton's charm or Rumsfeld's disdain for Europe, U.S. disengagement continued while the EU moved, step by step, toward security autonomy.

MENDING FENCES IN GEORGE W. BUSH'S SECOND TERM

Symbolic Mending of Fences

Europe was rediscovered as a useful ally early in the Bush administration's second term. When winning the war in Iraq was not quickly followed by the United States also winning the peace and when the costs in lives lost and dollars expended grew without an end of U.S. commitment in Iraq being in sight, unilateralism began to soften. Symbolic politics toward Europe changed, and efforts were made to improve the diplomatic climate.

In his first term, Bush's rhetoric and practice resembled closely the prescriptions articulated by the Project for the New American Century think tank and other neoconservative intellectuals. The dismissive attitude to Europe articulated by commentators such as R. Kagan found its practical counterpart in Secretary of Defense Rumsfeld's neglect of NATO, attempts to divide the EU into "old Europe" and "new Europe," and reliance on force rather than multilateral institutions and legitimacy by consensus. In Bush's first term, attitudes to Europe could be characterized as a combination of four responses. First, Europeans were lectured about their megalomania in overestimating their present or future potential. Second, they were told that their striving for autonomy demonstrated an immoral lack of gratitude for all the United States had done for them. Third, domestic discourse in the United States included a permanent putting down of Europeans. The fourth kind of response included the mobilization of a network of European allies and apologists as well as the deliberate attempt to divide the EU and to limit Europe's influence in the world.[17]

Yet by the end of Bush's first term, criticism of his approach to Europe was no longer confined to ex-Clinton staffers hibernating at the Brookings Institution. In late 2004, the influential Council on Foreign Relations published a task force report, *Renewing the Atlantic Partnership*, recommending diplomatic efforts to overcome the transatlantic rift. The task force included elder statesmen such as Henry Kissinger and Lawrence Summers and reminded U.S. leaders that the indispensable nation had an indispensable ally in Europe. Clashes of personalities and styles should be overcome by levelheaded leadership abstaining from polemics.[18] Considering their massive economic interdependence, the transatlantic partners should be able to find common ground in shared security interests.

In contrast to his earlier emphatic unilateralism, President Bush sought rapprochement with Europe early in his second term. In his address to the NATO summit in late February 2005, Bush acknowledged that the transatlantic alliance was the most important security relation of the United States. He also made an effort to mend fences with France and Germany, his most outspoken critics before the Iraq War. This new approach to transatlantic relations had started before the NATO summit with a charm offensive conducted by Secretary of State Condoleezza Rice in a whirlwind tour of several European capitals. Contrary to their earlier neglect of NATO, Secretary of Defense "Rumsfeld and Secretary of State Condoleezza Rice have gone out of their way in their visits to Europe and NATO to convince U.S. allies that despite differences inside NATO over the U.S.-led war against Iraq, the United States still views NATO as the main trans-Atlantic forum for discussing political issues and resolving crises."[19]

The new approach of Bush was reciprocated by the European governments critical of the Iraq War in 2003. The transatlantic rift had narrowed in early 2005 as the Bush administration learned to appreciate that a preeminent power such as the United States still needed close cooperation with an indispensable ally of the size of the EU. European leaders accommodated U.S. demands to contribute to postwar stabilization in Iraq, although there were still significant differences in the degree of involvement. "As a sign that differences over Iraq have been set aside, all 26 Allies are now contributing to NATO's training of Iraqi security forces, either in Iraq, outside of Iraq, through financial contributions or donations of equipment."[20] France and Germany still signaled their distance from the U.S. approach by contributing to the training of Iraqis only outside Iraq. The transatlantic rift continued, but there was enough goodwill on all sides to refrain from exacerbating differences.

NATO No Longer the Primary Forum?

Yet this improvement in transatlantic relations from their low in 2003 did not mean that nothing had changed since 1949 or 1991. At the 2005 NATO summit, leaders acknowledged the developing security role of the EU ("We intend to develop further our strategic partnership with the EU. A stronger

EU will further contribute to our common security."), and they agreed to give the alliance an enhanced political function: "We are committed to strengthening NATO's role as a forum for strategic and political consultation and coordination among Allies, while reaffirming its place as the essential forum for security consultation between Europe and North America."[21] While increasing its political significance, this also confirmed NATO's declining military relevance. The gradual transformation of NATO from a collective defense organization toward a security community continued. The grand strategy of the United States still prioritized the Middle East and the East Asian Littoral, although Europe had regained some attention. On the other hand, the EU was still developing its security role by forming its new "battle groups" for crisis management. The transatlantic partners mended fences in early 2005 but only to the extent of improving the diplomatic climate. The renegotiation of the transatlantic roles of 1949 continued nevertheless.

Further adjustments of the respective roles of the alliance partners were demanded by German Chancellor Schröder. His speech, presented by Defense Minister Struck at the Munich Conference on Security Policy (February 12, 2005), indicated concerns about the future of NATO and the state of transatlantic relations. Schröder confirmed that "close transatlantic ties" were "in the interests of Germany, Europe and America." Yet, he argued, "we cannot look to the past . . . as is so often the case when transatlantic loyalty is professed. Rather, we must adapt to new circumstances." Tensions across the Atlantic, in Schröder's view, "were due . . . to the fact that this process of adjustment to a changed reality has still not been completed." The security environment had changed, and so had the roles "of the two states which, as it were, were the linchpins of this cooperation for many decades, namely the United States and Germany." The latter wanted to take on "responsibility for international stability" and demanded "a right to be involved in decision-making."[22] Schröder not only claimed a permanent seat for Germany in the UN Security Council but also demanded more input in decision making for the EU.

NATO as an institution serving the transatlantic partnership had to adapt further. Schröder acknowledged the continuing value of the alliance. It was attractive to new members, and its military organization was helpful in Afghanistan. "However, it is no longer the primary venue where transatlantic partners discuss and coordinate strategies."[23] This statement received an immediate indignant response by Atlanticist voices accusing the chancellor of wanting to dismantle NATO. Yet Schröder had merely drawn conclusions form the fact that the crisis over Iraq was never officially discussed in NATO. The alliance was indeed not functioning as a forum for the discussion of strategy.

His critics failed to understand that Schröder had not dismissed NATO but requested the alliance be taken more seriously. The chancellor had pointed out a reality not to be hidden behind assertions of NATO's continued centrality to European security. Schröder's remark implied that the United States had ignored and bypassed the NATO alliance when taking unilateral decision about the war on terrorism, intervention in Afghanistan, and the war in Iraq.

NATO was no longer the place for discussion of strategy because it had been sidelined by the United States, not because Schröder was stating the obvious. NATO Secretary-General Jaap de Hoop Scheffer admitted that he too had initially mistaken Schröder's remarks as attack on NATO. Yet he had come to see in the chancellor's remarks a shared concern "that the present structures—that is, NATO—have to be utilized better."[24] This implied that NATO could become more relevant only if the United States began to take the alliance and the European NATO members more seriously.

Schröder also stressed the need to enhance the dialogue between the EU and the United States, "which in its current form does justice neither to the Union's growing importance nor to the new demands on transatlantic cooperation." A future security role for the EU was, Schröder asserted, compatible with NATO. "The steps towards creating its own set of political and military instruments with the European Security and Defense Policy are therefore necessary. . . . The European Union is assuming an increasing number of security tasks in close coordination with NATO." Nevertheless, the emerging security role of the EU had the potential to replace NATO in spite of Schröder's assurance that "a strong European pillar guarantees Europe's loyal partnership in the transatlantic alliance and its willingness to share the burden."[25]

President Bush responded diplomatically to Schröder's statement, interpreting it as a proposal to strengthen the alliance and to safeguard the relevance of NATO. Indeed, Schröder had demanded not an end to NATO but an alliance of equal partners. "Schröder's recent calls for improved alliance consultations on a broad set of political questions" were "diplomatic expressions for this yearning of being treated as an equal partner in a leadership role. . . . The future of German-American relations, therefore, hinges to a large extent on the question of whether a new balance can be struck between Washington's desire for supportive partners and Berlin's desire for co-equal leadership."[26]

CONCLUSION: GEOPOLITICAL DIFFERENCES, NOT JUST STYLE AND PERSONALITIES

The Bush administration in its first term had treated Europe as negligible while NATO had been bypassed in favor of improvised coalitions of the willing. This unilateralist approach was very visible, but there was also the less visible attempt to retain leadership through NATO and to block EU claims for an independent security role. Both sides, Europe and the United States, had options outside NATO. The United States could disengage from Europe and pursue global interests unilaterally or in ad hoc coalitions of the willing. European powers could build an autonomous *Europe puissance*. Both also had the option of continuing and renewing NATO. However, there were significant differences between U.S. claims for continuing leadership and French–German ambitions to rebalance NATO. All these options were being pursued simultaneously, with the United States sometimes neglecting NATO and sometimes halfheartedly continuing a leadership role, whereas Europeans would combine halfhearted participation in NATO with gradual development of the EU's security role.

NATO's strength as a military organization was also a limitation. While NATO provided an avenue for U.S. influence in Europe, it could only discuss military solutions for security challenges. Consequently, by limiting NATO to military issues, it was bound to lose relevance as a transatlantic forum only to be replaced eventually by a dialogue of the EU and the United States. On the other hand, by importing a broader political agenda, NATO would be overloaded and diluted as a military organization.

The charm offensive of Bush, Rice, and Rumsfeld in early 2005 improved the diplomatic climate between the United States and Europe. However, it was unlikely to prevent a gradual widening of the transatlantic rift. After four years of neglect, Bush's visit did not convince Europeans that it was more than an attempt to share the costs of the Iraq War when results were not achieved as easily as expected earlier. To return from open unilateralism to instrumental multilateralism only signaled that the Bush administration preferred unilateral methods whenever possible but was interested in restoring some multilateral consultation when going it alone proved too expensive.

The unilateralism of President Bush's first term had damaged the standing of the United States in Europe. Yet, besides differences in style, the substance of Bush's policy toward Europe had just continued trends already existing under Clinton. American disengagement continued, and military presence in Europe had fallen well below the level previously regarded as the essential minimum to keep NATO cohesive. In spite of this diminishing presence, the United States was still claiming security leadership and rejected an autonomous EU security role. Yet it was also leaving it to the EU to stabilize the Balkans, allowing the United States to concentrate on East Asia and the Middle East. NATO had been expanded further as President Bush continued de facto the transformation of the collective defense organization into a security community. And the United States had, in spite of gestures of protest, accepted the accumulation of steps toward EU security autonomy, as long as NATO's primacy was not challenged visibly.

All three U.S. presidents since the end of the Cold War had ascribed to Europeans a regional role and to the United States a global role, including security leadership in Europe. Yet in this broad frame, subtle shifts had occurred. The regional role of the EU had grown while U.S. involvement in Europe had diminished. In its global role, the United States had found that Europe had limited value as a military auxiliary. As Europe was consolidating its regional role, it was reluctant to get involved in faraway out-of-area crisis management under U.S. leadership. Yet at the same time, the EU was also extending its global reach by economic and diplomatic means.

The main difference between the Clinton and Bush periods was that the same trends had gone further. NATO was even larger, and the U.S. military presence in Europe was even smaller. The out-of-area power projection in Bosnia and Kosovo had caused tensions in NATO, but the long-distance intervention in Afghanistan and Iraq had challenged alliance cohesion even more. During the presidency of George H. W. Bush, Europeans had made an initial role claim in putting the CFSP on the EU's agenda in 1991 and in giving the WEU the Petersberg Tasks in 1992. This had turned, during George W. Bush's first term, into actual EU armed forces and the first small military missions. To be sure, unilateralism and Bush's quasi-religious rhetoric about the axis of evil and the war on terrorism damaged the transatlantic climate after September 2001. However, the main cause for substantial change in transatlantic relations was not presidential style but the change in the security environment after the 1991 collapse of the Soviet Union and the transformation of Europe's political landscape due to half a century of European integration. The election of Al Gore in 2000 or John Kerry in 2004 might have prevented some acrimony in transatlantic relations. However, the renegotiation of roles in the transatlantic relationship had become necessary not just because President Bush and President Chirac were not best friends but rather because of large-scale historical changes, including the end of the Soviet Union, the end of Europe's division by the Iron Curtain, German unification, and the growth of the EU, an economic giant claiming a geostrategic role.

Atlanticists among U.S. Democrats argued that the transatlantic value gap was not as deep as it appeared to be under President Bush. Following this logic, Atlanticists should have hoped for the election of a Democrat as U.S. president. Yet it was questionable whether a victory for Senator John Kerry in the 2004 presidential election would have resulted in more than an improved diplomatic climate. A hypothetical President Kerry might have modified U.S. unilateralism and taken the European NATO partners more seriously, making concessions to multilateralism and to the transatlantic alliance. A less abrasive style of communicating with Europeans would have preserved goodwill for the United States to a greater extent. Nevertheless, the structural reasons for transatlantic tensions would have continued even after a hypothetical Kerry victory in 2004.

In the transatlantic relationship, "structural and cultural gaps that have existed for a long time have been widened . . . ; if these differences are mishandled the result could be a transatlantic divide deeper than any seen in more than 50 years. Yet structure is not destiny, and it would be as wrong to exaggerate the gaps between Americans and Europeans as it would be to ignore them."[27] Insisting on outdated role allocations or improvising short-term solutions would fall short of the necessary redefinition of roles in the transatlantic partnership. Since the end of the Cold War, U.S. presidents asserted U.S. leadership in European security while making concessions to EU claims for security autonomy. One defining aspect of the post-1945 international system ended in 1991 with the collapse of the Soviet Union. Another aspect of the post-1945 international system has been changing more slowly and quietly. In the relation between the two most powerful economies, the asymmetrical post-1945 role allocation is coming to an end. In the transatlantic partnership, security dependency is being replaced by a new security partnership. Three U.S. presidents, since the end of the Cold War, have made hesitant concessions to European claims for security autonomy while asserting, as much as possible, continuing U.S. leadership in European security. The transatlantic partnership would benefit if U.S. policy toward Europe moved beyond hesitant adaptation and, indeed, welcomed a new role allocation. Europe's post-1945 security was not meant to last forever, and since 1991 a new security partnership is emerging.

CHAPTER 7

Emancipated Europe—United States without European Entanglements

RENEGOTIATING ROLES IN THE TRANSATLANTIC RELATIONSHIP

Renegotiation of Roles Required

The original allocation of roles in the transatlantic relationship had no more than residual justification six decades later. The habits of a lifetime should not prevent a renegotiation of roles required by the changed security environment since the end of the Soviet Union and the change in the balance of power between the United States and NATO–Europe since 1949. Old Atlanticists in Western Europe and new Atlanticists in Eastern Europe still expected continued U.S. leadership and involvement in European security to provide security against Russia, to act as balancer against German or Franco-German predominance in Europe, and to provide an attractive role in a special relationship with the hegemon. American Atlanticist Elizabeth Pond even claimed that the transatlantic alliance should continue because the United States was still needed in Europe "for the same reasons that required American engagement when NATO was formed half a century ago."[1] Yet, in reality, it was not possible to continue the Atlanticism of the late 1940s after the Soviet threat vanished in 1991. Since then, U.S. troops have been decamping from Europe for more than a decade, whereas the European Union (EU) became able to relieve the United States of the burden of stabilizing Europe. NATO–Europe did not need the United States in the same way as in 1949, but the advantages of good relations were still so massive that the transatlantic partners needed one another. After the rather benign hegemony of the Cold War decades had become unsustainable, there were still convincing reasons for a new partnership based on economic interdependence and shared interest in global stability. Indeed, "the ongoing construction of Europe's identity" was "giving the United States an increasingly valuable partner."[2]

Tomorrow's roles in a renegotiated transatlantic partnership have to recognize changes in potential power that have already taken place and take into account predictable change resulting from the EU's potential power. Europe's uneven emancipation from post-1945 dependence began with economic recovery and integration. For 40 years during the Cold War, Western Europe regained economic strength but remained under the U.S. military protectorate. By 1991, however, the gradual change in the relative power of the transatlantic partners had reached a new threshold. "Washington's preeminence began in the context of a Western Europe that was devastated and demoralized by World War II. . . . It is hard to believe that more than half a century later, a prosperous, capable and confident European Union will forever defer to the United States."[3] The EU's economic strength and a favorable security environment made possible the EU's turn to a Common Foreign and Security Policy (CFSP).

Over five decades, European economic integration has deepened enough to allow a CFSP. It has been argued in the preceding chapters that the outcome of these developments will be a powerful Europe in a multipolar world with the United States enjoying a preeminent role albeit a diminished one compared to the unique supremacy of 1945. After the end of the Soviet Union, the global military role of the United States gave the impression of unprecedented and unlimited supremacy. Yet in other respects, U.S. supremacy was substantially diminished because the most important part of its post-1945 sphere of influence, that is, Western Europe, had become an economic competitor, left the dollar zone, and established a second world currency. Last but not least, security was becoming European responsibility again while the United States was disengaging from Europe. To be sure, it is not claimed here that the U.S. hegemon is about to face "the challenger." Instead, it has been argued that a renegotiation of roles within the alliance was required because a shift in relative power had already occurred whose implications were still unfolding. The transatlantic relationship could no longer be based on the balance of power that had existed in 1945 and on the asymmetrical roles built into NATO's structure since 1949.

Some aspects of further change are fairly predictable. Enlargement of the EU will continue but has come close to its limits. With the admission of ten new members in May 2004, the EU population increased from 375 million to 450 million, and it may reach almost 600 million with new members joining. Consequently, the EU will be preoccupied with internal matters, securing economic development for 500 million to 600 million people, acting as security community for all member states, and mastering the complexities of multilevel governance for about 30 member states. The enlarged and consolidated EU will exercise a crisis management role ranging from crisis prevention to peacekeeping and peace enforcement. The United States will find itself relieved from the burden of protecting and pacifying Europe and will benefit from burden sharing with Europe in international crisis management. These predictions are not speculative but based on observable trends, including EU membership applications and the development of the common European Security and Defense Policy (ESDP).

The renegotiation of roles in the transatlantic relationship can go wrong. The transatlantic rift can deepen if one side insists on continuing a leadership role beyond its use-by date and if Europeans react to it by antihegemonic counterbalancing. This can be aggravated by polemical rhetoric about weak and meddlesome Europeans or arrogant Americans. Limited differences can be blown up out of proportion, but remembering the sheer magnitude of transatlantic economic interdependence should be a solid foundation for the renegotiation of roles. After transatlantic security dependency, a new security partnership is possible with a division of labor beneficial to both sides.

Beyond Atlanticist and Gaullist Visions of Europe

Four broad visions of Europe's future interacted for half a century. Three of them were "the Common Market's Federalist Europe," "de Gaulle's Europe of Nations," and "America's Atlantic Europe," in the words of historian David Calleo.[4] One might add, as a fourth model of some relevance, "Britain's European Free Trade Association." In de Gaulle's "Europe of Nations," Europe was meant to acquire independence from the superpowers the United States and the Soviet Union to become a global actor itself. This Europe would be a club of nation-states led by France. However, there were inherent contradictions in the Gaullist vision. The ambition to create a power rivaling the United States was achievable only by overcoming the "Europe of Nations" in favor of a more integrated Europe. The last thing de Gaulle would have wanted was sacrificing France's autonomy in defense policy to European integration. Yet this was required to create *Europe puissance:* for example, only by merging French state-owned armament enterprises into the EADS company was it possible to maintain any European Defense Industrial and Technological Base (EDITB).

There were also inherent weaknesses in Britain's vision of Europe as a free trade association. In the 1960s, the European Economic Community (EEC) with its federalist potential was more successful than the European Free Trade Association (EFTA) objective of creating just a free market for industrial goods, without tariff barriers but also without any further integration. The logic of the free trader argument led beyond Europe as a free trade area to a transnational "domestic" market with unintended implications for national sovereignty.

The contradictions in the Atlanticist position have become more visible since 1991. Atlantic Europe defined itself, through the transatlantic link, as part of a unified West. Europe as junior partner of the United States, this asymmetrical relationship was simply a geostrategic reality after 1945. The United States was so much more powerful than European powers, be it defeated Germany or the United Kingdom and France, victorious but exhausted. European leaders also welcomed the United States as benevolent hegemon, as protector against the Soviet threat, and as balancer between Western European powers and especially as a check on German ambitions. The transatlantic alliance was, above all, a security link institutionalized in NATO, although there was also economic interdependence and the discourse of the transatlantic community of values.

It was only after 1991 that the internal contradictions in the Atlanticist position became more evident. With the end of Soviet Union and the Warsaw Pact, the United States had become less indispensable for Europe. And the more Germany was tied into deepening European integration, the less the United States was required as balancer in Europe. The benefits of U.S. hegemony were diminishing compared to the inconvenience of having an overwhelming senior partner in NATO.

The cohesion of the transatlantic alliance was also affected by the change from Cold War deterrence to the post-1991 emphasis on power projection. During the Cold War, the disparity between U.S. and European forces could be accommodated in a viable division of labor. However, under the post–Cold War requirements of power projection, the transatlantic capabilities gap became more relevant, and the potential mission gap threatened the very existence of the alliance. Atlanticists intent on closing the capabilities gap and strengthening NATO–Europe as a credible ally had no instruments available other than those that would also create *Europe puissance*. For the purpose of saving the viability of NATO, European powers had to upgrade their defense capabilities, either as European Security and Defense Identity (ESDI) within NATO or as European Security and Defense Policy (ESDP) outside NATO. This ambiguity was brought closer to resolution by the disengagement of the United States from Europe. While Atlanticists hurried to strengthen Europe in order to keep the United States involved, the *Quadrennial Defense Review* of the Bush administration of 2001 pointed to new geostrategic priorities, and Europe was not one of them.

The Atlanticist effort to strengthen Europe as capable NATO partner will, in its effective outcome, strengthen Europe as independent power. In the Iraq War of 2003, "preserving the Atlantic link was one of the key motivations inducing Britain, Spain, Italy, and most Central European countries to side with the Bush administration. But now that the Atlantic alliance appears to be irreversibly headed toward demise, an Atlanticist Europe is no longer an option."[5]

Atlanticist reliance on U.S. leadership in European security has lost its objective base. American involvement in European security has diminished to make involvement in European crises optional and to reduce U.S. military presence down to a tenth of the Cold War level. At the same time, the Gaullist vision of Europe has also lost its viability: a strong Europe with its own geostrategic role could not be built as a Europe of nation-states led by

France but only as a much more integrated Europe with a common CFSP, ESDP, and EDITB. The other two visions for Europe have not been fulfilled either. Neither has the European federation arrived nor has the EU become an extended version of EFTA, the free trade area preferred by British leaders in the 1950s. Instead, the EU has become a unique model of multilevel governance, achieving greater integration through closer intergovernmental cooperation and through the allocation of responsibilities to the European level of governance.

Because of this peculiar nature of European integration, Atlanticist dependency has become as outdated as the Gaullist club of nations or the free trade area model. Instead, the European semifederation has become a unitary economic actor and is becoming a security actor relying on a mixture of intergovernmental cooperation, integrated defense industries, coordinated defense policies, a minimum of EU-level institutions, and EU intervention forces coexisting with national forces.

De Facto U.S. Disengagement Accelerates European Rethinking

American involvement in Europe in a continuing manner began in the 1940s in very specific circumstances. For two generations, the U.S. presence in Europe was a self-evident fact making it hardly conceivable that this was, historically, unusual. "The formation of NATO nevertheless represented a turning point in history, both of the United States and of the Atlantic powers as a whole. For the first time in peacetime, the United States had engaged in a permanent alliance linking itself to Western Europe in both a military and a political sense."[6] The magnitude of this shift also meant that it would not come to a sudden halt when it had lost its primary purpose. Yet the continuation of U.S. involvement beyond 1991 did not mean it would last forever, although retrenchment was more gradual than the arrival in the 1940s had been.

After the Cold War, Atlanticists were expecting the United States to stay in Europe, and the United States proclaimed the continuity of NATO. However, the actual disengagement of the United States from Europe continued quietly since 1991 and became very visible after September 11, 2001. "With the war on terrorism not just topping, but defining, America's strategic agenda, Europe is moving to the periphery of American grand strategy. The alliance is also of declining relevance to Europe. . . . Europe no longer needs its American pacifier."[7] And there had been enough evidence of disengagement in the 1990s, well before September 2001. For example, "America's effort in the Balkans was at best half-hearted and enjoyed only razor-thin political support."[8]

President George H. W. Bush contributed to stability during a time of dramatic transformation by proclaiming the continuity of U.S. engagement and of the transatlantic alliance. At the same time, however, U.S. military presence in Europe was already decreasing. Under President Clinton, defense budgets were cut and U.S. troops withdrawn from Europe. On the surface, "the events of the 1990s suggest that the United States will remain Europe's chief protector and peacemaker long into this new century.... NATO's intervention in Yugoslavia demonstrated that, in President Clinton's words, America is 'the indispensable nation,' and that American power and purpose are alive and well in Europe. Beneath the surface, however, a different picture is emerging."[9] In spite of the leading role of the United States in the war against Serbia, "America's behavior in Kosovo was indicative of a broader retrenchment in U.S. foreign policy that will become more pronounced in the years ahead."[10]

Decoupling in the transatlantic security relation has been happening over a long time. European economic integration established the EU as economic actor competing with the United States. The EEC began leaving the dollar zone in response to the floating of the dollar by President Nixon in 1971. Plans for a European monetary system emerged in the 1970s, although it took until 1999 for them to come to fruition with the introduction of the euro. American actions also contributed to decoupling with the Strategic Defense Initiative (SDI) plans of the 1980s intending to overcome the nuclear stalemate of mutually assured destruction, in which everyone shared nuclear risks, by creating an SDI shield for the United States while leaving Europe on the outer. After 1991, in the post–Cold War situation, the United States decoupled further by moving most of its troops out of Europe. This troop withdrawal was only interrupted but not reversed by the U.S. engagement in Bosnia and then in Kosovo. After these campaigns, U.S. forces did not stay but left the administration of the post-Yugoslav military protectorates to the Europeans. The "war on terrorism" and the war in Iraq further advanced disengagement from Europe. It was clear soon after September 11, 2001, that "the demands of the war in Afghanistan may provide the pretext for removing U.S. troops from the Balkans, and they are unlikely to go back when the crisis is over. In effect, this step means that the United States will be turning responsibility for Europe's security back to the Europeans."[11] The Iraq War of 2003 has only reinforced this trend.

Frightening consequences of U.S. disengagement were imagined by some Atlanticists. "The end of NATO could lead to the breakdown of the Schengen accord and other elements of the European Union, . . . various border and ethnic conflicts could reappear, and . . . national rivalries could be reborn."[12] The United States "as a superpower counterbalance for Germany from across the Atlantic" was still needed to ensure "that Germany does not seek a special relationship with Russia or a level of military power (perhaps including nuclear weapons) that its neighbours would find threatening."[13] When Mearsheimer, in 1990, predicted the renationalization of European security, the revival of German great-power ambitions, and the end of European integration,[14] he did not yet have the benefit of observing the 1990s. However, a decade later, Yost's fears were much less justified after the deepening of European integration since Maastricht and the continuation of German multilateralism. Germany's allies were not criticizing excessive German striving for military power; instead, the United States, the United Kingdom, and France were deploring cuts in German defense budgets.

On the one hand, U.S. politicians and experts were admonishing Europeans not to decouple by forming EU forces and setting up EU headquarters. On the other, the United States was reducing troop numbers stationed in Europe while engaging in conflicts outside Europe without consulting the NATO alliance. "But now that the Atlantic alliance appears to be irreversibly headed toward demise, an Atlanticist Europe is no longer an option."[15] As the security order of Europe was changing only very slowly, fears of change could also be alleviated gradually.

Changing the Habits of a Lifetime: Adjusting Transatlantic Roles

Transatlantic relations offered the United States and Western Europe stable roles during the Cold War. The United States exercised a rather benign hegemony over the European military protectorate, while European NATO members enjoyed U.S. security guarantees and acted as junior allies. Over time, such roles became firm habits, embedded in the identity of participants. Such stable subjective dispositions made it difficult to adjust perceptions and behavior even when reality changed dramatically. Yet a change of roles in the transatlantic alliance has been on the agenda since 1991 and was made more urgent, especially for the United States, by the terrorist attacks of September 11, 2001.

The United States had four broad options for the future transatlantic relationship. One was to try continuing the habit of half a century by claiming U.S. leadership through NATO. Second, the United States could pursue supremacy through unilateralism, discarding cumbersome alliances and sidelining NATO. Third, for those concerned about the costs of unilateralism and Bush's squandering of soft power, there was the option of renewing the transatlantic alliance between the United States, the indispensable nation, and Europe, the indispensable ally, perhaps also making some concessions to ESDP autonomy. A fourth option was to prepare for a transition to a multipolar world with the United States and Europe as equal partners. This last option presupposed an acknowledgment of the EU's geostrategic potential and an acceptance of the end of U.S. leadership regarding European security.

On the European side, there was the Atlanticist option of seeking security against external threats by welcoming continuing U.S. leadership. On the other hand, there was the Europeanist option of seeking autonomy from the United States through the EU's CFSP and ESDP. This option had superseded the Gaullist option of seeking European autonomy through a looser "Europe of nations" led by France. In a confrontational version of the Europeanist option, the distance to the hyperpower United States was to be achieved by overt counterbalancing in the transition to a multipolar world. In a more diplomatic version of the Europeanist option, such polemic was unnecessary because diminishing U.S. interest in European security was foreclosing the Atlanticist option anyhow. The transition to an autonomous ESDP was taking place in small steps while NATO was being discreetly transformed from a functioning military alliance into a security community, offering peaceful relations among members and reassurance for the unlikely case of a major war.

THE EU'S GEOPOLITICAL POTENTIAL: UNITING THE WESTERN END OF EURASIA

A transatlantic security partnership for the future has to take into account the transformation of NATO–Europe's role from a geostrategic bridgehead of the United States at the western end of Eurasia into an autonomous strategic actor uniting an enormous economic potential and a population of 500 million to 600 million, depending on the extent of EU expansion. Of course, the more the EU expanded, the more difficult it would be to build an appropriate political framework. "The European Community, if it were to become politically cohesive, would have the population, resources, economic wealth, technological and actual and potential military strength to be the preeminent power of the 21st century."[16] This claim, made by Samuel P. Huntington in 1988, is even more relevant two decades later. Yet Huntington's attempt to identify the most likely global hegemon is more speculative than the more modest claim made here that the EU clearly has the potential to become one of several major global players. Without replacing the United States as global hegemon, the weight of an integrated EU is changing the transatlantic relationship, replacing U.S. leadership of European junior allies by a partnership of two global powers.

NATO–Europe as U.S. Bridgehead in Western Eurasia

The political map of Eastern Europe had changed almost overnight in 1989–91, whereas the map of Western Europe had changed gradually because of several decades of integration. The most visible result was the expansion of NATO and EU into Central and Eastern Europe (CEE). Another less visible result was the gradual loss by the United States of a geostrategic bridgehead at the western end of Eurasia. Instead, Europe had become an economic competitor with geostrategic ambitions of its own. Forty years earlier, French author Jean-Jacques Servan-Schreiber had suggested in *The American Challenge* that Europe had the choice of becoming either an appendix of the United States or an autonomous center of power. The latter would require a closing of the technological gap between the United States and Western Europe that was possible only in a larger domestic market enabling European business to operate on a scale similar to U.S. business.[17] After 1991, the vision of Servan-Schreiber was becoming a reality. The Soviet Union had relinquished its sphere of influence in Eastern Europe, Western European integration had formed a unit strong enough to attract Eastern Europe, and the EU had become an economic superpower developing its own foreign and security policy.

NATO–Europe had been a strategic bridgehead for the United States at the western end of the Eurasian landmass, more valuable in the rivalry with the Soviet Union than the East Asian bridgehead because the latter consisted of islands (except for South Korea), whereas NATO–Europe was larger and located on the mainland. The worst nightmare scenario of U.S. geostrategists was the control of the entire Eurasian landmass by one central power, uniting an economic and demographic potential much greater than that of the Western Hemisphere. "Eurasia's power vastly overshadows America's. Fortunately for America, Eurasia is too big to be politically one."[18] For a short time, it had been imaginable in the late 1940s that the Soviet Union might combine this Eurasian potential, moving beyond its CEE sphere of influence and its (temporary) alliance with communist China. However, the United States quickly included Japan at the eastern and NATO–Europe at the western end of Eurasia into a global network of alliances and greatly reduced the influence of communist parties in both regions. The Sino–Soviet split in the 1960s ended this remote possibility of a united Eurasian bloc well before the collapse of the Soviet Union in 1991.

Nevertheless, U.S. strategists were still concerned about the effects of a possible loss of the NATO bridgehead at the western end of Eurasia: "Any ejection of America by its Western partners from its perch on the western periphery would automatically spell the end of America's participation in the game on the Eurasian chessboard, even though that would probably also mean the eventual subordination of the western extremity to a revived player occupying the middle space."[19] This fear of a Russian revival as great power in the center of Eurasia ignored the fact that much of Eurasia's population and economic potential was concentrated at its extremities, in East Asia, South Asia, and Europe. Thus, the shape of the emerging multipolar world will be determined by the economic potential and political unity achieved in these regions. Given the limitations of North America's potential, just uniting either the eastern or the western end of Eurasia would greatly affect the international balance of power. Had Japan's 1930s conquest of China become permanent, East Asia's combined potential could have become a formidable competitor. In the long run, China, on its own or in combination with Japan's economic potential, could still outweigh the United States. However, political unity between these East Asian powers remains a remote prospect. It will be much more difficult for China and Japan to put aside historical grievances and to combine their potential than it was for France and Germany since the 1950s. On the other hand, the western end of Eurasia has made substantial steps toward integration. Great-power rivalries between France, Germany, Italy, and the United Kingdom subsided after 1945. The EU developed as a formidable economic bloc, the division of Europe by the Iron Curtain ended in 1989–91, and most of CEE was integrated into EU and NATO by 2004. An autonomous security role for this European bloc would end U.S. control over the western Eurasian bridgehead.

The claim by Charles A. Kupchan that the EU was the main challenger to U.S. primacy may be overstated: "The near-term challenger to America is not a single country trying to play catch-up—which takes time—but a European Union that is in the process of aggregating the impressive economic resources that is member nations already possess." However, there is no doubt about a less far reaching claim: "Whether or not the United States likes it, Europe is becoming a new center of global power. America's sway will shrink accordingly."[20] The balance of relative power between the United States and NATO–Europe was no longer what it was in 1949, and a renegotiation of roles was taking place in a new security environment, without the Soviet threat perpetuating the original role allocation within NATO.

Potential EU Expansion and Economic Weight

To understand the change in the transatlantic partners' roles over the next two decades, one has to assess the EU's geopolitical potential, determined by its size, economic potential, and level of political unity. Contrasting the EEC of 1957 to the likely membership and geographic extension of the EU in 2017 can illustrate the magnitude of change more strikingly than a recapitulation of the gradual widening of European integration. In 1957, the EEC was a grouping of six Western European countries, with a population of 167 million, trying to recover economically from the war and relying on the United States for protection. By 2017, the EU could be a bloc of possibly 580 million people, an economic giant, and a powerful regional strategic actor. In 1957, it was the EEC's role to consolidate the economies of junior NATO allies. By contrast, in 2017, the EU will be the biggest economic actor globally, with responsibility for security within and beyond this space of 580 million. Its membership will include the entire region from Ireland in the west to Finland in the northeast and, possibly, Turkey in the southeast. Its immediate neighbors will include not only Russia but probably also Iran, Iraq, and Syria.

Beginning from six members in 1957, with about two-thirds of the U.S. population at that time, the EU had grown to 15 members in the 1990s, matching U.S. gross domestic product (GDP) and outnumbering the U.S. population by a quarter. From May 1, 2004, the EU had 25 members and about one and a half times the U.S. population and a GDP slightly bigger than the U.S. GDP. Romania and Bulgaria were expected to join in 2007. This could be rounded off by the inclusion of the successor states of Yugoslavia (other than Slovenia, which had joined in 2004), bringing the EU's population to 500 million. Furthermore, the inclusion of Turkey would bring the EU's population to 580 million, almost doubling U.S. population figures for 2000.

Geopolitical Impact of EU Expansion

In geostrategic terms, EU expansion implied a reversal of some U.S. gains of World War II. The European bridgehead, acquired in the 1940s, was being lost and had turned into a competitor. American influence in the eastern Mediterranean weakened when Greece became a member of the EU in 1981. Turkish EU membership would signal another step in the retreat of the United States from positions gained after 1945, when the United Kingdom could not retain influence in Greece and Turkey. The former West Asian sphere of influence of the United States, held together by the CENTO Pact in the 1950s, had turned into a Turkey linked with the EU, a fiercely independent Iran, with Iraq and Syria in between, neither of them convenient for the United States.

The inclusion of the entire Balkan as well as Turkey into the EU and the linking of North Africa by association treaties will widen the EU's regional influence. With Turkey's accession, Syria, Iraq, and Iran would be neighbors of the EU. The inclusion of Cyprus in May 2004 has already brought the EU very close to Lebanon, Israel, and Palestine. The EU's influence as immediate neighbor could rival the distant influence of the United States in North Africa, the eastern Mediterranean, and the Caucasus.

With the expansion of the EU to almost 600 million inhabitants, security in Europe will be transformed from an international issue between competing nation-states to a quasi-domestic internal task of the EU, not quite a federation but a deeply integrated security community. A larger EU will also influence its neighbors through soft power. On the other hand, the EU's use of military power will remain limited because of the difficulties of decision making. Nevertheless, an EU of 500 million to 600 million people and a GDP matching the United States can afford to tackle all Petersberg Tasks of crisis management at the periphery of Europe and beyond.

The Danger of Institutional Paralysis

"The key question, of course, is whether the European Community will develop enough political cohesion to act as one on a wide range of international issues, or whether it will remain a customs union of twelve nations with strongly different nationalisms and foreign policies."[21] The question of sufficient political cohesion had become even more important with the growth of the EU to 15 members in 1995 and to 25 in 2004. To become a challenger to U.S. hegemony, the EU only had to unite an economic potential that already existed, whereas China or India would have to sustain several decades of continued economic growth to match U.S. power. However, achieving unity of political will in the EU was difficult enough.

To become a strategic actor with a functioning CFSP, the EU will have to overcome the danger of institutional paralysis. Its institutions were capable of making decisions when the EEC had a membership of six and a compromise could be reached by extended negotiations. Every accession of members, especially the increase from 15 to 25 in May 2004, made institutional reform more urgent. For example, the voting procedure requiring unanimity in the Council of Ministers was viable for six neighbors making deals in the EEC of 1957; however, for 25 or more members, unanimity is virtually impossible, and rules of majority voting will have to be adopted.

The Treaty of Nice of 2000 found imperfect, transitional solutions, including rules for qualified majority voting in the Council of Ministers. The Convention for the Future of Europe of 2002–03 was meant to find more permanent solutions in its draft constitution for the EU. For the CFSP and ESDP, two provisions of the draft constitution would be relevant. The EU was to have a foreign minister and a common diplomatic service implementing the CFSP. Furthermore, the draft constitution included a mutual defense guarantee for EU members.[22]

However, the ratification of this document by all 25 member countries was unlikely after it had been rejected by the electorate in France and the Netherlands in June 2005. If a constitution for the EU cannot be found by either ratifying the draft of 2003 or adopting a modified version, the EU can still become a security actor through intergovernmental cooperation. Without a constitution, the EU could continue integration through intergovernmental treaties. Core groups of member countries willing to integrate security and defense policies could take initiatives without all EU members participating, whereas previously defense policy had been excluded from such "enhanced cooperation."[23] Yet cumbersome decision making and lack of political unity remained a serious handicap in security and defense policy, more so than in the EU's history of economic integration where member countries could allow themselves time to arrive at compromises.

With or without a constitution, the EU will be not a federation but rather a model of multilevel governance with slow central decision making. With its complex institutions, the EU can be a powerful, unitary actor in the world economy but will remain less effective as a strategic actor. The EU cannot wage major wars, but it can handle the Petersberg Tasks of crisis intervention. Thus, the EU can use its massive economic weight and its diplomatic resources to influence outcomes, it can provide security in its internal space of 25 to 30 member countries, and it can provide crisis management in the periphery of Europe and in failed or failing states in Africa.

NEW SECURITY PARTNERSHIP U.S.-EUROPE: RENEWING THE TRANSATLANTIC ALLIANCE

Observable Changes in the Division of Labor between NATO and the EU

"While they have the luxury of doing so, the United States and its main regional partners should begin to imagine life after Pax Americana."[24] Yet it was difficult to change the thought habits of a lifetime. In the late 1990s, an unchanged division of labor between NATO and the EU could still be imagined by commentators. "NATO has emerged as the key security institution governing and maintaining order in the European geostrategic space;

the EU has emerged as the key economic institution governing and maintaining order in the European geoeconomic space."[25] Yet the same author also presented factors likely to upset this continuity. While proposing a parallel extension of the EU and NATO in CEE, he also wanted "the EU to emerge as an independent European actor capable of cooperating with the United States (or Russia) or acting alone." This "EU speaking with a single voice on foreign policy and defence issues would provide a counter to American power in Europe."[26] These passages exemplify the German attempt to reconcile Atlanticism and Europeanism by practicing both and presenting them as compatible. However, in the five years after the Kosovo crisis, change accelerated, and a new division of labor emerged.

Observable changes were modifying the division of labor between the United States, NATO, and the EU regarding European security. NATO and U.S. involvement were no longer required as protection from a Soviet threat, although perceptions of a residual Russian threat still justified U.S. involvement, at least as reassurance for an unlikely case. As protection from hypothetical German threats, NATO was hardly required since Germany was deeply integrated into the EU and did not spend more on defense than either France or the United Kingdom. Nevertheless, there were psychological benefits for European integration in having the United States acting as offshore balancer and staying linked to Europe through NATO.

Future U.S. intervention in small European crises was highly unlikely after it had become optional during the 1990s. While the United States intervened in Bosnia and Kosovo decisively, though late and reluctantly, steps were also taken to delegate such tasks to European Combined Joint Task Forces (CJTF). From the ESDI under President George H. W. Bush to President Clinton's CJTF concept, European forces were becoming more detachable from the formerly monolithic NATO military structures. Europeans were allowed and encouraged to manage crises on their own, while the United States was also becoming more detachable from European crises as U.S. involvement became optional. Extrapolating this trend, the result would be EU responsibility for crisis management in Europe, especially once almost all European countries (except Russia) had become members of the EU.

Projecting stability to CEE was a combined effort of NATO providing security and of the EU offering economic integration. Further to the east, NATO exercised influence beyond the reach of the EU in the Partnership for Peace links with the countries of the Commonwealth of Independent States (CIS). Regarding CEE, however, security was becoming an internal matter for the EU, to be managed through civilian instruments.

Power projection out of area had become a priority for NATO, but most EU members were hesitant to follow the U.S. lead. The war on terrorism guided U.S. attention to regions far away from Europe, whereas the EU found it easier to cooperate with the United States in antiterrorist policing than in distant wars. Out-of-area missions resulted in optional cooperation, in disagreements over Iraq, and in the United States acting without NATO in Afghanistan, although the alliance was called on to assist in stabilizing the country after the war. The autonomous security role of the EU has also developed since the first claims were made in the adoption of the EU's CFSP in 1991 and of the Petersberg Tasks of the West European Union (WEU) in 1992. Since then, the EU has advanced the integration of defense industries, formed its own armed forces on a small scale, and conducted its first military missions.

Aspects of a Future Transatlantic Security Partnership

The trends observable over 15 years since the end of the Cold War have been reshaping the security partnership between the United States and Europe. The new security environment allowed the United States to withdraw troops from Europe and extricate itself from involvement in European crises. The EU, on the other hand, was acting as stabilizer of a region, forming a security community for its members, and practicing crisis management at its periphery. While this reduced the indispensability of the United States for European security, compared to the post-1945 period, there were clear benefits in this new situation for both sides of the transatlantic relationship. Extrapolating the trends of the post–Cold War period allows a broad characterization of the future security partnership between the United States and Europe.

A Balanced Partnership

The Cold War security partnership had clearly come to an end, with its asymmetrical allocation of roles between the hegemonic United States providing the nuclear umbrella and NATO–Europe providing auxiliary conventional forces. The discussion about the capabilities gap in NATO still revolved around this old division of labor where superior U.S. military forces would be supplemented by the limited but useful contributions of European junior allies. This arrangement worked for Cold War deterrence, but for the power projection required by post-1991 threats, it could work only if the European contribution was useful enough to support U.S. missions but not strong enough to challenge U.S. leadership. Too small a European effort would exacerbate the capabilities gap and lead to a mission gap. The United States would not need such incapable allies, and for Europeans a "Nintendo-like America with Europeans as cannon fodder" would be "politically unsustainable."[27] On the other hand, very substantial European capabilities would either encourage European claims for equality in the alliance or bolster demands for an autonomous ESDP. This balancing act between NATO–Europe being too weak to be useful and too strong to be obedient could destroy the alliance in the long run. Furthermore, the emerging autonomous security role of the EU was moving beyond the Cold War allocation of roles anyhow. "A more balanced relationship between the United States and Europe, and a European security order that is more European and less Atlantic, holds out the best hope for preserving a cohesive transatlantic community."[28]

Not Just "Doing Windows"

A conceivable but unlikely division of labor was that between the United States acting as military superpower and Europe exclusively relying on "soft power" or "civilian power." This could be regarded as division of labor between a strong United States and weak Europe without other choices, where the United States would refuse to do menial tasks such as peacekeeping. "Superpowers don't do windows," whereas Europeans might be relegated to "doing the dishes" after U.S. military power had sorted out crises such as Bosnia and Kosovo. On the other hand, this division of labor could be a positive option: "Each side would profit from being responsible for what it does best. Complementarity is the key to transatlantic reconciliation."[29] Instead of trying to match U.S. defense expenditure, the EU should maximize its use of soft power, practicing crisis prevention as the largest donor of economic aid. "And when it comes to the essential instruments for avoiding chaos or quagmire once the fighting stops—trade, aid, peace-keeping, international monitoring, and multilateral legitimacy—Europe remains indispensable."[30] In this case, the United States could still win wars alone (and would not ask Europe how to run them), but the United States could not win the peace alone and would definitely need Europe after conflicts and might therefore even consult Europe before conflicts. Yet the European trends of the past 15 years do not point in the direction of exclusive reliance on nonmilitary instruments, whether out of weakness or as positive choice. While the EU continued to rely heavily on economic and diplomatic instruments, it has also developed the military capabilities for crisis management, including peace enforcement.

Europeans are not accepting a division of labor in which "the United States retreats ever more forcefully into the role of a technological super-warrior." Reducing the EU to the exercise of soft power would create a division of labor "Europeans must sternly resist if they are to avoid ceding control of the strategic agenda to the United States."[31] If the United States leaves peacekeeping to Europeans, it is not only because the latter are too weak for high-intensity warfare but also because of an American inability. "A principal British concern is that role specialization may prompt the US to reduce its relatively high-technology forces to the point where they can no longer carry out more labour-intensive peace-support operations." Taking role specialization too far can make it impossible "to ensure that political cohesion is maintained in all phases of a coalition operation."[32]

EU Peacekeeping in the Western Balkans

The EU's predominant role in the stabilization of the western Balkans since 1999 was an indicator of the future division of labor between NATO and the EU. NATO's military interventions in Bosnia in 1995 and in Kosovo in 1999 caused transatlantic tensions but also gave the alliance a new purpose and consolidated U.S. leadership in European security, at least in the short term. However, after the end of the military conflicts, U.S. military presence was reduced in spite of earlier assurances to the contrary. In the late 1990s, European NATO members had still insisted that they would provide ground troops only if the United States stayed and even threatened to withdraw if the United States left ("all-in-all-out"). However, within a few years, U.S. presence was down to symbolic numbers, and Europeans were largely left on their own. Furthermore, responsibility for the stabilization of the region (including the successor states of Yugoslavia as well as Albania) had been handed over by NATO to the EU.

In the military conflicts in Bosnia and Kosovo, the United States had still been the indispensable nation. However, the terrorist attacks of September 11, 2001, had reinforced the tendency for the United States to disengage from Europe after the end of the Cold War. On the other hand, for the EU "the Balkans represent the principal testing ground of Europe's CFSP and evolving ESDP," and "for the states of the Balkans, the EU represents the only viable option if the region is to escape its recent past and its retarded development."[33] NATO as a military alliance could not provide what the region needed, whereas the EU had available the necessary combination of civilian and military instruments to assist with peacekeeping and nation building.

The EU and the countries of the western Balkans have embarked on a "Stabilization and Association Process" that prepares these countries for the prospect of eventually joining the EU. Individual countries have concluded Stabilization and Association Agreements (SAA) with the EU. Unlike the agreements concluded between the EU and the membership applicants in CEE, the SAA do not envisage EU membership at the end of this process but are regarded as a preliminary process. Nevertheless, the EU has had significant impact on the western Balkans through a combination of military peacekeeping, administrative and economic support for nation building, and the attraction of future membership in the EU.

While the EU does still not have the military means to conduct a war the size of NATO's Kosovo campaign of 1999, it has the armed forces for peacekeeping and enforcement according to the Petersberg Tasks, and it has the administrative and economic means to assist with nation building for many years. In the 1990s, NATO and the EU treated Bosnia and Kosovo as security problems outside, as interventions "out of area." However, as the EU takes over responsibility from NATO, security in the western Balkans becomes more and more an internal issue. In the 1990s, Bosnia and Kosovo were objects for the security role of NATO under U.S. leadership. The long-term prospect, however, is the inclusion of the western Balkans into the EU zone of security and stability.

EU as Security Community for Europe

Responsibility for stability in Europe has shifted to the EU in its function as security community after almost half a century of stability through bloc confrontation and superpower leadership. Although neoconservative critics questioned European visions of transforming the international system into a peaceful Kantian community of states integrated by institutions and rules, this is exactly what was happening in Europe. It can be questioned whether the European model of stability through institutions can be exported to other parts of the world anytime soon; however, the European Union has brought France and Germany so close together that wars, as in 1870–71, 1914–18, and 1939–45, have become inconceivable. Adversaries of two world wars, such as Britain, France, Germany, and Italy, are integrating their defense industries and planning joint military forces under the EU's CFSP. This transformation also applies to CEE, where the EU has prevented any violent settlement of outstanding issues between Romania and Hungary, for example. There is a real prospect that the EU as zone of peace and stability will include the successor states of Yugoslavia as well to prevent any repeat of the Bosnian and Kosovo crisis, thus relegating memories of past Balkan wars to the history books and overcoming the hurtful memories of interethnic strife during German occupation in the 1940s. This achievement should not be dismissed by neoconservative complaints that a Kantian Europe was preoccupied with internal affairs and prone to illusions about their applicability to the wider world. Instead, it should be acknowledged as a contribution to a new transatlantic security partnership. The EU is stabilizing a region of 25 to 30 countries that had been the source of two global wars in the twentieth century and regional crises in the 1990s. "Indeed, the question whether Europe is prepared to project power abroad, which had been a major US objective for several years, must not obscure the necessity, first, for Europe to project power within Europe itself."[34] Even if this task limits the ability of Europeans to play a role in other regions, it is still a necessary and valuable contribution to global security. It allows the United States to withdraw 300,000 troops from Europe and leave crisis management in Europe to the EU.

NATO as Reassurance and Large Security Community

The task of territorial defense was clearly a prerogative of NATO during the Cold War and remained so after 1991. When the WEU claimed a crisis management role in the Petersberg Tasks of 1992, it included peacekeeping and peace enforcement but clearly excluded territorial defense. This was confirmed in the Amsterdam Treaty, when the EU incorporated the WEU's Petersberg Tasks into its remit but still left territorial defense to NATO. It was only with the mutual defense clause of the 2004 draft constitution that the EU envisaged a territorial defense role. However, the likelihood of an attack on EU countries by state actors and the need for territorial defense was extremely low in the post-1991 security environment. No state, except the United States and Russia, was capable of a serious conventional invasion of the EU. Residual fears of Russia served to justify the territorial defense role of NATO, but this role was reduced to that of reinsurance for extremely unlikely situations. The reduction of U.S. military presence in Europe was a strong indication that NATO regarded the need for territorial defense as extremely unlikely.

"With the war against terrorism not just topping but defining America's strategic agenda, Europe is moving to the periphery of America's grand strategy. The alliance is also of declining relevance to Europe. . . . Europe no longer needs its American pacifier."[35] As NATO has outlived its old functions of territorial defense and as a vehicle of U.S. leadership, the alliance was growing into a new role. Thus, in the future security partnership, NATO has a political role anchoring a large security community, bringing together North America, Western Europe, CEE, Russia, and other CIS states either as alliance members or associates. Its military role in Europe will be that of a reinsurance, comforting but unlikely to be called on in earnest.

Partnership as U.S.–EU Dialogue

The post-1945 involvement of the United States is coming to an end without, however, resulting in an isolationist withdrawal from Europe. In the future security partnership, the United States will no longer claim leadership in European security but will step back to a role as offshore balancer, still involved in NATO as security community but not required for crisis management in Europe. The intense economic interdependence of the transatlantic partners should prevent any disinterest in European stability, and the benefits of cooperation with the EU for global stability should ensure continued interest in a new form of security partnership.

The transatlantic security partnership will increasingly operate as U.S.–EU or NATO–EU dialogue, gradually diminishing but not replacing bilateral relations and the NATO framework. As U.S. military presence in Europe declined, NATO's integrated military structure made less sense. Therefore, the "NATO-first" approach to Europe is of diminishing value. On the other hand, as EU defense industries and defense equipment markets integrate, defense policies are being integrated as well. The EU will still not be a unitary actor, and the nation-states will retain considerable scope of national decision making in foreign and security policy. Therefore, the United States can still use bilateral relations to individual European countries, but closer European caucusing can be expected. Nevertheless, relating to the EU as a whole is becoming increasingly useful besides maintaining bilateral relations. The NATO–EU dialogue could be institutionalized in the participation of NATO's secretary-general in EU top committees and of the EU representative for CFSP in the NATO Council.

EU as Crisis Manager, with and without the United States

A European capability to manage crises in Europe without U.S. involvement has been encouraged since NATO adopted the CJTF concept in 1994.

President Clinton's support for the CJTF concept did not envisage the extent of EU autonomy achieved a decade later; however, relinquishing leadership in European crisis management is a small price to pay for the benefit of getting the United States out of European entanglements, as in Bosnia and Kosovo. The security partnership takes on the form of a clear geographic division of labor.

This geographic separation also applies to Africa, where the EU is claiming a postcolonial sphere of influence. The battle groups of the EU are likely to act without U.S. involvement but in cooperation with the United Nations and with African regional organizations, such as the African Union and the Economic Community of West African States. Just as the United States will never ask the EU to participate in military interventions in the Americas, the United States is likely to stay out of the EU's sphere of influence. This leaves only a limited area where joint U.S.–European intervention is likely. Out-of-area intervention will not be the mainstay of a future transatlantic security partnership, contrary to Senator Lugar's dictum that NATO will go out of area or out of business. "The notion that NATO should be turned into a vehicle for global military operations . . . should also be abandoned. . . . Washington should encourage Europe to shoulder more of the burden in its own neighborhood."[36]

Fields of U.S.–EU Cooperation

Security interdependence between the transatlantic partners has diminished compared to the Cold War period, whereas economic interdependence has remained as intensive as ever. A new security relationship is emerging "in which Europeans recognize that America is going to do its own security 'thing,' and Americans recognize that Europe will do its own security 'thing' whilst preserving the ability of the two security 'things' to do things together."[37] Instead of involving the United States closely in European security, a future security partnership will be based on a shared interest in global stability outside Europe. In spite of the buildup of the European Rapid Response Forces and the battle groups, neither the EU nor individual EU members have the capacity to conduct major wars abroad like the United States. This, together with disagreements about objectives and strategies as in the Iraq War of 2003, will exclude U.S.–EU cooperation in major wars but not participation of individual EU members in U.S.-led coalitions of the willing. More likely fields of cooperation include police and intelligence cooperation against terrorism and international crime. While European views differ from the Bush administration's military approach to the war on terrorism, U.S.–EU cooperation is occurring in intelligence, policing, and financial controls directed against terrorism. "From Washington's perspective, conducting a dialogue with a single European interlocutor on international crime is preferable to doing so with fifteen. That view is reflected in Washington's enthusiasm for EUROPOL, the nascent European police force."[38]

The EU also has capabilities in preventive security measures. This includes the military and police personnel required for peacekeeping but also the economic, diplomatic, and administrative means to support nation building in failed or failing states. The EU also has economic and diplomatic means to influence outcomes. "Indeed, the greatest potential for agreement and reinforcement of action in the transatlantic world falls in the area of advance effort, of trying to prevent the emergence of threats in common to the United States and Europe." Rather than dismissing the use of nonmilitary instruments, R. Hunter argues that "this U.S.-EU strategic partnership would not primarily be about military relations . . . but rather about marshalling the economic strengths, talents, leadership, and commitments that are common to these nations."[39] Thus, contrary to unilateralist polemics against European policies allegedly born out of weakness and aiming to undermine U.S. freedom of action, the EU has much to offer to a new transatlantic security partnership.

CONCLUSION

As a new transatlantic division of labor emerges from this protracted renegotiation of roles, Europeans are completing the second part of their emancipation from post-1945 dependency as the asymmetrical roles in the alliance are transformed into an U.S.–EU dialogue. If the transition can be managed with a minimum of animosity, economic interdependence will underpin good transatlantic relations even after the end of security dependency. And a shared interest in global security should underpin a division of labor in security matters.

The transition to this new division of labor can be made more painful by overstated role claims and overheated rhetoric. On the other hand, more precise understanding of changing relative power and an awareness of lasting common interests could make the transition more manageable. The unilateralist option of ignoring and alienating Europe could be costly, and the attempt to continue the asymmetrical relationship of the past 50 years without adjustment is bound to fail. Instead, *Renewing the Atlantic Partnership*, as recommended by Council on Foreign Relations task force report, could create a climate in which future cooperation is not threatened by unnecessary rhetoric. Roles could be renegotiated with awareness that economic interdependence and shared benefits are more important than disputed issues. Regarding world trade and economic stability, "transatlantic interdependence and joint responsibility for global leadership have grown rapidly for both economic superpowers."[40] Such joint economic leadership should facilitate a rebalancing of the security roles of the United States and the EU.

With NATO forming a very large security community and with the United States acting as overseas balancer and as reinsurance for territorial defense in conceivable but highly unlikely situations, the United States can leave Europe in the hands of the EU. The new partnership will rely more on economic interdependence than on shared fears of external threats, and the security dependence of half a century can be replaced by a division of responsibilities within a continuing transatlantic partnership, within a wider security community including North America, Europe, and Russia.

"In place of traditional aspects of security and defence, tomorrow's strategic partnership should, and probably will, be dominated by trade, international politics, global crisis management, safeguarding common interests and commodities, arms control, non-proliferation and export-control regimes, counter-terrorism, international crime and strategic defences."[41] This widening of the agenda of cooperation would reduce the role of NATO as the historical centerpiece of the transatlantic relationship. For the United States, "the EU will be a more interesting partner in global crisis management than the European pillar within NATO" except for the purpose of "European collective defence and high-end peace enforcement in Europe."[42]

This gives NATO a long-term role as security community for the wider North Atlantic space, including North America, Western Europe, CEE, and post-Soviet space. NATO will also retain a transitional role "as long as . . . the EU-US relationship is embryonic, and until such time as the EU has addressed key flaws in its crisis management capabilities and ended its dependence on US assets and capabilities for high-end military operations."[43]

Since 1991, the West has been undergoing a slow but profound redefinition. The roles allocated in the late 1940s to the United States and NATO–Europe in the transatlantic relationship were affected quietly by European economic recovery from post-1945 weakness and by integration into a powerful economic bloc. The collapse of the Soviet Union in 1991 changed the security environment for the United States and Europe. In the post-1991 situation, the EU was able to begin translating its economic potential into a limited but autonomous security role. The asymmetrical security partnership of the Cold War period has endured beyond 1991 because the roles allocated in 1949 were structurally entrenched and had become part of the identity of political and military personnel. Yet renegotiating roles in the transatlantic partnership requires an acceptance of post-1991 realities and a break with a lifetime of post-1945 habits. The economic interdependence between the two most powerful economies and a shared interest in global stability should make a redefined and rebalanced security partnership not only desirable but also achievable.

Notes

PREFACE

1. Christoph Bertram, *Europe in the Balance: Securing the Peace Won in the Cold War* (Washington, D.C.: Carnegie Endowment for International Peace, 1995), 40.

2. Joseph S. Nye, *Soft Power: the Means to Success in World Politics* (New York: Public Affairs, 2004), 4.

3. Charles F. Doran, "Economics, Philosophy of History, and the 'Single Dynamic' of Power Cycle Theory: Expectations, Competition, and Statecraft," *International Political Science Review* 24, no. 1 (2003): 13–49.

4. Peter Shearman and Matthew Sussex, eds., *European Security after 9/11* (Aldershot: Ashgate, 2004).

INTRODUCTION

1. Christoph Bertram, *Europe in the Balance: Securing the Peace Won in the Cold War* (Washington, D.C.: Carnegie Endowment for International Peace, 1995), 4.

2. David Calleo, *The Atlantic Fantasy: The US, NATO, and Europe* (Baltimore: The Johns Hopkins University Press, 1970), 27–28.

3. Robert Kagan, "Power and Weakness," *Policy Review*, no. 113 (June/July 2002): 22–23.

4. Joseph S. Nye, *Bound to Lead: The Changing Nature of American Power* (New York: Basic Books, 1990), 21.

5. Ibid., 7.

6. Deutsche Welle, "U.S. Confirms Troop Reductions in Germany," June 16, 2004, http://www.dw.world.de; *Financial Times Deutschland*, "US-Armee dampft Truppenpräsenz in Deutschland ein," April 12, 2005, http://www.ftd.de/pw/eu/2942.html?mode = print.

7. Zbigniew Brzezinski, *Game Plan: A Geostrategic Framework for the Conduct of the U.S.-Soviet Contest* (Boston: Atlantic Monthly Press, 1986), 196–97.

8. Henry Kissinger, *The Troubled Partnership: A Re-appraisal of the Atlantic Alliance* (Garden City, N.Y.: Anchor Books, 1966), 6.

9. Zbigniew Brzezinski, *The Grand Chessboard: American Primacy and Its Geostrategic Imperatives* (New York: Basic Books, 1997), 40.

10. Ibid., 50.

11. Ibid., 59.

12. NATO, "The Alliance's Strategic Concept," Rome, November 8, 1991, sec. 8, p. 3.

13. Kagan, "Power and Weakness," 6; Joseph S. Nye, *The Paradox of American Power* (Oxford: Oxford University Press, 2002), 39.

14. Young-Kwan Yoon, "Introduction: Power Cycle Theory and the Practice of International Relations," *International Political Science Review* 24, no. 1 (2003): 6; see also Charles F. Doran, "Economics, Philosophy of History, and the 'Single Dynamic' of Power Cycle Theory: Expectations, Competition, and Statecraft," *International Political Science Review* 24, no. 1 (2003): 13–49.

15. Yoon, "Introduction," 8.

16. For a discussion of the concept, see Joseph S. Nye, *Soft Power: The Means to Success in World Politics* (New York: Public Affairs, 2004).

17. "But it is far wiser to get ahead of the curve and shape structural design than to find unipolarity giving way to chaotic multipolarity by default." Charles A. Kupchan, "The Rise of Europe, America's Changing Internationalism, and the End of U.S. Primacy," *Political Science Quarterly* 118, no. 2 (2003): 231.

18. Nye, *Soft Power,* 4.

19. Geir Lundestad, *"Empire" by Invitation: The United States and European Integration 1945–1997* (Oxford: Oxford University Press, 1998), 168.

CHAPTER 1

1. Zbigniew Brzezinski, *The Grand Chessboard: American Primacy and Its Geostrategic Imperatives* (New York: Basic Books, 1997), 59.

2. Henry A. Kissinger, *The Troubled Partnership: A Re-appraisal of the Atlantic Alliance* (Garden City, N.Y.: Anchor Books, 1966), 6–7, 25.

3. Anthony Laurence Gardner, *A New Era in US-EU Relations? The Clinton Administration and the New Transatlantic Agenda* (Aldershot: Ashgate, 1997), 4.

4. Henry A. Kissinger, "The Year of Europe. Address to the Associated Press Annual Luncheon, New York, April 23, 1973," in *American Foreign Policy,* 3rd ed. (New York: W. W. Norton, 1977), 104–5.

5. Henry A. Kissinger, *Does America Need a Foreign Policy? Toward a Diplomacy for the 21st Century* (New York: Simon and Schuster, 2001), 80–81.

6. Robert Kagan, "Power and Weakness," *Policy Review,* no. 113 (June/July 2002): 7–8; Robert Wilkie, "Fortress Europe: European Defense and the Future of the Atlantic Alliance," *Parameters* 32, no. 4 (winter 2002–03): 46.

7. Kagan, "Power and Weakness," 6.

8. Project for the New American Century, "Statement of Principles," June 3, 1997, http://www.newamericancentury.org/statementofprinciples.htm.

9. G. John Ikenberry, "The End of the Neo-Conservative Moment," *Survival* 46, no. 1 (spring 2004): 12.

10. Charles A. Kupchan, "The Rise of Europe, America's Changing Internationalism, and the End of U.S. Primacy," *Political Science Quarterly* 118, no. 2 (2003): 206.

11. Samuel P. Huntington, "The Lonely Superpower," *Foreign Affairs* 78, no. 2 (March/April 1999): 37.

12. Ibid., 49.

13. Samuel P. Huntington, "The Clash of Civilizations?" *Foreign Affairs* 72, no. 3 (summer 1993): 22.

14. Kissinger, *Does America Need a Foreign Policy?*, 81.

15. Ikenberry, "The End of the Neo-Conservative Moment," 12.

16. G. John Ikenberry, *After Victory: Institutions, Strategic Restraints, and the Rebuilding of Order after Major Wars* (Princeton, N.J.: Princeton University Press, 2001), 265.

17. Joseph S. Nye, *Soft Power: The Means to Success in World Politics* (New York: Public Affairs, 2004).

18. Brzezinski, *The Grand Chessboard*, 76.

19. Ivo Daalder and James M. Goldgeier, "Putting Europe First," *Survival* 43, no. 1 (spring 2001): 71–91.

20. Brzezinski, *The Grand Chessboard*, 199.

21. Stephen M. Walt, *The Origins of Alliances* (Ithaca, N.Y.: Cornell University Press, 1987), 283.

22. Charles A. Kupchan, "Kosovo and the Future of U.S. Engagement in Europe: Continued Hegemony or Impending Retrenchment?," in *Alliance Politics, Kosovo and NATO's War: Allied Forces or Forced Allies?*, ed. Pierre Martin and Mark R. Brawley (Houndmills, Basingstoke: Palgrave, 2000), 87.

23. Ted Galen Carpenter, "NATO's New Strategic Concept: Coherent Blueprint or Conceptual Muddle?," in *NATO Enters the 21st Century*, ed. Ted Galen Carpenter (London: Frank Cass, 2001), 24.

24. Charles A. Kupchan, *The End of the American Era: U.S. Foreign Policy and the Geopolitics of the Twenty-first Century* (New York: Alfred A. Knopf, 2003), 263.

25. Ibid., 119.

26. Council on Foreign Relations, *Renewing the Atlantic Partnership*, Task Force Report No. 51 (New York: Council on Foreign Relations Press, March 2004).

27. Ibid., 7; Judy Dempsey, "U.S. Rebuffs Germany on Plan for NATO," *International Herald Tribune*, February 15, 2005, http://www.iht.com/bin/print_ipub.php?file=/articles/2005/02/14/news/munich.html.

28. Ikenberry, *After Victory*, 226; such fears of a renewable German threat were also shared by David S. Yost, "Transatlantic Relations and Peace in Europe," *International Affairs* 78, no. 2 (April 2002): 277–300, and in the novel by Alain Crémieux, *Quand les "Ricains" repartiront: Le journal imaginaire du nouveau millénaire* (Boofzheim: ACM Edition, 2000).

29. Rob de Wijk, "Transatlantic Relations: A View from the Netherlands," *International Journal* 59, no. 1 (winter 2003–04): 185.

30. Robert Wilkie, "Fortress Europe: European Defense and the Future of the North Atlantic Alliance," *Parameters* 32, no. 4 (winter 2002–03): 45.

31. William Wallace, "The Collapse of British Foreign Policy," *International Affairs* 82, no. 1 (2005): 55.

32. Ibid., 65–68.

33. Jiri Sedivy and Marcin Zaborowski, "Old Europe, New Europe and Transatlantic Relations," *European Security* 13, no. 3 (2004): 209.

34. Ibid., 206.

35. Olaf Osica, "Poland: A New European Atlanticist at a Crossroads?," *European Security* 13, no. 4 (2004): 320.

36. Marcin Zaborowski and Kerry Longhurst, "America's Protégé in the East? The Emergence of Poland as Regional Leader," *International Affairs* 79, no. 5 (2003): 1028.

37. Ibid., 1011.

38. Kerry Longhurst and Marcin Zaborowski, "The Future of European Security," *European Security* 13, no. 4 (2004): 385.

39. Osica, "Poland," 309, 312, 311.

40. Olaf Osica, "A Secure Poland in a Better Union? The ESS as Seen from Warsaw's Perspective," in *The European Security Strategy: Paper Tiger or Catalyst for Joint Action. Part II*, ed. Marco Overhaus, Hanns W. Maull, and Sebastian Harnisch. *German Foreign Policy in Dialogue* 5, no. 14 (October 14, 2004): 14.

41. Quoted in Craig R. Whitney, "France Presses for a Power Independent of the US," *New York Times*, November 7, 1999, A5.

42. Council on Foreign Relations, *Renewing the Atlantic Partnership*, 15.

43. Pierre Hassner, *The United States: The Empire of Force or the Force of Empire?*, Chaillot Papers, no. 54 (Paris: Institute for Strategic Studies of the European Union, September 2002), 46.

44. Hassner, *The United States*, 30, quoting John Hillen, "Superpowers Don't Do Windows," *Orbis* 41, no. 2 (spring 1997): 241–58.

45. Hassner, *The United States*, 8.

46. Emmanuel Todd, *Weltmacht USA: Ein Nachruf* (Munich: Piper, 2003), 38 (German translation of *Après l'empire: Essai sur la décomposition du système américain* [Paris: Éditions Gallimard, 2002]).

47. Ibid., 114.

48. Gregor Schöllgen, *Die Außenpolitik der Bundesrepublik Deutschland* (Munich: Beck, 1963), 72.

49. Thomas Fuller, "EU's 'Big Three' Agree on Defense," *International Herald Tribune*, November 29, 2003, http://www.iht.com/cgi-bin/generic.cgi?template=atriclepr int.tmp.

50. de Wijk, "Transatlantic Relations," 185; Osica, "Poland," 302, 321.

51. Ivo H. Daalder, "The End of Atlanticism." *Survival* 45, no. 2 (summer 2003): 147–66.

52. Longhurst and Zaborowski, "The Future of European Security," 389.

53. Kupchan, "The Rise of Europe," 208.

54. Ibid., 225.

CHAPTER 2

1. G. John Ikenberry, *After Victory: Institutions, Strategic Restraints, and the Rebuilding of Order after Major Wars* (Princeton, N.J.: Princeton University Press, 2001), 164: "The United States sought to take advantage of the postwar juncture to lock in a set of institutions that would serve its interests well into the future."

2. Zbigniew Brzezinski, *Game Plan: A Geostrategic Framework for the Conduct of the U.S.-Soviet Contest* (Boston: Atlantic Monthly Press, 1986), 22.

3. Peter F. Drucker, "Trading Places," *The National Interest*, spring 2005, 101.

4. Ibid., 104.

5. John McCormick, *Understanding the European Union: A Concise Introduction*, 2nd ed. (Houndmills, Basingstoke: Palgrave, 2002), 12–18.

6. Alain Monnier, "The European Union at the Time of Enlargement," *Population-E* 59, no. 2 (2004): 318, 334 (figures for the United States, Russia, and Japan for 2000).

7. Council on Foreign Relations, *Renewing the Atlantic Partnership*, Task Force Report No. 51 (New York: Council on Foreign Relations Press, March 2004), 16.

8. Organization for Economic Cooperation and Development, *National Accounts of OECD Countries* (Paris: Organization for Economic Cooperation and Development, 1976), 118–19.

9. Drucker, "Trading Places," 107.

10. Vladislav Inozemtsev, "The U.S., EU and Russia in the 21st Century," *International Affairs* 48, no. 6 (2002): 128, quoting Eurostat, *Europe in Figures*, 5th ed. (London: The Stationery Office, 2000), 115.

11. Robert C. Pozen, "Mind the Gap: Can the New Europe Overtake the U.S. Economy?," *Foreign Affairs* 84, no. 2 (March/April 2005): 8, 11.

12. Ibid., 10.

13. Council on Foreign Relations, *Renewing the Atlantic Partnership*, 16.

14. Pozen, "Mind the Gap," 11.

15. William Drozdiak, "The North Atlantic Drift," *Foreign Affairs* 84, no. 1 (January/February 2005): 89.

16. Desmond Dinan, *Ever Closer Union: An Introduction to European Integration*, 2nd ed. (Houndmills, Basingstoke: Palgrave, 1994), 483–503 (on common commercial policy).

17. Ibid., 503–8 (on development policy).

18. Martin Holland, "Development Policy: Paradigm Shifts and the 'Normalization' of a Privileged Partnership?," in *Developments in the European Union 2*, ed. Maria Green Cowles and Desmond Dinan (Houndmills, Basingstoke: Palgrave, 2004), 276.

19. David Calleo, "The Strategic Implications of the Euro," *Survival* 41, no. 1 (spring 1999): 5.

20. Fred C. Bergsten, "The Dollar and the Euro," *Foreign Affairs* 76, no. 4 (July/August 1997): 83.

21. Dinan, *Ever Closer Union*, 464.

22. Drucker, "Trading Places," 103.

23. Joseph S. Nye, *Bound to Lead: The Changing Nature of American Power* (New York: Basic Books, 1990), 77.

24. Drucker, "Trading Places," 102.

25. Kenneth Katzman, "The Iran-Libya Sanctions Act (ILSA)," *CRS Report for Congress*, RS20871 (Washington, D.C.: Congressional Research Service, Library of Congress, April 19, 2005), 3–5.

26. Katia Vlachos-Dengler, *Off Track? The Future of the European Defense Industry* (Santa Monica, Calif.: RAND Corporation, 2004), 5.

27. Inozemtsev, "The U.S., EU and Russia in the 21st Century," 131.

28. Council on Foreign Relations, *Renewing the Atlantic Partnership*, 16–17.

CHAPTER 3

1. NATO, "The Alliance's Strategic Concept," Rome, November 8, 1991, sec. 11.

2. Anthony Forster and William Wallace, "What Is NATO For?," *Survival* 43, no. 4 (winter 2001–02): 108.

3. Dieter Mahncke, "The Changing Role of NATO," in *Redefining Transatlantic Security Relations: The Challenge of Change*, ed. Dieter Mahncke, Wyn Rees, and Wayne C. Thompson (Manchester: Manchester University Press, 2004), 54.

4. For example, John Mearsheimer, "Back to the Future: Instability in Europe after the Cold War," *International Security* 15, no. 1 (summer 1990): 5–56.

5. Ibid., 6.

6. Stephen M. Walt, *The Origin of Alliances* (Ithaca, N.Y.: Cornell University Press, 1987), 5.

7. Ibid., 283.

8. Karl Deutsch et al., *Political Community and the North Atlantic Area: International Organization in the Light of Historical Experience* (Princeton, N.J.: Princeton University Press, 1957), 5.

9. Mahncke, "The Changing Role of NATO," 53.

10. Ibid., 54.

11. Philip H. Gordon, "Bridging the Atlantic Divide," *Foreign Affairs* 82, no. 1 (January/February 2003): 75–77. Gordon argues that, in spite of the election of President Bush in 2001, the values of U.S. voters have not shifted fundamentally away from European values (76).

12. G. John Ikenberry, *After Victory: Institutions, Strategic Restraint, and the Rebuilding of Order after Major Wars* (Princeton, N.J.: Princeton University Press, 2001), 273.

13. Zbigniew Brzezinski, *Game Plan: A Geostrategic Framework for the Conduct of the U.S.-Soviet Contest* (Boston: Atlantic Monthly Press, 1986), 24.

14. Bruno Tertrais, "The Changing Nature of Military Alliances," *Washington Quarterly* 27, no. 2 (spring 2004): 136.

15. Ikenberry, *After Victory*, 258; Zbigniew Brzezinski, *The Grand Chessboard: American Primacy and Its Geostrategic Imperative* (New York: Basic Books, 1997), 40.

16. Mearsheimer, "Back to the Future," 54–55.

17. Tertrais, "The Changing Nature of Military Alliances," 143.

18. Ibid., 139.

19. Ibid., 141.

20. Council on Foreign Relations, *Renewing the Atlantic Partnership*, Task Force Report No. 51 (New York: Council on Foreign Relations Press, March 2004).

21. Dirk Nabers, "Transregional Security Cooperation after September 11, 2001," National Europe Centre Paper, no. 18 (Canberra: Australian National University, July 3–4, 2002), 9.

22. Ibid., 13.

23. Council on Foreign Relations, *Renewing the Atlantic Partnership*, 13.

CHAPTER 4

1. Elizabeth Pond, *The Rebirth of Europe*, 2nd ed. (Washington, D.C.: Brookings Institution Press, 2002), 196.

2. Anthony Forster and William Wallace, "What Is NATO For?," *Survival* 43, no. 4 (winter 2001–02): 108.

3. Peter Duignan, *NATO: Its Past, Present, and Future* (Stanford, Calif.: Hoover Institution Press, Stanford University, 2000), 69.

4. Henning Tewes, *Germany, Civilian Power and the New Europe: Enlarging NATO and the European Union* (Houndmills, Basingstoke: Palgrave, 2001), 152, 160–66.

5. Ibid., 180–81.

6. NATO, "Founding Act on Mutual Relations, Cooperation and Security between NATO and the Russian Federation," Paris, May 27, 1997, http://www.nato.int/docu/basictxt/fndact-a.htm.

7. Desmond Dinan, *Ever Closer Union: An Introduction to European Integration*, 2nd ed. (Houndmills, Basingstoke: Palgrave, 1999), 190–94.

8. Olaf Osica, "Poland: A New European Atlanticist at the Crossroads?," *European Security* 13, no. 4 (2004): 321.

9. James Sperling, "Two Tiers or Two Speeds? Constructing a Stable European Security Order," in *Two Tiers or Two Speeds? The European Security Order and the Enlargement of the European Union and NATO*, ed. James Sperling (Manchester: Manchester University Press, 1999), 187.

10. Richard Rupp, "NATO 1949 and NATO 2000: From Collective Defence toward Collective Security," in *NATO Enters the 21st Century*, ed. Ted Galen Carpenter (London: Frank Cass, 2001), 154, 172.

11. Julian Lindley-French, *Terms of Engagement: The Paradox of American Power and the Transatlantic Dilemma Post-September 11*, Chaillot Papers, no. 52 (Paris: Institute for Strategic Studies of the European Union, April 2003), 54.

12. NATO, "Founding Act on Mutual Relations, Cooperation and Security between NATO and the Russian Federation," Paris, May 27, 1997, http://www.nato.int/docu/basictxt/fndact-a.htm.

13. Pond, *The Rebirth of Europe*, 58.

14. Duignan, *NATO*, x.

15. Charles A. Kupchan, "Kosovo and the Future of U.S. Engagement in Europe: Continued Hegemony or Impending Retrenchment?," in *Alliance Politics, Kosovo, and NATO's War: Allied Force or Forced Allies?*, ed. Pierre Martin and Mark R. Brawley (Houndmills, Basingstoke: Palgrave, 2000), 75.

16. Ibid., 79.

17. David S. Yost, "The NATO Capabilities Gap and the European Union," *Survival* 42, no. 4 (winter 2000–01): 118: "The DCI involves 58 areas for the improvement of NATO's capabilities."

18. Ibid., 110.

19. Gregor Schöllgen, *Die Außenpolitik der Bundesrepublik Deutschland* (Munich: Beck, 1999), 72.

20. Pond, *The Rebirth of Europe*, 204.

21. Charles A. Kupchan, "The Rise of Europe, America's Changing Internationalism, and the End of U.S. Primacy," *Political Science Quarterly* 118, no. 2 (2003): 220.

22. Philip H. Gordon, "NATO after 11 September," *Survival* 43, no. 4 (winter 2001–02): 92.

23. Christoph Bertram, *Europe in the Balance: Securing the Peace Won in the Cold War* (Washington, D.C.: Carnegie Endowment for International Peace, 1995), 19.

24. Rupp, "NATO 1949 and NATO 2000," 175.

25. NATO, "The Alliance's Strategic Concept," Rome, November 8, 1991, sec. 6.

26. Ted Galen Carpenter, "NATO's New Strategic Concept: Coherent Blueprint or Conceptual Muddle?," in Carpenter, *NATO Enters the 21st Century*, 7–11.

27. Gordon, "NATO after 11 September," 93.

28. Ibid., 94.

29. Kupchan, "The Rise of Europe, America's Changing Internationalism, and the End of U.S. Primacy," 226.

30. John Mearsheimer, "Back to the Future: Instability in Europe after the Cold War," *International Security* 15, no. 1 (summer 1990): 6.

31. G. John Ikenberry, *After Victory: Institutions, Strategic Restraint, and the Rebuilding of Order after Major Wars* (Princeton, N.J.: Princeton University Press, 2001), 226.

32. Dinan, *Ever Closer Union,*133.

33. Christopher Layne, "Offshore Balancing Revisited," *Washington Quarterly* 25, no. 2 (spring 2002): 233–48.

34. David S. Yost, "Transatlantic Relations and Peace in Europe," *International Affairs* 78, no. 2 (April 2002): 291.

35. Ibid., 295.

36. Ibid., 298.

37. Ibid., 299.

38. Tewes, *Germany, Civilian Power and the New Europe*, 145.

39. Emil J. Kirchner, "Second Pillar and Eastern Enlargement: The Prospects for a European Security and Defence Identity," in *Two Tiers or Two Speeds? The European Security Order and the Enlargement of the European Union and NATO*, ed. James Sperling (Manchester: Manchester University Press, 1999), 47.

40. Sperling, "Two Tiers or Two Speeds?," 185.

41. Ibid.

42. Bertram, *Europe in the Balance*, 79.

43. Shaun Gregory, *French Defence Policy into the Twenty-first Century* (Houndmills, Basingstoke: Macmillan, 2000), 114.

44. Duignan, *NATO*, 60.

45. James P. Thomas, *The Military Challenges of Transatlantic Coalitions*, Adelphi Paper, no. 333, International Institute for Strategic Studies (Oxford: Oxford University Press, 2000), 66.

46. Kirchner, "Second Pillar and Eastern Enlargement," 51.

47. Bertram, *Europe in the Balance*, 85.

48. Dieter Mahncke, "The Changing role of NATO," in *Redefining Transatlantic Security Relations: The Challenge of Change*, ed. Dieter Mahncke, Wyn Rees, and Wayne C. Thompson (Manchester: Manchester University Press, 2004), 119.

49. Henry Kissinger, *Does America Need a Foreign Policy? Toward a Diplomacy for the 21st Century* (New York: Simon and Schuster, 2001), 81.

50. Bertram, *Europe in the Balance*, 85.

51. Frédéric Bozo, "La relation transatlantique et la 'longue' guerre contre le terrorisme," *Politique Étrangère* 67, no. 2 (April–June 2002): 346.

52. Ibid., 348.

53. Ibid., 349.

54. Forster and Wallace, "What Is NATO For?," 107.

55. Ibid., 111.

56. Ibid., 119.

CHAPTER 5

1. Desmond Dinan, *Ever Closer Union: An Introduction to European Integration*, 2nd ed. (Houndmills, Basingstoke: Palgrave, 1999), 133.

2. NATO, "The Alliance's Strategic Concept," Rome, November 8, 1991, sec. 8.

3. Gregor Schöllgen, *Die Außenpolitik der Bundesrepublik Deutschland* (Munich: Beck, 1999), 176.

4. Stephen M. Walt, "Why Alliances Endure or Collapse," *Survival* 39, no. 1 (spring 1997): 159.

5. NATO, "Declaration of the Heads of State and Government," Ministerial Meeting of the North Atlantic Council/North Atlantic Cooperation Council, NATO Headquarters, Brussels, January 10–11, 1994, 2, http://www.nato.int/docu/comm/49–95/c940111a.htm.

6. Ibid., 1.

7. Christoph Bertram, *Europe in the Balance: Securing the Peace Won in the Cold War* (Washington, D.C.: Carnegie Endowment for International Peace, 1995), 24.

8. Patrick McCarthy, "The Franco-German Axis from de Gaulle to Chirac," in *Europe's Franco-German Engine*, ed. David P. Calleo and Eric R. Staal (Washington, D.C.: Brookings Institution Press, 1998), 115.

9. Martin Ortega, "Petersberg Tasks, and Missions for the EU Military Forces," Briefing Paper (Paris: Institute for Strategic Studies of the European Union, February 2005), 1.

10. Emil J. Kirchner, "Second Pillar and Eastern Enlargement: The Prospects for a European Security and Defence Identity," in *Two Tiers or Two Speeds? The European Security Order and the Enlargement of the European Union and NATO*, ed. James Sperling (Manchester: Manchester University Press, 1999), 49.

11. Jean-Yves Haine, "ESDP: An Overview," Briefing Note (Paris: Institute for Strategic Studies of the European Union, 2004), 3.

12. Antonio Missiroli, "The Constitutional Treaty: 'Enabling Text' for Foreign Policy and Defence," Analysis Paper (Paris: Institute for Strategic Studies of the European Union, 2004).

13. Seven heads of states of EU member countries signaled the political will to overcome the setback of the referendums in France and the Netherlands in a joint statement: "Getting the Ship Back on Course," *International Herald Tribune*, July 15, 2005, http://www.iht.com/bin/print_ipub.php?file = /atricles/2005/07/14/o ...

14. Hans-Christian Hagmann, *European Crisis Management and Defence: The Search for Capabilities*, Adelphi Paper, no. 353, International Institute for Strategic Studies (Oxford: Oxford University Press, 2002), 40.

15. Jean-Yves Haine, "Berlin Plus," Briefing Paper (Paris: Institute for Strategic Studies of the European Union, 2003), 2.

16. European Union, *A Secure Europe in a Better World: European Security Strategy*, Document proposed by Javier Solana and adopted by the Heads of State and Government at the European Council in Brussels on 12 December 2003 (Paris: Institute for Strategic Studies of the European Union, 2003).

17. Katia Vlachos-Dengler, *Off Track? The Future of the European Defense Industry* (Santa Monica, Calif.: RAND Corporation, 2004), 5.

18. Burkard Schmitt, "European and Transatlantic Defense Industrial Strategies: A European Perspective," Analyses (Paris: Institute for Strategic Studies of the European Union, 2005), http://www.iss-eu.org/new/analysis/analy036.html.

19. Burkard Schmitt, "Armaments Cooperation in Europe," Briefing Paper (Paris: Institute for Strategic Studies of the European Union, January 2005), 1–2.

20. François Heisbourg, "French and German Approaches to Organizing Europe's Future Security and Defense: A French Perspective," in *Europe's Franco-German*

Engine, ed. David P. Calleo and Eric R. Staal (Washington, D.C.: Brookings Institution Press, 1998), 60.

21. Mary Elise Sarotte, *German Military Reform and European Security*, Adelphi Paper, no. 340, International Institute for Strategic Studies (Oxford: Oxford University Press, 2001), 51.

22. Yves Boyer, "The Next Phase of ESDP and the Key Role of the Military—A French View," in *The European Security Strategy: Paper Tiger or Catalyst for Joint Action*, ed. Marco Overhaus, Hanns W. Maull, and Sebastian Harnisch. *German Foreign Policy in Dialogue* 5, no. 13 (June 24, 2004): 21.

23. Ibid., 21–22.

24. Ibid., 18–19.

25. G. Lindström, with Giovanni Gasparini, "The Galileo Satellite System and Its Security Implications," Occasional Papers, no. 44 (Paris: Institute for Strategic Studies of the European Union, April 2003), 21–22.

26. Project for the New American Century, "Statement of Principles," June 3, 1997, http://www.newamericancentury.org/statementofprinciples.htm.

27. Compiled from International Institute for Strategic Studies, *The Military Balance, 2000–2001* (London: Oxford University Press/International Institute for Strategic Studies, 2000), 297–98.

28. Compiled from International Institute for Strategic Studies, *The Military Balance, 2004–2005* (London: Oxford University Press/International Institute for Strategic Studies, 2004), 353–54.

29. Kirchner, "Second Pillar and Eastern Enlargement," 57–58.

30. This was the subtitle of Burkhard Schmitt, *The European Union and Armaments: Getting a Bigger Bang for the Euro*, Chaillot Papers, no. 63 (Paris: Institute for Strategic Studies of the European Union, August 2003).

31. Elizabeth Pond, *The Rebirth of Europe*, 2nd ed. (Washington, D.C.: Brookings Institution Press, 2002), 208.

32. Rob de Wijk, "Transatlantic Relations: A View from the Netherlands," *International Journal* 59, no. 1 (winter 2003–04): 185–86.

33. Schmitt, *The European Union and Armaments*, 26.

34. Sarotte, *German Military Reform and European Security*, 54.

35. Lindström, "The Galileo Satellite System," 3.

36. Mark John, "EU Boosts New Battle Groups," Reuters, May 23, 2005, http://today.reuters.co.uk/PrinterFriendlyPopup.aspx?type = worldNews&storyID = uri:2005

37. Charles Grant, "EU Defence Takes a Step Forward," Briefing Note (London: Centre for European Reform, December 2003), 2–3.

38. Bradley Graham, "Rumsfeld Criticizes EU Defense Plan," *Washington Post*, December 3, 2003, A18; Laurent Zecchini, "Deux visions de l'Europe et de sa défense," *Le Monde*, October 7, 2003.

39. Hagmann, *European Crisis Management and Defence*, 50.

40. Dov Lynch and Antonio Missiroli, "ESDP Operations," Briefing Paper (Paris: Institute for Strategic Studies of the European Union, 2005), 1–4.

41. Hagmann, *European Crisis Management and Defence*, 25.

42. Kirchner, "Second Pillar and Eastern Enlargement," 46–47.

43. Ted Galen Carpenter, "NATO's New Strategic Concept: Coherent Blueprint or Conceptual Muddle?," in *NATO Enters the 21st Century*, ed. Ted Galen Carpenter (London: Frank Cass, 2001), 20.

44. Ibid., 21–22.

45. Geir Lundestad, *"Empire" by Invitation: The United States and European Integration 1945–1997* (Oxford: Oxford University Press, 1998), 169.

46. Carpenter, "NATO's New Strategic Concept," 24.

47. Ibid., 21.

48. Katia Vlachos-Dengler, *Off Track?*, iii.

49. Ibid., xviii–xxi, 110–17, 123–24.

50. Christoph Grams, *Das Medium Extended Air Defense System (MEADS)—Ein Prüfstein für Deutschlands Streitkräftetransformation?* DGAP Analyse, no. 2 (Berlin: Forschungsinstitut der Deutschen Gesellschaft für Auswärtige Politik, February 2005), 8–9.

51. Ethan B. Kapstein, "Capturing Fortress Europe: International Collaboration and the Joint Strike Fighter," *Survival* 46, no. 3 (autumn 2004): 138.

52. Ibid., 143.

53. Ibid., 147.

54. Ibid., 149.

55. Sarotte, *German Military Reform and European Security*, 70.

56. Hanns W. Maull, "Germany and the Use of Force: Still a 'Civilian Power'?" *Survival* 42, no. 2 (summer 2000): 56–80.

57. Adrian Hyde-Price, "'Of Dragons and Snakes': Contemporary German Security Policy," in *Developments in German Politics 2*, ed. Gordon Smith et al. (Houndmills, Basingstoke: Palgrave, 1996): 189.

58. Sarotte, *German Military Reform and European Security*,14.

59. Ibid., 44.

60. American Institute of Contemporary German Studies, "Redefining German Security: Prospects for *Bundeswehr* Reform," *German Issues* 25 (Baltimore: American Institute of Contemporary German Studies, The Johns Hopkins University, September 2001), 8–9.

61. Ibid., 45.

62. Ibid., 7.

63. Sarotte, *German Military Reform and European Security*, 28.

64. American Institute of Contemporary German Studies, "Redefining German Security," 3.

65. Ibid., 8.

66. Sarotte, *German Military Reform and European Security*, 37.

67. Ibid., 40.

68. Ibid., 41.

69. American Institute of Contemporary German Studies, "Redefining German Security," 42–43.

70. Ibid., 5–6.

71. Sarotte, *German Military Reform and European Security*, 62.

72. Michael Meimeth, "Deutsche und französische Perspektiven einer Gemeinsamen Europäischen Sicherheits- und Verteidigungspolitik," *Aus Politik und Zeitgeschichte*, no. B3–4 (2003): 28, referring to Minister Struck's speech in the Bundestag, December 5, 2002.

73. Ibid.,

74. Peter Struck, "Die neue Bundeswehr—Auf dem richtigen Weg. Erklärung der Bundesregierung durch den Bundesminister der Verteidigung, Dr. Peter Struck, am 11. März in Berlin," March 12, 2004, 2–3, http://www.bmvg.de/archiv/reden/minister/print/040311_regierung . . .

75. American Institute of Contemporary German Studies, "Redefining German Security," 27, commenting on General Kujat's *Material- und Ausrüstungskonzept.*

76. Ibid., 41.

77. Richard Rupp, "NATO 1949 and NATO 2000: From Collective Defence toward Collective Security," in Carpenter, *NATO Enters the 21st Century,* 175.

78. Christoph Bertram, *Europe in the Balance: Securing the Peace Won in the Cold War* (Washington, D.C.: Carnegie Endowment for International Peace, 1995), 19.

79. Nicole Gnesotto, "Reacting to America," *Survival* 44, no. 4 (winter 2002–03): 103.

80. Joseph S. Nye, *Bound to Lead: The Changing Nature of American Power* (New York: Basic Books, 1990), 4.

81. Deutsche Welle, "U.S. Confirms Troop Reductions in Germany," June 16, 2004, http://www.dw.world.de; *Financial Times Deutschland,* "US-Armee dampft Truppenpräsenz in Deutschland ein," April 12, 2005, http://www.ftd.de/pw/eu/2942.html?mode = print.

82. Hagmann, *European Crisis Management and Defence,* 56.

CHAPTER 6

1. Thomas L. Friedman, "NATO Tries to Ease Military Concerns in Eastern Europe," *New York Times,* June 7, 1991, A8.

2. Henning Tewes, *Germany, Civilian Power and the New Europe: Enlarging NATO and the European Union,* (Houndmills, Basingstoke: Palgrave, 2001), 152.

3. Anthony Laurence Gardner, *A New Era in US-EU Relations? The Clinton Administration and the New Transatlantic Agenda* (Aldershot: Ashgate, 1997), 65.

4. Ibid., 22.

5. Charles A. Kupchan, *The End of the American Era: U.S. Foreign Policy and the Geopolitics of the Twenty-first Century* (New York: Alfred A. Knopf, 2003), 65.

6. Ted Galen Carpenter, "NATO's New Strategic Concept: Coherent Blueprint or Conceptual Muddle?," in *NATO Enters the 21st Century,* ed. Ted Galen Carpenter (London: Frank Cass, 2001), 21.

7. Robert Kagan, "Power and Weakness," *Policy Review,* no. 113 (June/July 2002): 6.

8. Philip H. Gordon, "NATO after 11 September," *Survival* 43, no. 4 (winter 2001–02): 94.

9. Charles Grant, "EU Defence Takes a Step Forward," Briefing Note (London: Centre for European Reform, December 2003), 2–3. Jean-Yves Haine, "Berlin Plus," Briefing Paper (Paris: Institute for Strategic Studies of the European Union, 2003).

10. Robert Wilkie, "Fortress Europa: European Defense and the Future of the North Atlantic Alliance," *Parameters* 32, no. 4 (winter 2002–03): 45.

11. Gordon, "NATO after 11 September," 75.

12. Ibid., 81.

13. Ibid., 78.

14. Kupchan, *The End of the American Era,* 267.

15. Olaf Osica, "Poland: A New European Atlanticist at a Crossroads?," *European Security* 13, no. 4 (2004): 302.

16. Deutsche Welle, "U.S. Confirms Troop Reductions in Germany," June 16, 2004, http://www.dw.world.de; *Financial Times Deutschland,* "US-Armee dampft Truppenpräsenz in Deutschland ein," April 12, 2005, http://www.ftd.de/pw/eu/2942.html?mode = print.

17. Norman Birnbaum, "Bush zum Zweiten," *Blätter für deutsche und internationale Politik* 50, no. 2 (February 2005): 170–71.

18. Council on Foreign Relations, *Renewing the Atlantic Partnership*, Task Force Report No. 51 (New York: Council on Foreign Relations Press, March 2004), 7.

19. Judy Dempsey, "U.S. Rebuffs Germany on Plan for NATO," *International Herald Tribune*, February 15, 2005, http://www.iht.com/bin/print_ipub.php?file = / articles/2005/02/14/news/munich.html.

20. NATO Update, "NATO Leaders Express Unity on Iraq, Reaffirm Values," February 22, 2005, http://www.nato.int/docu/update/2005/02-february/e0222a.htm.

21. NATO, "Statement Issued by the Heads of State and Government Participating in a Meeting of the North Atlantic Council in Brussels," February 22, 2005, http://www.nato.int/docu/pr/2005/p05–022e.htm.

22. Gerhard Schröder, "Speech on [*sic*] the 41th Munich Conference on Security Policy," February 12, 2005, 2, http://www.securityconference.de/konferenzen/ rede.php?menu_2005 = &menu_konferenzen = &sprache = en&id = 143&print = &.

23. Ibid.

24. Jeanne Rubner and Christian Wernicke, "Wir brauchen keinen Dritten Weg," *Süddeutsche Zeitung*, April 20, 2005, http://www.sueddeutsche.de/ausland/ artikel/642/51591/print.html.

25. Schröder, "Speech," 2, 4.

26. Gunther Hellmann, "American Needs Meet German Ambitions," *International Herald Tribune*, February 23, 2005, http://www.iht.com/bin/print_ipub.php?file = / articles/2005/02/22/opinion/edhell.html.

27. Philip H. Gordon, "Bridging the Atlantic Divide," *Foreign Affairs* 82, no. 1 (January/ February 2003): 72.

CHAPTER 7

1. Elizabeth Pond, *The Rebirth of Europe*, 2nd ed. (Washington, D.C.: Brookings Institution Press, 2002), 204.

2. Anthony J. Blinken, "The False Crisis over the Atlantic," *Foreign Affairs* 80, no. 3 (May/June 2001): 45.

3. Ted Galen Carpenter, "NATO's New Strategic Concept: Coherent Blueprint or Conceptual Muddle?," in *NATO Enters the 21st Century*, ed. Ted Galen Carpenter (London: Frank Cass, 2001), 24.

4. David P. Calleo, *Europe's Future: The Grand Alternatives* (New York: W. W. Norton, 1967), chaps. 3–5.

5. Charles A. Kupchan, "The Rise of Europe, America's Changing Internationalism, and the End of U.S. Primacy," *Political Science Quarterly* 118, no. 2 (summer 2003): 226.

6. Peter Duignan, *NATO: Its Past, Present, and Future* (Stanford, Calif.: Hoover Institution Press, Stanford University, 2000), 4.

7. Kupchan, "The Rise of Europe," 226.

8. Ibid., 219.

9. Charles A. Kupchan, "Kosovo and the Future of U.S. Engagement in Europe: Continued Hegemony or Impending Retrenchment?," in *Alliance Politics, Kosovo, and NATO's War: Allied Force or Forced Allies?*, ed. Pierre Martin and Mark R. Brawley (Houndmills, Basingstoke: Palgrave, 2000), 75.

10. Ibid., 79.

11. Stephen M. Walt, "Beyond Bin Laden: Reshaping U.S. Foreign Policy," *International Security* 26, no. 3 (winter 2001/02): 77.

12. David S. Yost, "Transatlantic Relations and Peace in Europe," *International Affairs* 78, no. 2 (April 2002): 286.

13. Ibid., 294.

14. John J. Mearsheimer, "Back to the Future: Instability in Europe after the Cold War," *International Security* 15, no. 1 (summer 1990): 5–56.

15. Kupchan, "The Rise of Europe," 226.

16. Samuel P. Huntington, "The U.S.—Decline or Renewal?" *Foreign Affairs* 67, no. 2 (winter 1988–89): 93.

17. Jean-Jacques Servan-Schreiber, *Le Défi Américain,* (Paris: Denoel, 1967), English translation: *The American Challenge* (New York: Atheneum, 1968).

18. Zbigniew Brzezinski, *The Grand Chessboard: American Primacy and Its Geostrategic Imperatives* (New York: Basic Books, 1997), 31.

19. Ibid., 35.

20. Charles A. Kupchan, *The End of the American Era: U.S. Foreign Policy and the Geopolitics of the Twenty-first Century* (New York: Alfred A. Knopf, 2003), 62, 63.

21. Joseph S. Nye, *Bound to Lead: The Changing Nature of American Power* (New York: Basic Books, 1990), 143–44.

22. Antonio Missiroli, "The Constitutional Treaty: 'Enabling Text' for Foreign Policy and Defence," Analysis Paper (Paris: Institute for Strategic Studies of the European Union, October 2004), 1, http://www.iss-eu.org/new/analysis/analy097.html.

23. Ibid.,

24. Kupchan, "Kosovo and the Future of U.S. Engagement in Europe," 87.

25. James Sperling, "Two Tiers or Two Speeds? Constructing a Stable European Security Order," in *Two Tiers or Two Speeds? The European Security Order and the Enlargement of the European Union and NATO,* ed. James Sperling (Manchester: Manchester University Press, 1999), 185.

26. Ibid., 195.

27. American Institute of Contemporary German Studies, "Redefining German Security: Prospects for *Bundeswehr* Reform," *German Issues* 25 (Baltimore: American Institute of Contemporary German Studies, The Johns Hopkins University, September 2001), 25.

28. Kupchan, "Kosovo and the Future of U.S. Engagement in Europe," 88.

29. Andrew Moravcsik, "Striking a New Transatlantic Bargain," *Foreign Affairs* 82, no. 4 (July/August 2003): 84.

30. Ibid., 74.

31. Julian Lindley-French, *Terms of Engagement: The Paradox of American Power and the Transatlantic Dilemma Post-September 11,* Chaillot Papers, no. 52 (Paris: Institute for Strategic Studies of the European Union, May 2002), 15, 14.

32. James P. Thomas, *The Military Challenges of Transatlantic Coalitions,* Adelphi Paper, no. 333, International Institute for Strategic Studies (Oxford: Oxford University Press, 2000), 72, 77.

33. Dimitrios Triantaphyllou, "The Balkans between Stabilisation and Membership," in *Partners and Neighbours: A CFSP for a Wider Europe,* ed. Judy Batt et al., Chaillot Papers, no. 64 (Paris: Institute for Strategic Studies of the European Union, September 2003), 63.

34. Robert E. Hunter, "Europe's Leverage," *Washington Quarterly* 27, no. 1 (winter 2003–04): 96.

35. Kupchan, "The Rise of Europe," 226.

36. Kupchan, "Kosovo and the Future of U.S. Engagement in Europe," 84.

37. Lindley-French, *Terms of Engagement*, 16.

38. Anthony Laurence Gardner, *A New Era in US-EU Relations? The Clinton Administration and the New Transatlantic Agenda* (Aldershot: Ashgate, 1997), 56.

39. Hunter, "Europe's Leverage," 106, 107.

40. Fred C. Bergsten, "America and Europe: Clash of the Titans?," *Foreign Affairs* 78, no. 2 (March/April 1999): 21.

41. Hans-Christian Hagmann, *European Crisis Management and Defence: The Search for Capabilities*, Adelphi Paper, no. 353, International Institute for Strategic Studies (Oxford: Oxford University Press, 2002), 57.

42. Ibid., 58.

43. Ibid., 59.

Bibliography

Allin, Dana H. *NATO's Balkan Interventions.* Adelphi Paper, no. 347. International Institute for Strategic Studies. Oxford: Oxford University Press, 2002.

American Institute of Contemporary German Studies. "Redefining German Security: Prospects for *Bundeswehr* Reform." *German Issues* 25. Baltimore: American Institute of Contemporary German Studies, The Johns Hopkins University, September 2001.

Andréani, Giles. "L'Europe de la défense: y a-t-il encore une ambition française?" *Politique Étrangère* 67, no. 4 (winter 2002–03): 983–1000.

Andréani, Giles, Christoph Bertram, and Charles Grant. *Europe's Military Revolution.* London: Centre for European Reform, 2001.

Becher, Klaus. "Has-Been, Wannabe, or Leader: Europe's Role in the World after the 2003 European Security Strategy." *European Security* 13, no. 4 (2004): 345–59.

Bereuter, Doug, and John Lis. "Broadening the Transatlantic Relationship." *Washington Quarterly* 27, no. 1 (winter 2003–04): 147–62.

Bergsten, Fred C. "America and Europe: Clash of the Titans?" *Foreign Affairs* 78, no. 2 (March/April 1999): 20–34.

———. "The Dollar and the Euro." *Foreign Affairs* 76, no. 4 (July/August 1997): 83–95.

Bertram, Christoph. *Europe in the Balance: Securing the Peace Won in the Cold War.* Washington, D.C.: Carnegie Endowment for International Peace, 1995.

Binnendijk, Hans, and Richard Kugler. "Transforming European Forces." *Survival* 44, no. 3 (autumn 2002): 117–32.

Birnbaum, Norman. "Bush zum Zweiten." *Blätter für deutsche und internationale Politik* 50, no. 2 (February 2005): 164–72.

Blinken, Anthony J. "The False Crisis over the Atlantic." *Foreign Affairs* 80, no. 3 (May/June 2001): 35–48.

Borwaski, John. "NATO beyond 2000: A New Flashpoint for European Security." *European Security* 9, no. 2 (summer 2000): 1–12.

Boyer, Yves. "The Next Phase of ESDP and the Key Role of the Military—A French View." In *The European Security Strategy: Paper Tiger or Catalyst for Joint Action*, ed. Marco Overhaus, Hanns W. Maull, and Sebastian Harnisch. *German Foreign Policy in Dialogue* 5, no. 13 (24 June 2004): 15–23.

Bozo, Frédéric. "La relation transatlantique et la 'longue' guerre contre le terrorisme." *Politique Étrangère* 67, no. 2 (April–June 2002): 337–51.

Brenner, Michael. *Terms of Engagement: The United States and the European Security Identity*. Published with the Center for Strategic and International Studies, Washington D.C. Westport, Conn.: Praeger, 1998.

Brzezinski, Zbigniev. *Game Plan: A Geostrategic Framework for the Conduct of the U.S.-Soviet Contest*. Boston: Atlantic Monthly Press, 1986.

———. *The Grand Chessboard: American Primacy and Its Geostrategic Imperatives*. New York: Basic Books, 1997.

Burwell, Frances G. "Cooperation in US-European Relations." In *The United States and Europe in the Global Arena*, ed. Frances G. Burwell and Ivo H. Daalder, 276–302. Houndmills, Basingstoke: Macmillan, 1999.

Calleo, David P. *The Atlantic Fantasy*. Baltimore: The Johns Hopkins University Press, 1970.

———. *Europe's Future: The Grand Alternatives*. New York: W. W. Norton, 1967.

———. "The Strategic Implications of the Euro." *Survival* 41, no. 1 (spring 1999): 5–19.

Calleo, David P., and Eric R. Staal, eds. *Europe's Franco-German Engine*. Washington, D.C.: Brookings Institution Press, 1998.

Campbell, Kurt M. "The End of Alliances? Not So Fast." *Washington Quarterly* 27, no. 2 (spring 2004): 151–63.

Carpenter, Ted Galen. *NATO Enters the 21st Century*. London: Frank Cass, 2001.

———. "NATO's New Strategic Concept: Coherent Blueprint or Conceptual Muddle?" In *NATO Enters the 21st Century*, ed. Ted Galen Carpenter, 7–28. London: Frank Cass, 2001.

Cornish, Paul "NATO: The Practice and Politics of Transformation." *International Affairs* 80, no. 1 (2004): 63–74.

Council on Foreign Relations. *Renewing the Atlantic Partnership*. Task Force Report No. 51. New York: Council on Foreign Relations Press, March 2004.

Daalder, Ivo H. "The End of Atlanticism." *Survival* 45, no. 2 (summer 2003): 147–66.

Daalder, Ivo, and James M. Goldgeier. "Putting Europe First." *Survival* 43, no. 1 (spring 2001): 71–91.

Dassu, Marta, and Nicholas Whyte. "America's Balkan Disengagement?" *Survival* 43, no. 4 (2001): 123–36.

Dempsey, Judy. "U.S. Rebuffs Germany on Plan for NATO." *International Herald Tribune*, February 15, 2005, http://www.iht.com/bin/print_ipub.php?file = / articles/2005/02/14/news/munich.html.

Deutsch, Karl W., et al. *Political Community and the North Atlantic Area: International Organisation in the Light of Historical Experience*. Princeton, N.J.: Princeton University Press, 1957.

Deutsche Welle. "U.S. Confirms Troop Reductions in Germany." June 16, 2004, http://www.dw.world.de.

Dinan, Desmond. *Ever Closer Union: An Introduction to European Integration.* 2nd ed. Houndmills, Basingstoke: Palgrave, 1999.

Doran, Charles F. "Economics, Philosophy of History, and the 'Single Dynamic' of Power Cycle Theory: Expectations, Competition, and Statecraft." *International Political Science Review* 24, no. 1 (2003): 13–49.

Drozdiak, William. "The North Atlantic Drift." *Foreign Affairs* 84, no. 1 (January/February 2005): 88–98.

Drucker, Peter F. "Trading Places." *The National Interest*, no. 79 (spring 2005): 101–07.

Duignan, Peter. *NATO: Its Past, Present, and Future.* Stanford, California: Hoover Institution Press, Stanford University, 2000.

European Union. *A Secure Europe in a Better World: European Security Strategy.* Document proposed by Javier Solana and adopted by the Heads of State and Government at the European Council in Brussels on 12 December 2003. Paris: Institute for Strategic Studies of the European Union, 2003.

Financial Times Deutschland. "US-Armee dampft Truppenpräsenz in Deutschland ein." April 12, 2005, http://www.ftd.de/pw/eu/2942.html?mode = print.

Forster, Anthony, and William Wallace. "What Is NATO For?" *Survival* 43, no. 4 (winter 2001–02): 107–22.

Friedman, Thomas L. "NATO Tries to Ease Military Concerns in Eastern Europe." *New York Times*, June 7, 1991, A8.

Fuller, Thomas. "EU's 'Big Three' Agree on Defense." *International Herald Tribune*, November 29, 2003, http://www.iht.com/cgi-bin/generic.cgi?template = atricleprint.tmp.

Gaertner, Heinz. "European Security, the Transatlantic Link and Crisis Management." In *Europe's New Security Challenges*, ed. Heinz Gaertner, Adrian Hyde-Price, and Erich Reiter, 125–48. Boulder, Colo.: Lynne Rienner Publishers, 2001.

Gardner, Anthony Laurence. *A New Era in US-EU Relations? The Clinton Administration and the New Transatlantic Agenda.* Aldershot: Ashgate, 1997.

Giegerich, Bastian, and William Wallace. "Not Such a Soft Power: The External Deployment of European Forces." *Survival* 46, no. 2 (summer 2004): 163–82.

Gnesotto, Nicole. "Reacting to America." *Survival* 44, no. 4 (winter 2002–03): 99–106.

Gordon, Philip H. "Bridging the Atlantic Divide." *Foreign Affairs* 82, no. 1 (January/February 2003): 70–83.

———. "NATO after 11 September." *Survival* 43, no. 4 (winter 2001–02): 89–106.

Graham, Bradley. "Rumsfeld Criticizes EU Defense Plan." *Washington Post*, December 3, 2003, A18.

Grams, Christoph. *Das Medium Extended Air Defense System (MEADS)—Ein Prüfstein für Deutschlands Streitkräftetransformation?* DGAP Analyse, no. 2. Berlin: Forschungsinstitut der Deutschen Gesellschaft für Auswärtige Politik, February 2005.

Grant, Charles. "EU Defence Takes a Step Forward." Briefing Note. London: Centre for European Reform, December 2003.

Gregory, Shaun. *French Defence Policy into the Twenty-first Century.* Houndmills, Basingstoke: Macmillan, 2000.

Hagmann, Hans-Christian. *European Crisis Management and Defence: The Search for Capabilities.* Adelphi Paper, no. 353. International Institute for Strategic Studies. Oxford: Oxford University Press, 2002.

Haine, Jean-Yves Haine. "Berlin Plus." Briefing Paper. Paris: Institute for Strategic Studies of the European Union, 2003.

———. "ESDP: An Overview." Briefing Note. Paris: Institute for Strategic Studies of the European Union, 2004.

Ham, Peter van. "Europe's Common Defense Policy: Implications for the Trans-Atlantic Relationship." *Security Dialogue* 31, no. 2 (June 2000): 215–28.

Hassner, Pierre. "The United States: The Empire or Force or the Force of Empire?" Chaillot Papers, no. 54. Paris: Institute for Strategic Studies of the European Union, September 2002.

Heisbourg, François. "French and German Approaches to Organizing Europe's Future Security and Defense: A French Perspective." In *Europe's Franco-German Engine*, ed. David P. Calleo and Eric R. Staal, 47–70. Washington, D.C.: Brookings Institution Press, 1998.

Hillen, John. "Superpowers Don't Do Windows." *Orbis* 41, no. 2 (spring 1997): 241–58.

Holland, Martin. "Development Policy: Paradigm Shifts and the 'Normalization' of a Privileged Partnership?" In *Developments in the European Union 2*, ed. Maria Green Cowles and Desmond Dinan, 275–95. Houndmills, Basingstoke: Palgrave, 2004.

Howorth, Jolyon. "Britain, France and the European Defence Initiative." *Survival* 42, no. 2 (summer 2000): 33–55.

———. "France, Britain and the Euro-Atlantic Crisis." *Survival* 45, no. 4 (winter 2003–04): 173–92.

Hunter, Robert E. "Europe's Leverage." *Washington Quarterly* 27, no. 1 (winter 2003–04): 91–110.

Huntington, Samuel P. "The Clash of Civilizations?" *Foreign Affairs* 72, no. 3 (summer 1993): 22–49.

———. "The Lonely Superpower." *Foreign Affairs* 78, no. 2 (March/April 1999): 35–49.

———. "The U.S.—Decline or Renewal?" *Foreign Affairs* 67, no. 2 (winter 1988–89): 76–96.

Hyde-Price, Adrian. "'Of Dragons and Snakes': Contemporary German Security Policy." In *Developments in German Politics 2*, ed. Gordon Smith et al., 173–91. Houndmills, Basingstoke: Palgrave, 1996.

Ikenberry, G. John. *After Victory: Institutions, Strategic Restraints, and the Rebuilding of Order after Major Wars*. Princeton, N.J.: Princeton University Press, 2001.

———. "The End of the Neo-Conservative Moment." *Survival* 46, no. 1 (spring 2004): 7–22.

Inozemtsev, Vladislav. "The U.S., EU and Russia in the 21st Century." *International Affairs* 48, no. 6 (2002): 126–38.

International Institute for Strategic Studies. *The Military Balance, 2000–2001*. London: Oxford University Press/International Institute for Strategic Studies, 2000.

———. *The Military Balance, 2004–2005*. London: Oxford University Press/International Institute for Strategic Studies, 2004.

Kagan, Robert. "Power and Weakness." *Policy Review*, no. 113 (June/July 2002): 3–28.

Kaplan, Lawrence S. *The Long Entanglement: NATO's First Fifty Years*. Westport, Conn.: Praeger, 1999.

Kapstein, Ethan B. "Capturing Fortress Europe: International Collaboration and the Joint Strike Fighter." *Survival* 46, no. 3 (autumn 2004): 137–60.

Kirchner, Emil J. "Second Pillar and Eastern Enlargement: The Prospects for a European Security and Defence Identity." In *Two Tiers or Two Speeds? The European Security Order and the Enlargement of the European Union and NATO*, ed. James Sperling, 46–62. Manchester: Manchester University Press, 1999.

Kissinger, Henry A. *Does America Need a Foreign Policy? Toward a Diplomacy for the 21st Century*. New York: Simon and Schuster, 2001.

———. *The Troubled Partnership: A Re-appraisal of the Atlantic Alliance*. Garden City, N.Y.: Anchor Books, 1966.

———. "The Year of Europe. Address to the Associated Press Annual Luncheon, New York, April 23, 1973." In *American Foreign Policy*, 3rd ed., 99–103. New York: W. W. Norton, 1977.

Krauthammer, Charles. "The Unipolar Moment." *Foreign Affairs* 70, no. 1 (1991): 23–33.

Kupchan, Charles A. *The End of the American Era: U.S. Foreign Policy and the Geopolitics of the Twenty-first Century*. New York: Alfred A. Knopf, 2003.

———. "Kosovo and the Future of U.S. Engagement in Europe: Continued Hegemony or Impending Retrenchment?" In *Alliance Politics, Kosovo, and NATO's War: Allied Force or Forced Allies?*, ed. Pierre Martin and Mark R. Brawley, 75–90. Houndmills, Basingstoke: Palgrave, 2000.

———. "The Rise of Europe, America's Changing Internationalism, and the End of U.S. Primacy." *Political Science Quarterly* 118, no. 2 (2003): 205–31.

Lantis, Jeffrey S. "American Perspectives on the Transatlantic Security Agenda." *European Security* 13, no. 4 (2004): 361–80.

Layne, Christopher. "Offshore Balancing Revisited." *Washington Quarterly*, 25, no. 2 (spring 2002), 233–48.

Lindley-French, Julian. *Terms of Engagement: The Paradox of American Power and the Transatlantic Dilemma Post-September 11*. Chaillot Papers, no. 52. Paris: Institute for Strategic Studies of the European Union, May 2002.

Lindström, Gustav, with Giovanni Gasparini. "The Galileo Satellite System and Its Security Implications." Occasional Papers, no. 44. Paris: Institute for Strategic Studies of the European Union, April 2003.

Longhurst, Kerry, and Marcin Zaborowski. "The Future of European Security." *European Security* 13, no. 4 (2004): 381–91.

Lundestad, Geir. *"Empire" by Invitation: The United States and European Integration 1945–1997*. Oxford: Oxford University Press, 1998.

Lynch, Dov, and Antonio Missiroli. "ESDP Operations." Briefing Paper. Paris: Institute for Strategic Studies of the European Union, 2005.

Mahncke, Dieter. "The Changing Role of NATO." In *Redefining Transatlantic Security Relations: The Challenge of Change*, ed. Dieter Mahncke, Wyn Rees, and Wayne C. Thompson, 52–83. Manchester: Manchester University Press, 2004.

Maull, Hanns W. "Germany and the Use of Force: Still a 'Civilian Power'?" *Survival* 42, no. 2 (summer 2000): 56–80.

McCarthy, Patrick. "The Franco-German Axis from de Gaulle to Chirac." In *Europe's Franco-German Engine*, ed. David P. Calleo and Eric R. Staal, 101–35. Washington, D.C.: Brookings Institution Press, 1998.

McCormick, John. *Understanding the European Union: A Concise Introduction*. 2nd ed. Houndmills, Basingstoke: Palgrave, 2002.

Mearsheimer, John J. "Back to the Future: Instability in Europe after the Cold War." *International Security* 15, no. 1 (summer 1990): 5–56.

Meimeth, Michael. "Deutsche und französische Perspektiven einer Gemeinsamen Europäischen Sicherheits- und Verteidigungspolitik." *Aus Politik und Zeitgeschichte*, no. B3–4 (2003): 21–30.

Menon, Anand. "From Crisis to Catharsis: ESDP after Iraq." *International Affairs* 80, no. 4 (2004): 631–48.

Meyer, Steven E. "Carcass of Dead Politics: The Irrelevance of NATO." *Parameters* 33, no. 4 (winter 2003–04): 83–97.

Missiroli, Antonio. "The Constitutional Treaty: 'Enabling Text' for Foreign Policy and Defence." Analysis Paper. Paris: Institute for Strategic Studies of the European Union, 2004.

———. "EU-NATO Cooperation in Crisis Management: No Turkish Delight for ESDP." *Security Dialogue* 33, no. 1 (2002): 9–26.

Monnier, Alain. "The European Union at the Time of Enlargement," *Population-E* 59, no. 2 (2004): 315–36.

Moravcsik, Andrew. "Striking a New Transatlantic Bargain." *Foreign Affairs* 82, no. 4 (July/August 2003): 74–89.

Nabers, Dirk. "Transregional Security Cooperation after September 11, 2001." National Europe Centre Paper, no. 18, Canberra: Australian National University, July 3–4, 2002.

NATO. "The Alliance's Strategic Concept." Rome, November 8, 1991.

———. "Declaration of the Heads of State and Government." Ministerial Meeting of the North Atlantic Council/North Atlantic Cooperation Council, NATO Headquarters, Brussels, January 10–11, 1994, http://www.nato.int/docu/comm/49–95/c940111a.htm.

———. "Founding Act on Mutual Relations, Cooperation and Security between NATO and the Russian Federation." Paris, May 27, 1997, http://www.nato.int/docu/basictxt/fndact-a.htm.

———. "Statement issued by the Heads of State and Government Participating in a Meeting of the North Atlantic Council in Brussels." February 22, 2005, http://www.nato.int/docu/pr/2005/p05–022e.htm.

NATO Update. "NATO Leaders Express Unity on Iraq, Reaffirm Values." February 22, 2005, http://www.nato.int/docu/update/2005/02-february/e0222a.htm.

New York Times. "Excerpts from Pentagon's Plan: Prevent the Re-Emergence of a New Rival." March 8, 1992, sec. 1, p. 14L.

Nye, Joseph S. *Bound to Lead: The Changing Nature of American Power.* New York: Basic Books, 1990.

———. *The Paradox of American Power: Why the World's Only Superpower Can't Go It Alone.* Oxford: Oxford University Press, 2002.

———. *Soft Power: The Means to Success in World Politics.* New York: Public Affairs, 2004.

Olsen, Gorm Rye. "The EU and Conflict Management in African Emergencies." *International Peacekeeping* 9, no. 3 (autumn 2002): 87–102.

Ortega, Martin. "Petersberg Tasks, and Missions for the EU Military Forces." Briefing Paper. Paris: Institute for Strategic Studies of the European Union, February 2005.

Osica, Olaf. "Poland: A New European Atlanticist at a Crossroads?" *European Security* 13, no. 4 (2004): 301–22.

———. "A Secure Poland in a Better Union? The ESS as Seen from Warsaw's Perspective." In *The European Security Strategy: Paper Tiger or Catalyst for Joint*

Action. Part II, ed. Marco Overhaus, Hanns W. Maull, and Sebastian Harnisch. *German Foreign Policy in Dialogue*, 5, no. 14 (October 14, 2004): 9–15.

Overhaus, Marco. "In Search of a Post-Hegemonic Order: Germany, NATO and the European Security and Defence Policy." *German Politics* 13, no. 4 (December 2004): 551–68.

Parmentier, Guillaume. "Redressing NATO's Imbalances." *Survival* 42, no. 2 (summer 2000): 96–112.

Pond, Elizabeth. "Kosovo: Catalyst for Europe." *Washington Quarterly* 22, no. 4 (autumn 1999): 77–92.

———. *The Rebirth of Europe*. 2nd ed. Washington, D.C.: Brookings Institution Press, 2002.

Posen, Barry R. "ESDP and the Structure of World Power." *The International Spectator* 39, no. 1 (2004): 5–17.

Pozen, Robert C. "Mind the Gap: Can the New Europe Overtake the U.S. Economy?" *Foreign Affairs* 84, no. 2 (March/April 2005): 8–12.

Project for the New American Century. "Statement of Principles." June 3, 1997.

Rasmussen, Mikkel V. "Turbulent Neighbourhoods: How to Deploy the EU's Rapid Reaction Force." *Contemporary Security Policy* 23, no. 2 (August 2002): 39–60.

Rupp, Richard. "NATO 1949 and NATO 2000: From Collective Defence toward Collective Security." In *NATO Enters the 21st Century*, ed. Ted Galen Carpenter, 154–76. London: Frank Cass, 2001.

Sarotte, Mary Elise. *German Military Reform and European Security*. Adelphi Paper, no. 340. International Institute for Strategic Studies. Oxford: Oxford University Press, 2001.

Schmitt, Burkard. "Armaments Cooperation in Europe." Briefing Paper. Paris: Institute for Strategic Studies of the European Union, January 2005.

———. "European and Transatlantic Defense Industrial Strategies: A European Perspective." Analyses. Paris: Institute for Strategic Studies of the European Union, 2005, http://www.iss-eu.org/new/analysis/analy036.html.

———. *The European Union and Armaments. Getting a bigger bang for the Euro*. Chaillot Papers, no. 63. Paris: Institute for Strategic Studies of the European Union, August 2003.

Schmitt, Burkard, ed. *Between Cooperation and Competition: The Transatlantic Defence Market*. Chaillot Paper, no. 44. Paris: Institute for Strategic Studies of the European Union, January 2001.

Schmitt, Gary. "NATO and EU Defense Plans." *Project for a New American Century*, October 17, 2003, http://www.newamericancentury.org/nato-20031017.htm.

Schöllgen, Gregor. *Die Außenpolitik der Bundesrepublik Deutschland*. Munich: Beck, 1999.

Schröder, Gerhard. "Speech on [*sic*] the 41th Munich Conference on Security Policy." February 12, 2005, 2, http://www.securityconference.de/konferenzen/rede.php?menu_2005 = &menu_konferenzen = &sprache = en&id = 143&print = &.

Sedivy, Jiri, and Marcin Zaborowski. "Old Europe, New Europe and Transatlantic Relations." *European Security* 13, no. 3 (2004): 187–213.

Servan-Schreiber, Jean-Jacques. *Le Défi Américain*. Paris: Denoel, 1967; English translation: *The American Challenge*. New York: Atheneum, 1968.

Sharp, Jane M. O. "Tony Blair, Iraq and the Special Relationship". *International Journal* 59, no. 1 (winter 2003–04): 59–86.

Sikorski, Radek. "NATO Has Not Perished Yet while We Are Still Alive." *The National Interest*, no. 75 (spring 2004): 69–72.

Smith, Martin A., and Graham Timmins. *Building a Bigger Europe: EU and NATO Enlargement in Comparative Perspective.* Aldershot: Ashgate, 2000.

Sperling, James. "Two Tiers or Two Speeds? Constructing a Stable European Security Order." In *Two Tiers or Two Speeds? The European Security Order and the Enlargement of the European Union and NATO*, ed. James Sperling, 181–98. Manchester: Manchester University Press, 1999.

Steinberg, James B. "An Elective Partnership: Salvaging Transatlantic Relations." *Survival* 45, no. 2 (summer 2003): 113–46.

Struck, Peter. "Die neue Bundeswehr—Auf dem richtigen Weg. Erklärung der Bundesregierung durch den Bundesminister der Verteidigung, Dr. Peter Struck, am 11. März in Berlin." Berlin, March 12, 2004, http://www.bmvg. de/archiv/reden/minister/print/040311_regierung.

Tertrais, Bruno. "The Changing Nature of Military Alliances." *Washington Quarterly* 27, no. 2 (spring 2004): 135–50.

Tewes, Henning. *Germany, Civilian Power and the New Europe.* Houndmills, Basingstoke: Macmillan, 2001.

Thomas, James P. *The Military Challenges of Transatlantic Coalitions.* Adelphi Paper, no. 333. International Institute for Strategic Studies. Oxford: Oxford University Press, 2000.

Thomson, James. "US Interests and the Fate of the Alliance." *Survival* 45, no. 4 (winter 2003–04): 207–20.

Todd, Emmanuel. *Weltmacht USA: Ein Nachruf.* Munich: Piper, 2003 (German translation of *Après l'empire: Essai sur la d écomposition du système américain.* Paris: Éditions Gallimard, 2002).

Triantaphyllou, Dimitrios. "The Balkans between Stabilisation and Membership." In *Partners and Neighbours: A CFSP for a Wider Europe*, ed. Judy Batt et al., 60–76. Chaillot Papers, no. 64. Paris: Institute for Strategic Studies of the European Union, September 2003.

Vlachos-Dengler, Katia. *Off Track? The Future of the European Defense Industry.* Santa Monica, Calif.: RAND Corporation, 2004.

Voigt, Karsten D. "Begründung eines neuen Atlantizismus: Von Partnerschaft zu euroatlantischer Gemeinschaft." *Internationale Politik*, no. 3 (2000): 3–10.

Wallace, William. "The Collapse of British Foreign Policy." *International Affairs* 82, no. 1 (2005), 53–68.

———. "Europe, the Necessary Partner." *Foreign Affairs* 80, no. 3 (May/June 2001): 16–34.

Wallander, Celeste A., and Robert O. Keohane. "Risk, Threat, and Security Institutions." In *Imperfect Unions: Security Institutions over Time and Space*, ed. Helga Haftendorn, Robert O. Keohane, and Celeste A. Wallander, 21–47. Oxford: Oxford University Press, 1999.

Walt, Stephen M. "Beyond Bin Laden: Reshaping U.S. Foreign Policy." *International Security* 26, no. 3 (winter 2001/02): 56–78.

———. "NATO's Future (in Theory)." In *Alliance Politics, Kosovo, and NATO's War*, ed. Pierre Martin and Mark R. Brawley, 11–25. Houndmills, Basingstoke: Palgrave, 2000.

———. *The Origins of Alliances.* Ithaca, N.Y.: Cornell University Press, 1987.

———. "Why Alliances Endure or Collapse." *Survival* 39, no. 1 (spring 1997): 156–79.

Whitney, Craig R. "France Presses for a Power Independent of the US." *New York Times*, November 7, 1999, A5.

Wijk, Rob de. "European Military Reform for a Global Partnership." *Washington Quarterly* 27, no. 1 (winter 2003–04): 197–210.

———. "Transatlantic Relations: A View from the Netherlands." *International Journal* 59, no. 1 (winter 2003–04): 167–86.

Wilkie, Robert Wilkie. "Fortress Europa: European Defense and the Future of the North Atlantic Alliance." *Parameters* 32, no. 4 (winter 2002–03): 34–47.

Yoon, Young-Kwan. "Introduction: Power Cycle Theory and the Practice of International Relations." *International Political Science Review* 24, no. 1 (2003): 5–12.

Yost, David S. "The NATO Capabilities Gap and the European Union." *Survival* 42, no. 4 (winter 2000–01): 97–128.

———. "Transatlantic Relations and Peace in Europe." *International Affairs* 78, no. 2 (April 2002): 277–300.

Zaborowski, Marcin, and Kerry Longhurst. "America's Protégé in the East? The Emergence of Poland as a Regional Leader." *International Affairs* 79, no. 5 (2003): 1009–28.

Zecchini, Laurent. "Deux visions de l'Europe et de sa défense." *Le Monde*, October 7, 2003.

Zelikow, Philip, and Condoleezza Rice. *Germany Unified and Europe Transformed: A Study in Statecraft*. Cambridge, Mass.: Harvard University Press, 1995.

Index

About the Author

FRANZ OSWALD is Associate Professor of European Politics and International Relations at Curtin University of Technology, Perth, Western Australia, and the author of *The Party That Came Out of the Cold War: The Party of Democratic Socialism in United Germany* (Praeger, 2002).